GOVERNANCE OF INDIA

BEING A COMMETRY ON THE GOVERNMENT OF INDIA

GOVERNANCE OF INDIA

BEING A COMMETRY ON THE GOVERNMENT OF INDIA

KHUSHAL TALAKSI SHAH

GYAN

Published by

Gyan Publishing House
5, Ansari Road
Daryaganj, New Delhi-110002
Phone: 011-47034999, 9811692060
E-mail: books@gyanbooks.com

Distribution Network
gyanbooks.com
India, USA, Canada, UK, Australia

ISBN: 978-93-7225-047-3 (PB)

First Published, 1917

2nd Impression 2025

Printed at: Gyan Press, Delhi.

GOVERNANCE OF INDIA
Author: KHUSHAL TALAKSI SHAH

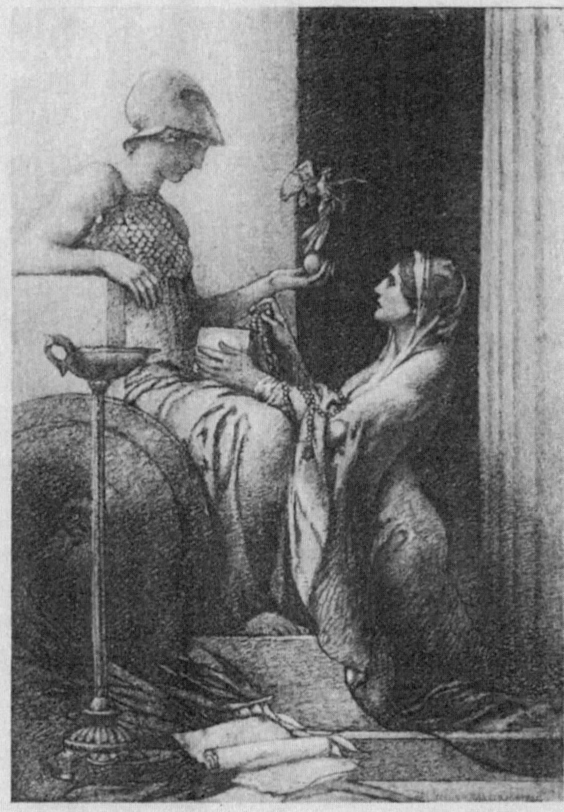

Governance of India

BEING

A commentary on the "Government of India" Acts of 1915 and 1916, with additional chapters on the Indian Local Government, Indian Army, Indian Finance and the Native States of India.

BY

KHUSHAL T. SHAH,

B. A., B. Sc. (Econ., London); Bar-at-law;

Professor of Economics, St. Xavier's College; Lecturer in Administration, Sydenham College of Commerce and Economics; University Post-Graduate Lecturer on the Agrarian and Industrial Problems of India, 1916-17.

PUBLISHED BY:

RAMCHANDRA GOVIND & SON,

Kalbadevi Road, BOMBAY.

1917.

Contents.

CHAPTER IV.

Local Government.

CHAPTER V.

Indian Legislatures.

APPENDIX TO CHAPTERS II, III, IV & V.

Indian Finance.

CHAPTER VI.

Public Services in India.

CHAPTER VII.

Judicial Administration.

CHAPTER VIII.

Church in India.

CHAPTER IX.

Local Government in India.

CHAPTER X.

The Indian Army.

CHAPTER XI.

The Native States of India.

CHAPTER XII.

Miscellaneous.

INTRODUCTION.

Difficulties of a writer on political subjects.

To attempt a full description of the political institutions of a country is a very difficult, and often a thankless task. The entirety of administrative organs, with all their complexity of structure and variety of functions, is seldom described in a single instrument. In many countries, like Hungary, or Russia, or England, no such document at all exists. Even in the countries—like the United States or France—where all constitutional provisions are supposed to be contained in one document—the silent growth of usage, the accumulated force of indefinite but well-known precedent, render the letter of the constitution incomplete if not obsolete, unreliable if not altogether fictitious. Change and progress is the one law of human life to which all human institutions must submit, and political institutions, far from being an exception to the rule, are amongst the most unstable of our achievements. The experience of France alone suffices to show that a constitutional instrument, if it aims at immutability, attempts an impossible task. For the functions and importance of administrative authorities vary even while the constitution which instituted them remains itself unchanged. Only, in the absence of specific amendments of the constitution, the ingenuity of constitutional lawyers, sharpened by the exigencies of an unthought of situation, will suggest interpretations, which, because they were never intended by the authors, will not be the less approved and accepted. Such interpretations make the original, unaltered constitution a mere fiction, a standing, solemn satire on those who intended it to be unalterable. Besides, in describing political institutions an honest author has often to wrestle—consciously or unconsciously—against the influences of his own education, and environment. He has eternally to be on his guard against losing sight of the perspective between the past and the present. Living in the present, thinking always of the present he often unwillingly, unconsciously exposes himself to the charge of partisanship. To avoid that charge altogether ought to be the aim, but it is often an impossible ideal. To outline all the aspects of a question would be the safest rule of conduct, but for the risk of undue prolixity. To present one's own opinion on a question, and to support it, when necessary, by examining and exposing the opposite opinion is possible to every writer and not entirely reprehensible.

Special difficulties of an Indian writer: (a) variety of sources of political authority in India: (i) Acts of Parliament.

These difficulties, common to all writers on political subjects, are particularly hard to overcome for a writer on the Indian polity. The powers of the Government of India are derived from several sources, and of these the Acts of Parliament are the most important to-day. An Act of Parliament seldom deals exhaustively with a topic, but even when it does, English legislators delight in fashioning each Act so far as to suit only the exigency of the moment. They fancy themselves to be of an eminently practical bent of mind, because they exclude logic and system in the conception and finish of their creations. One cannot quarrel with a people who serenely accept their obvious defects as the undisputed hall-mark of their genius. But since Acts of Parliament—even the best of them—leave ample room for forensic construction and judicial interpretation, the student is bewildered by the number alone of the statutes—each explanatory, amendatory or abrogatory of the previous ones—through which he has to pursue his investigations. In the case of the Government of India, for instance, the last consolidating Act–the Act of 1915–had to repeal, or amend 47 previous statutes. All these several Acts were passed as and when an occasion arose, and always with reference to that occasion only. Attempts were made from time to time to collect this medley of provisions into one consolidating enactment; but soon the Consolidating Act itself had to be amended, either because the growing needs of administration demanded an expansion, or because of the obscurity or imperfection that had been overlooked while framing the main Act. Thus the Regulating Act was superseded by Pitt's act, and that again by the various Charter Acts. The Government of India Act of 1858 was materially amended by the India Councils Act of 1861, by the Indian High Courts Act, and by the Reforming Acts of 1892, 1909, 1912. Even the latest Consolidating Act (5 & 6 Geo. V. Ch. 61) was itself amended within less than a year after its passage.

Acts of Parliament have to be supplemented by reports of Parliamentary Committees, dispatches of Directors and speeches in Parliament.

Acts of Parliament, even when they are logical, systematic and comprehensive, do not tell the whole tale. At most they can provide the bare skeleton; the breath of life has to be infused from other sources. Under the Company two distinct agencies tried to fill up the inevitable gap left by an Act of Parliament. Great pieces of legislation, like the Charter Acts, were preceded by exhaustive inquiries by Parliamentary Committees, and the Acts were based on the reports of those committees. These reports, therefore, served as an unfailing guide to the motives actuating the authors of that legislation. And when a new Act was passed the comments of the Court of Directors, embodied in their dispatches to the authorities in India, served to explain and illustrate the changes made in the status quo. The dispatch of the Directors, for instance, on the Charter Act of 1833, is even now regarded as an authority on the principles governing the relations between the supreme government and its provincial lieutenants in India. Valuable light may also be thrown on the scheme of the governance of India under the Company by the pages of Hansard, though this last becomes particularly important only after India had passed to the Crown. More important than these is the voluminous literature comprising the biographies and private correspondence of some of the leading personages in the story of India under the British rule.

(ii) Prerogative of the Crown and (iii) acts of local legislatures.

With the aid of these several agencies of Parliamentary reports and Directors' dispatches and the lives and correspondence of men like Clive and Hastings, and Burke and Dundas, and Canning and Wellington, we may indeed succeed in animating the bare skeleton provided by parliamentary enactments. But, as already observed, these are not the only source of the powers of the Government of India. The prerogative of the Crown—vague and extensive in England—is not insignificant in India. And a still greater portion of the governmental machinery depends upon the acts and ordinances of the local legislatures and authorities. The entire scheme of local self-governing institutions in India, or the great code regulating the conduct of public servants in India is the result of such action. These local acts, ordinances and resolutions are more numerous than the statutes of Parliament, and need external commentaries as much. The force of custom and precedent, ever very powerful, is particularly important in the bureaucratic atmosphere of India. To explain this mass of local acts, to render precise the indefinite sway of usage, the student must seek the help of the published volumes of dispatches and correspondence, as well as that of the speeches and writings of eminent men connected with the administration. Authors and administrators like Sir R. Temple, Sir J. Strachey, Sir H. Maine, Sir W. Hunter have left ample material for a student to work upon. Reports of Royal Commissions—which in India as in England are the *ultima ratio* of embarrassed officials—and resolutions of policy issued by the Imperial Government on these reports are also indispensable.

(iv) Heritage of the past.

The mere mention of the necessity to consult such a variety of authorities would suffice to give an idea of the difficulties of a student of Indian political institutions, even in that portion of them which has been the subject of definite legal enactments. A not insignificant portion of the powers of government in India is derived from the ancient rulers of the country. This is a heritage of the days when there was no constitution, and when the personal genius or caprice of the ruler was all-in-all. The whole of the Indian system of finance, if we exclude the most recent changes; the chief sources of public revenues; the constitutional position and practical importance of the army—all alike bear witness to this heritage of our past. In this respect the greatest difficulty is the lack of any authoritative pronouncement guiding the policy. As an instance in point we may mention the position of the Native States in India. The relations between the British Government and the Native States have formed the subjects of numberless treaties and engagements and sanads. These have been collected by an industrious official, the late Sir Charles Aitchison, and have been brought up-to-date. But many of the treaties, even when they have not been specifically annulled or abrogated are often obsolete owing to the ever increasing mass of custom and precedent, and not less to the changed atmosphere of the times. The older treaties contemplate the relations of equal allies; the more recent ones seem to suggest the position of sovereign and feudatories. We are at a loss to determine the exact principles governing this subject—in spite of an illuminating treatise by the late Sir W. Lee-Warner—because it has ever been the policy of the Government of India to regard these relations as confidential. In the absence of official, authoritative pronouncements, rumours and conjectures, unsound inferences deduced from exploded theories, have more than their due share; and the student, already bewildered by the mass of conflicting legislation, is at last completely mystified by this last aspect of the powers of the Government of India.

(b) India in transition.

Yet another difficulty is raised by the admitted fact of political transition in India to-day. The European War, an unmitigated disaster for mankind in general, has yet proved serviceable to India in as much as the claims of Indians have begun to obtain recognition, thanks to the services of India to the British Empire in the hour of its utmost need. Our soldeirs have fought and bled and died for the Empire in France and Egypt and Mesopotamia. Our Government has offered a free gift of £ 100,000,000, to the Government of the King, besides subscribing heavily to the English loans from our various Reserves. The Indian people—the poorest in the world—have breathed not a murmur against the increasing burden of taxation, and our princes have hesitated not a moment to place their purse and their sword at the disposal of the King-Emperor. In return England has admitted the claims of India to a fuller recognition as an equal member of the Empire, and her Colonies have not protested. We are conscious of impending, radical changes. The acknowledged representatives of the people have put forth definite proposals, while even the leading officers of the state in India have admitted the necessity of a change in the democratic direction. For all these sentiments to materialise time must no doubt be allowed; though it is to be hoped, time will not serve to make the powers that be forgetful of the services as also of the needs of India. Be that as it may, the point remains, that Indian polity being admittedly in a state of transition, the student's task is as delicate as it is otherwise difficult.

The signs of a rapid and radical transition are not confined to India alone. Even the staid and sober old England is undergoing a revolution, all the more formidable because it is so silent. A Curzon-Milner-Lloyd George-Henderson combination would have been simply inconceivable three years ago, and is the most palpable reality of to-day. We must not, indeed, generalise too hastily upon the basis of the events forced by the War. We cannot say, for instance, if the military and industrial conscription necessitated by the War will be maintained in times of peace; we may doubt if the press censorship required to-day for obvious reasons, will continue when those reasons no longer exist; we may even question, in spite of the declaration of Mr. Lloyd George to the contrary, if the party spirit has vanished from the English politics never to return. Nevertheless we may be sure that every one of the War measures—from the "Business Government" and Directory of Five to the military and industrial conscription—have been accepted because they pointed out some flaws in the political and national organisation of England before the war, and that their spirit will not be lost sight of even if they do not endure in the exact shape they have to-day.

The Constitution of the British Empire in transition.

Corresponding to these changes in England the rest of the Empire has also felt the effects of the war. Till this war the English self-governing Colonies were intent upon developing their local resources. New countries with an almost virgin soil, they gave ample opportunities to every class of their inhabitants; and the best of the colonials were consequently unable to see beyond the horizon of the Colonies. This is, perhaps, the only explanation of South Africa deliberately creating a tension with India, Canada negotiating a Reciprocity Treaty with the United States, and Australia affronting China and Japan by her labour legislation. The Imperial Government was often embroiled with its neighbours and embarrassed vis-a-vis its dependants because the colonial statesmen simply could not realise their imperial and other obligations. But the war, we may hope, has made them realise these responsibilities, even though the field for local development has not appreciably contracted. Without the Colonies of England understanding these duties there could never be a sound and durable Federation of the Empire, perhaps not even a durable reconstruction of Europe.

India and Imperial Federation.

In the following pages I have discussed only the domestic problems of India from the standpoint of an Indian statesman. But the aspect of India as a unit of the British Empire has, by recent events, acquired an importance which no student of Indian political institutions can ignore; and this is perhaps as fit a place as any in the body of book to discuss that aspect. No one can write now, as Prof. Lowell wrote only a few years ago, that the question of Imperial Federation can have reference only to the self-governing colonies and England. If we are to believe the highest authorities in England, and if we may accept some of the recent events as an earnest of their intentions, we may take it as settled that no scheme of Imperial Federation will now be entertained which does not incorporate India as an integral part of the Federation. The question, then, to discuss is how the idea of Federation, if realised, will affect India, and what ought to be India's position in that Federation.

Case for federation in other parts of the Empire.

It may be observed at the outset that there is not —and there cannot be—that unanimity of sentiment in favour of a closer union which we in India are at first sight apt to imagine. A closer union of the various self-governing members of the Empire would necessarily result in a surrender, to some extent, of the power of self-government now so fully enjoyed. That there is at all a sentiment for a closer union—and that not in England alone—is explained by the fact that under the existing state of things, on all occasions of the greatest moment, England could virtally compel her self-governing colonies to forego some of the powers of local autonomy. Said Mr. Hughes the Australian Premier, on the eve of his departure from England last year, "The conseqences of the War to the Dominions are not confined to contributions of men to fight the battles of the Empire, nor to their maintenance; but extend in such a way as in effect to reduce the self-governing powers of the Dominions, merely giving effect to the war policy determined by those who control it. And the effect of doing those things that had to be done will not cease when the war ends, but will remain for many years—in this case at least for a generation—to modify profoundly, if not actually to determine, the policy of the Dominions. It will hardly be denied that if Britain had a right to compel the Dominions to incur such a tremendous burden of debt as this war will impose upon all of them, it has, for all practical purposes, the power to compel them to impose heavy taxation upon themselves; and, if one nation has a right to tax another, it is perfectly clear that the sovereignty or quasi-sovereignty of the latter disappears." (*The Times, June* 1916.)

Opposition to Federation in Africa and Australia.

This long extract is given to show that the idea of a closer union of the Empire, stripped of its sentimentalism, is caused on the side of England because of the growing inability of England to meet single-handed the cost in men and money of a modern European War, as also the much greater cost of preparing for it; and on the side of the Dominions in a desire to control the foreign policy of England with a view to reap the economic and other advantages expected to result from a control of the external affairs. Where colonial politicians have not yet risen to the stature of Imperial statesmen, where the perception of advantages resulting from a co-ordination of foreign policy and defence is yet vague, the sentiment for union, involving a surrender in some measure of the powers of self-government, does not find favour with the public. Thus at a Nationalist Congress in South Africa, held at Worcester in September last, a resolution was moved and carried, "This Congress, having heard of the movement in the United Kingdom and its colonies in favour of a reconstruction of the British Empire, declares itself as strongly as possible against such reconstruction, which may have the effect of any reduction of the existing rights of colonial self-government, or any interference with the immediate power of the people of the Union, or our government, over matters of moment to the country." This resolution expresses the sentiments of a not insignificant portion of the people of that colony. The Nationalist vote at the last election amounted to 80,000 and there is no reason to believe that the Nationalist party is losing ground. Perhaps we may explain this opposition to federation in South Africa on the ground of the unfortunate race question between the Boer and the Briton. Such race differences exist even in other colonies. That French and English Canadians are at one in this war may be explained by the close alliance between England and France, but in the untoward event of a difference between England and France, or worse still, between England and the United States may not the the same opposition be apprehended in Canada? Even in the purely British Colony of Australia the sentiment in favour of a Federation is by no means so unanimous as the utterances of Mr. Hughes and other Imperialist politicians might suggest. An Australian correspondent of the New Statesman writes from Melbourne on February 16, "The opinion prevails in this country that Australia's real attitude towards the Imperial Federation has been seriously misrepresented by publications like the Round Table and the Quarterly Review and a certain group of officials and politicians who pose as authorities on Commonwealth affairs.........The truth is that outside a very limited circle there is nobody of opinion which favours Imperial Federation or any closer political bonds with the United Kingdom." In support of this view the same writer quotes the "Sydney Telegraph" writing as follows.—"Nothing exists to show that the system which has yielded such excellent results until the war and during the war, cannot continue to do so. It is quite unwarranted to assume that in its foreign policy the Imperial Government, as matters stand, does or can ignore, the interests of the Dominions, or that under a system of Imperial Federation, our influence upon the shaping of such policy would be greater than it is now. Any representation that you have in an Imperial Government would be insufficient to enable the Commonwealth view appreciably to affect its decisions." (*The New Statesman, April 21, 1917*).

Case for Federation in India.

Under such a state of public opinion in the colonies it would be presumptuous for an individual citizen of any one part of the Empire to pronounce upon the desirability of the Federation. Nor can it be said yet what powers and functions will be allotted to the Imperial Council proper—when one is constituted,—and what would be its relations with its constituents; though this much seems self-evident that at least the foreign affairs, defence, and some portion of financial powers will have to be made over to such a council. At this stage an Indian writer could with propriety discuss India's attitude towards Imperial Federation. The case for a closer union with the United Kingdom and her colonies is fairly strong in India, though some of the advantages supposed to result from such a union are likely to be exaggerated. Thus we are often told that India gains immensely in administrative efficiency by that class of her public servants who are trained in England. By severing her connection with the Empire, India might no doubt lose her English servants; but England is no longer the only country for training up young men in the rudiments of public service; nor are Indians altogether lacking in a turn for public service in every branch. On the other hand the necessity of public defence is yet too great for India to deny the value of England's co-operation in the defence of the country. The question whether India can ever be equal to her own defence is altogether a different one. But under the existing circumstances, and in view of the modern methods of warfare, it would be absurd to suggest that India could depend upon herself—unaided by England—at least for a generation. That her possible enemies on the frontier are weaker and cruder than herself is no reason to prove India's ability to meet all possible exigencies. In economic matters, too, membership of the Empire is fraught with decisive advantages for us. India is only just waking up to her vast industrial possibilities. These she cannot develop without capital. And capital she would find on much easier terms by participating in the joint credit of the Empire than on her own unsupported credit. Moreover, with the foreign affairs in the control of a truly Imperial Council in which India has her representatives, she might quite possibly succeed in securing for herself those advantages with which most treaties of the last generation were so fully occupied. The case for a closer union is, therefore, very strong on military and economic grounds.

Possible case against Federation in India, examined.

On the other hand we must not ignore the possible case on the other side. The unfortunate experience of the consequences of a difference in race may incline many Indian publicists to declare against a closer union. But the question of a closer union can only be discussed on the assumption that India is completely autonomous for all her local affairs; and, with a popular government in India which is given an equal recognition in the Council of the Empire, the fears of racial differences are apt to be exaggerated, if not entirely unfounded. The experience like the one Indians were meeting with in South Africa may not be quite impossible even under a federated Empire; but it may be safely said that such experiences will be rare and always likely to be effectively remedied by India herself or by the Imperial Council.

Another obstacle in the way of a closer union may be found in the current of the informed public opinion of to-day. Leaders of public opinion seem to have definitely accepted the idea of provincial autonomy; but the logical conclusion of such an idea may quite possibly be a desire like the one expressed by the "Sydney Telegraph" quoted above. An attempt has been made in the body of this book to show why a really self-governing India would not need provincial autonomy so urgently as leaders of public opinion seem to think to-day. In any case it is not unreasonable to believe that a fuller realisation of India's political and economic needs would prevent the turn of Indian nationalism in a channel which might lead to a desire for separation from the British Empire in the near future. As already observed the materialisation of all these advantages in conditional upon India's being admitted in the Council of the Empire on terms of perfect equality. Even so one might urge that no scheme of representation can ever give any single part of the Empire an appreciable influence in the joint

Council of the Empire. Such a line of argument is based on a misconception of the nature and functions of the Imperial Council. While admitting that the constitution of the common council is bound to tax heavily the resources of Imperial statesmanship; while confessing that the problem of securing proper representation to each unit according to the different principles of population and political and economic importance is a grave one, we may yet say that the Imperial Council will only deal with purely imperial questions. The Government of India, like those of other units, will be supreme in the local concerns of India; and Indian representatives, we may assume, will be allowed a preponderant voice in the Imperial Council even in those foreign questions which relate exclusively or preponderantly to India. As regards inter-state differences, the unbiassed opinion of a majority of the elect of the whole Empire may well be allowed to prevail, though such a device as a $\frac{2}{3}$ majority in all fundamental questions of imperial policy may be profitably adopted. And as for the burdens of the Empire, necessarily resulting as a corollary of the union, they will have to be accepted if the advantages of the union are at all commensurate.

In the face of all these obstacles I have ventured to present, in the following pages, a picture of the administrative machinery of India as it works to-day. The picture, it need hardly be added, is bound to be sketchy and perhaps incomplete. My only excuse for making an effort at all is the growing interest in an ever widening circle in political questions. It would be a pity if the awakening consciousness of the people of India to their political existence were left to be guided entirely by those amateur politicians who are frequently without any equipment to handel political questions save their commonsense. Eevn so I would have hesitated, but for the admirable opportunity for a systematic, scientific treatment of our polity, afforded by the Consolidating Act of 1915. I have endeavoured to make this little work interesting—and even useful—to a wider circle than the one embracing the undergraduates of our University, though, it must be confessed, the first impulse to write originated from my connection with the students. And in saying this I have no intention to underrate the merits of those eminent authors who had already endeavoured to enlighten the Indian and English public on the subject. Sir Courtney Ilbert's work is deservedly recognised as an authority; but it is a wrok more likely to interest constitutional lawyers than the ordinary public. Sir George Chesney's classic work on the Indian Polity has even now its own value, though since he wrote vast strides have been made in the development of the Indian Polity. Sir John Strachey has given us an admirable picture of India as a high official of a generation ago looked at it, and his successors and imitators like Sir B. Fuller have not corrected their angle of vision. The Imperial Gazetteer gives a colourless but clear and authoritative version of the administration of India, while foreign observers—like Mr. Joseph Chailley–reflect the prejudices and preconceptions of their informants. Writers, also, of a more recent date, with an altogether new belief regarding the destiny of India, are not unknown, and chief among these may be mentioned the late Sir H. Cotton, who, though an Anglo-

Indian official himself, was yet able to rise superior to the prejudices of Anglo-Indiana. Of indigenous writers there is not yet a superabundance Indian publicists are too busy criticising current topics to attempt a systematic work describing the Indian system of administration, though of late years there has been a notable and welcome change even in this respect. To single out individual writers for praise or censure would be individuous, but the general remark may be hasarded that they all appear to minister to the need of an important, but still a limited, section of the public, the undergraduate world.

Scope & Method of this work.

Working on the basis of a Parliamentary enactment, I had two alternative methods of treatment open to me. I might have followed Ilbert and made this book a handbook for the constitutional lawyer. I have preferred to take the law as a back-ground to trace upon it the outlines of the political institutions of our country. Designed originally for the undergraduate, the book in its present form will, I venture to think, be of use to a wider world of students of India. It has been my constant endeavour to discuss each question scientifically; it was inevitable, therefore, to take into consideration the important aspect of each controversial point. And though on many questions I have not hesitated to pronounce an opinion, I have on many another point refrained from pronouncing for obvious reasons of uncertainty in the question itself, or incompetency of the author. I may only add that the purpose of this book will not be misunderstood because, here and there, its outward form or some stray expression might lend itself to misconstruction.

My debt of gratitude is great to my friends Messrs. M. L. Tannan, B. Com., Bar-at-law, of the Sydenham College, and M. J. Mehta, B. A., LL. B., Bar-at law; the one for going through the index to this work and preparing a list of the errata, the other for looking over the proofs of some portions dealing with points of law. I also owe much to my students of the St. Xavier's College and of the Sydenham College, for their ingenuous difficulties have often suggested to me new aspects of a question. I trust they will not be the less benefited by this work because it is not designed exclusively as a help in passing examinations.

BOMBAY,
1st *June* 1917.

K. T. S.

Errata.

—:o:—

Page	Line (from top)		For	Read.
41	26	,,	resanons.	reasons.
44	19	,,	united.	United.
55	16	,,	Committe ewas.	Committee was.
68	26	,,	toontinent	Continent.
79	24	,,	representative.	Representative.
79	25	,,	government.	Government.
83	3	,,	Offic ia.	Official.
84	17	,,	Leat.	least.
88	7	,,	and.	an.
98	5	,,	Lientenant Governor	Lieutenant-Governor.
174	25	,,	geven.	given.
179	6	,,	Ligeslative.	legislative.
204	9	,,	vacancya. nd.	Vacancy,—and.
222	22	,,	and.	,
238	Last	,,	loca.	local.
269	,,	,,	town-snow.	Towns—now.
273	24	,,	property of.	property or
275	34	,,	borrow	raise
298	15	,,	wase Stablished.	was established.
318	3	,,	tasign.	resign.
326	Schedule 3	,,	India	Indian

CHAPTER I.

The British Parliament and the Government of India.

Government of India Act, 1915

(5 & 6 Geo, 5. ch. 61.).

An Act to consolidate enactments relating to the Government of India. (29th July 1915).

Be it enacted by the King's most Excellent Majesty, by and with the advice and consent of the Lords Spiritual and Temporal, and Commons, in this present Parliament assembled, and by the authority of the same, as follows.—

PART I

HOME GOVERNMENT.

The Crown.

1. The territories for the time being vested in His Majesty in India are governed by and in the name of His Majesty the King, Emperor of India, and all rights, which if the Government of India Act, 1858, had not been passed, might have been exercised by the East India Company in relation to any territories, may be exercised by and in the name of His Majesty as rights incidental to the Government of India.

COMMENTS.

I. The Growth of Parliamentary Sovereignty over India.

The East India Company was in its origin a creature of the Royal Prerogative, and as such dependent upon the good-will of the Executive for all its powers. "By virtue of our Prerogative Royal, which we will not in that behalf have argued or brought into question," says the Charter of Queen Elizabeth, the East India Company is constituted and its powers determined. Under the immediate successors of Elizabeth those who depended for their existence on the Royal Prerogative had some very great hardships to face; for the first half of the XVII century was marked in England by the great struggle between the Crown and Parliament for ultimate supremacy which did not end by the execution of one king. Though the legality of the monopolies granted by Royal Prerogative was questioned under Elizabeth herself, and still more seriously under her immediate successor, the East India Company continued to be a creature of the Crown, or rather of the executive authority. Even when the Civil War had ended in the death of Charles I, and the establishment of the Protectorate, the position of the Company remained unaffected in this respect. The Protector, appreciating the value of the Eastern trade, and recognising the utility of the Company, lent them his strong support in their quarrels with their European rivals in the East. Thus in 1654, by the Treaty of Westminster, he forced the Dutch to pay the Company a compensation of £ 85,000 for the massacre of Amboyna, and for their exclusion from the trade of the Spice Islands. Like his Royal predecessors, and his later Parliamentary successors, Cromwell did not give his aid for nothing; this very sum of £ 85,000 not being easy to be apportioned among the several joint stocks of which the capital of the Company consisted, Cromwell ".borrowed" £ 50,000, pending the settlement. He extended the prestige of the Company by another charter from himself incorporating a rival association with the East India Company. During the Restoration the position of the Company was quite satisfactory. Charter followed Charter in quick succession, each more lavish than the preceding in increasing the powers of the Company.

After the Revolution of 1689, however, the situation of the Company became very critical. On the throne was a king who had not forgotten his Dutch origin because he was made a king of England by a successful Revolution; and who could not help looking with a favourable eye on the Dutch rivals of the English Company. Moreover, the then head of the Company, Sir Josiah Child, had indentified himself and his Company far too much with the Stuart cause to be a *persona grata* with the ministers of William III. In the closing years of the XVII century the privileges of the Company were menaced by the growth of a New Company, which was encouraged by the ministers of the Crown, and which was given valuable rights by Acts of Parliament and Royal Charters. Though the Old Company managed to render nugatory, or at least innocuous, the privileges of their rivals by buying up a great portion of the stock of the latter, the situation became more critical than before, as the promoters of the New Company found their rights almost valueless to themselves. A coalition between the two Companies was the only means to remedy the situation; and it was effected by the intervention of Lord Godolphin in 1702. Further difficulties appeared in carrying out the arrangements of 1702. At last, therefore, an Act was passed in 1707, by which the New Company was required to advance to the Crown an additional loan of £ 1,200,000 without interest. In consideration of this the Company's exclusive privileges were continued till 1726; and Godolphin was empowered to settle the outstanding differences between the two Companies. Accordingly Lord Godolphin gave an Award in 1708, and in the following year the Old Company surrendered all its charters and its seperate existence came to an end. The original Charter of the New or the English Company became the source of all the powers of the Company,—the United Company,—and it remained unaltered upto the end of the Company in 1858, except by Acts of Parliament.

Though the sovereignty of Parliament was thus asserted as early as the beginning of the XVIII century, the first real attempt to regulate the government of the Company *in India* by Acts of Parliament did not come till more than two generations after. The acquisition by the Company of the Civil Administration of Bengal in 1765, and their constant engagement in wars in India had so completely changed their original character of traders, as determined by charters and Acts of Parliament, that the need for a wholesale revision of the powers and duties of the Company could no longer be ignored. Even so the reform might have been yet further delayed had it not been for the financial necessities of the Company. When they applied to the Treasury to advance them a loan, the Government of Lord North took the opportunity to revise the constitution of the Company by an Act of Parliament. The **Regulating Act** was the result; and for the first time the Government of the East India Company, both in England and in India, came to be regulated in all its entirety by an Act of Parliament. The principle seems to be from this time unquestionably established **that all changes in the structure of the Government in India as well as in England can only be made by an Act of Parliament.** The entire control of the Government in this country cannot, it would seem, be said to be under the sovereignty of Parliament from 1773. But even this doubt was removed by the **Act of 1784**, by which a **Board of Control was** established to superintend and control the affairs of India, and the President of which became responsible to Parliament. Even after the Act of 1784, though there was a regular machinery for the exercise of Parliamentary control, the authority of the Board, and therefore of the Parliament, was not the only authority concerned with the administration of India. The Court of Directors of the Company were still left considerable power, and very frequently it became exceedingly difficult to locate the responsibility for a particular act of the Government of India, as for instance in the first Afghan War. This situation was at last remedied by the transfer of the Government of India to the Crown in 1858, when **a Secretary of State was made solely responsible to Parliament for the Government of India, and was given power to superintend, control and direct the Government of India.**

II. Nature and Extent of Parliamentary Sovereignty over India.

In the theory of the law, Government by the Crown means Government by the British Parliament. In common with all the parts of the British Empire, the legal Sovereign of India is the King-in-Parliament. There is, however, this difference between the sovereignty of the King-in-Parliament in the Self-Governing colonies and in India:—that while in the Self-Governing colonies the delegation by the Imperial Parliament of legislative independence has gone so far that Parliament seldom interferes in the domestic affairs of, or legislates directly for, those colonies; in India, on the other hand, though there is no doubt a certain amount of delegation of legislative authority, the right of the British Parliament to legislate directly for British India is more than nominal. It is true India has a constitution granted by Parliament—a constitution which is codified by the present Consolidating Act; but in spite of some delegation of legislative autonomy, Parliament still retains a considerable field for legislation relating to India in which its authority is supreme and is frequently directly felt.

It must be noted, however, that though the sovereignty of the British Parliament over India is as complete as that over any part of the King's Dominions, the Government of India derive a substantial portion of their power from the Royal Prerogative as well as from the old Mogul Emperors of the country. (1) That the Royal Prerogative is by no means as obsolete in this country as in England or in the Self-Governing colonies—prerogatives such as legislating by Orders in Council or by Executive orders,—is evidenced by the practical repeal of the Partition of Bengal by a personal proclamation of the King-Emperor in Delhi in December 1911. (2) And that the Government of India exercise certain powers which can only be explained by their being regarded as successors of the old Mogul Emperors can be proved by many a revenue code, and by the complex mass of undefined regulations governing their relations with the Native States, But when these allowances have been made, it still remains true that the general constitution of the Government to-day, both in India and in England, has been created and regulated by Acts of Parliament. Thus the functions of the Governor-General, especially his relations with his Council and his supremacy over the Provinces; the powers of the local Legislatures; the constitution and jurisdiction of the several High Courts; the very existence of the Secretary of State and his Council—all alike are based upon Parliamentary enactments.

The supremacy of Parliament in legislation is unchallenged. But even in matters outside the legislative sphere, Parliamentary supremacy is very often directly felt by the Government of India. Thus in executive matters the Foreign relations of the Government of India are almost exclusively determined by the Home Government. And in so far as Parliament can be said to control the Foreign Policy of the Empire, the Foreign relations of India also are to that extent controlled by Parliament. Again, in matters financial, Parliament has laid down that the revenues of India may not be applied for military expeditions outside the frontiers of India without the consent of Parliament, except for preventing or repelling an actual invasion or any other sudden or urgent necessity; that detailed accounts of Indian revenues and expenditure must be laid annually before Parliament together with a Report on the Moral and Material progress of the country. In addition to all these, in accordance with constitutional usuage, the Secretary of State, as Minister of the Crown, is exposed to criticism in Parliament and to a vote of censure should an occasion arise.

This is the position in theory. In point of fact, however, the influence of Parliament in the conduct of Indian affairs is relatively insignificant. There are various reasons why Parliament cannot interfere frequently and directly in the actual task of administration. Chief among these are the following:—

1. The British Parliameut has neither the time nor the energy to superintend, much less to carry on directly, the Govern-

ment of a distant dependency like India. Even at Home, the practice has recently grown up of delegating a great deal of its legislative authority to the leading departments of State or to the King-in-Council. The so-called Statutory Orders are all framed under such delegated authority; and when they are approved of or notified to Parliament, they have as great a force as any law of the realm. The intricacy and complexity of modern legislation makes it inevitable for a body of amateur legislators to rely more and more upon expert advice both in the framing and working of those laws, reserving to itself only the power of criticism and approval. This dependence upon a subordinate authority becomes greater as the distance or dissimilarity of local conditions increases. In matters relating to India, therefore, though in the theory of the law Parliament is sovereign and is quite competent to legislate on any conceivable topic relating to this country, in point of fact, Parliament does not and cannot legislate for any and every topic. It confines itself usually to acts relating to the Political Constitution of the country, or those enabling the Secretary of State to raise moneys by loan in England.

2. The deliberate, settled policy of the statesmen of England, ever since the transferrence of the Government of India to the Crown, has been to keep all Indian questions entirely outside the pale of party politics. This is often regarded as a very wise maxim and people are not wanting who believe that India gains by it. All the same by being excluded altogether from party programmes, Indian questions never receive that searching, exhaustive, almost venomous criticism from the press and platform, from the opposition in and out of Parliament, which every question included in its programme by one of the leading parties in the State habitually receives in England. And even if we believe that the exclusion from party politics is a good thing for India, it cannot but be admitted that grave questions of imperial policy, in which India is vitally concerned, will never be thoroughly discussed if India is kept out of politics so determinedly in England. Party dominates the whole field of politics in England. Whatever their abuses, constitutional Govern-

ment would be impossible in England without parties. And however sound the theory of exclusion of India from party politics may seem, so long as the supremacy of the British Parliament over India is maintained, it is futile to expect any definite solution of our constitutional questions if our country is altogether kept out of politics in future as she has been in the past. We may conceivably lose by our political problems being brought on the party programme and being made party issues in England. But it is quite certain that Indian questions would receive much greater attention, and therefore much speedier solution, if they are brought on the party programme.

3. The expedients provided for maintaining the supremacy of Parliament have, in practice, either fallen into disuse, or ended in being mere formalities. Thus for instance, Parliament has laid down definite rules as regards the employment of the revenues of India. But such restrictions, from their very nature, are of a negative kind which can be, and have been, relaxed whenever necessary. Moreover it is common custom to present the finance accounts of the Government of India to Parliament towards the fag end of a Parliamentary session. The members at that time are more anxious to finish up the work, and enjoy their well-earned holidays, than to raise discussions or debates on such an uninteresting and intricate topic as the finance of India. Those who have attended in the visitors' gallery of the House of Commons on days when the accounts of the Government of India are laid on the table of the House, and when they ostensibly formed the subject of discussion for the day, could not but have been surprised at the scantiness of attention paid by Members of Parliament to the well-being of the peoples of an Empire which is described as the brightest jewel in the British Crown. Usually there are not more than half a dozen members all told in the whole House, including the Speaker and the Secretary or Under-Secretary of State who presents the accounts. The debate, if we may so dignify the proceedings, ends in a motion which amounts to saying that the accounts of the Government of India show what they show. Occasionally a member puts some questions

which the occupant of the almost empty treasury bench may answer or brush aside. For the salary of the Secretary of State, and the charges of his establishment, are paid out of the revenues of India, and not of England; and naturally the members have no interest to probe very deeply into Indian questions. The House of Commons never gets an opportunity to vote these charges as it does in the case of the Secretary of State for the Colonies. It has, therefore, no incentive to discuss or review the administration of India at a time when the attendance in the House is keen and regular.

4. Added to all these is the general ignorance, and in some cases total incompetence, of the Members of Parliament about questions relating to distant parts of the Empire which helps to perpetuate Parliamentary indifference to Indian questions. The average, Member of Parliament has his hands full with questions that relate to his own constituency or to the peculiar interest he represents. Whether he is a lawyer, a merchant, a landowner, or a retired civil servant, he has very little time and interest to take up subjects in Parliament which he can have no knowledge of, especially when he has more urgent questions nearer home requiring his immediate attention.

III. The Changing Situation and its Causes.

Of late, however, the situation as described above, has undergone some slight modification for the following reasons:—

(1) Ever since the Golden Jubilee of the late Queen in 1887, when British citizens from all over the globe assembled in London to celebrate the fiftieth anniversary of the reign of their beloved sovereign, English people began to take some direct interest in the greatness as well as in the latent powers of their vast Empire. Previous to that day, the great bulk of public opinion in England regarded colonies and distant depen-

dencies as costly luxuries, which England would lose nothing in giving up altogether. Perhaps the charters of Self-Government to the colonies, which were such a marked feature of the nineteenth century British imperial politics, were the result of this lurking distrust—itself the child of the experience gained from the American colonies in the eighteenth century—of distant and disconnected colonies, rather than of any avowed preference for or belief in the merits of Self-Government by the colonies. Even if this were not true it is a universally acknowledged fact that the interest of the average Britisher in the Empire on which the sun never sets was, to say the least, very slight before 1887. From that day, however, opinion has changed. The change is as far reaching in effects as it is revolutionary in character. It has been brought about by the keener realisation of the rivalry of foreign countries in the fields of trade and industry. Britain, once supreme for nearly the whole century, is already finding some of her practical monopolies threatened by the growth of new and vigorous powers like the United States of America or the German Empire. If England is to retain her old position as the workshop, the carrier and the Banker of the world, she must put forth all the efforts she is capable of. That she has resources much more vast than any of her rivals was realised for the first time when men from the different parts of the Empire met in London in 1887 to celebrate the Golden Jubilee of their common sovereign and to realise their common citizenship. The necessity to organise and exploit these resources, to co-ordinate and focus the efforts and energies of the whole Empire on the one task of maintaining the old supremacy made English people look closer into the problems of the Empire. Indirectly, therefore, since that date along with the colonies, India began to loom larger before the British public, not only as the most important part of the British Empire both in men and material, but also as a part whose problems were unique; and whose problems, unless they were solved satisfactorily, would prevent the closer welding together of the different parts of the Empire. The welcome that the first Indian member—Mr. Dadabhai Naoroji—met with in the British Parliament in 1892 was but an indication of the realisation of its imperial responsibility by the British Legislature.

(2) There are other factors also which have helped to increase in recent years Parliamentary attention to Indian questions. Among these, we may reckon as the chief the growing class of the retired servants of the Government of India in England, who cannot forget the fields of their early triumphs or griefs, and whose efforts, therefore, result in attracting more and more attention every day to Indian questions. Whatever side they adopt, whether in Parliament like the late Sir Henry Cotton, or in the Press, or as authors of more permanent literature relating to India, they all serve in their own several ways the land where their prime of manhood was passed. While this class of retired Anglo-Indian officials provides information relating to Indian problems, there is steadily growing up another class of English Members of Parliament who come to the same questions from altogether different motives, and who view these questions from altogether a different stand-point. Elected by the public who looks upon him as their own special deputy to the Imperial Parliament, the average M. P. is, however, shut out, by the growth of the party system, altogether from any chance of winning distinction in domestic politics. The field of domestic politics, in which the constituents are directly interested, is dominated, almost exclusively, by the towering personalities of the party leaders in England. If the average Member of Parliament has any ambition to be known to the constituency—if he has any idea to rise one day to the ministerial or cabinet rank, he must find some other fields of activity—new as well as useful—which he should make it his task to make interesting to his leaders and even to the British electorate. These fields of activity are supplied by the outlying parts of the Empire, chief among which is India, who is entirely voiceless in the councils of the Empire. Her interests, therefore, may well be championed, not without hope of profit to themselves, by this class of aspiring Members of Parliament. They receive not only considerable encouragement by the frequent demonstrations of gratitude by the peoples of India, but substantial help from those educated Indians who are visiting England for profit or pleasure or education in greater and greater numbers every year. Facilities in the means of communication have not only resulted in

bringing the different parts of the Empire together; they have made interchange of views and the combination of effort through the identity of interest much more feasible.

Hence at the present day, the interest taken in Indian questions by the British Parliament as well as by the English public is appreciably greater than ten years ago. There is no doubt a great deal of ignorance or indifference still prevailing among the average Members of Parliament on Indian questions. And there is still a much greater ignorance on these matters among the British public at large. It is also true that in some cases, and notably in some economic questions, the interests of India are apparently opposed to those of England. But when all allowance has been made for these factors, it must be admitted that India is trying more and more to attract the attention of the British Parliament. It is an interesting question as to what would be the relative position of the Government of India and the British Parliament, as representative institutions are introduced in this country in ever increasing proportions till India becomes as much a Self-Governing country as Australia or Canada. If representative institutions take a deep root in this country, and the Government of India becomes national in tone and in character as well as in name, their present position of complete subordination to the Government of England would be found to be impossible to maintain; and we shall cease to look for improvement from a distant, incompetent, partisan assembly, when all the improvements we desire we can effect ourselves.

IV. Means to attract Parliamentary Notice.

The realisation of the complete sovereignty of the English Parliament over India has made the problem of attracting greater and greater attention of that body to Indian questions of the utmost importance in Indian politics. It was realised long before the present aspirations for Self-Government had taken root that any change in the fundamental principles of Government in India could only come from England. In the days of the Company, when the princes and peoples of India had understood the real character of that body, appeals to Parliament or the Crown in England were not unknown. The impecunious Nawab of the Carnatic, for instance, even when he was defeated in a suit against the Company, could obtain a representative of the English Crown to his court, and thus frustrate many a design of Lord Wellesley (1793-99). In those days such an appeal to the ultimate source of all authority in India could, however, from the very nature of the case, be within the means of a very small section of the community in this country. With the transfer of the Government to the Crown, even this thin screen of independent authority vanished; and the governing authorities in India stood out directly as the servants of the British Crown, and as such under the control of the British Parliament. As education made progress among the people of India; as the ideals of Government cherished by the English people and taught by the English history began to be assimilated; and as the true position of the powers in India came to be fully realised, organised efforts were set afoot to reach at the very fountain-head, and there seek a change in the basic principles of government in this country.

The earliest and the most important of these efforts,—one not yet altogether abandoned,-was to try and educate the English public into a sense of India's growing needs, to meet which the established authorities of Government in India were alike unable and incompetent by their training, their temperament, and their general environment. With this view an organ of the advanced Indian opinion was established, and representative Indians were often sent to England to rouse the public in that country. This method, though intrinsically sound, could only yield results after a length of time. Besides, it was not impossible to misinterpret the object of such an agitation in sympathy with the corresponding agitation in India. The aim of such an activity was not, and could not have been, to induce Parliament to interfere in the details of administration in India: Parliament could not, from the nature of the case, interfere without belittling itself. What was desired was to induce Parliament to make such a radical alteration in the maxims of Government as would be more in harmony with the changed conditions of India, and as would save it from all subsequent appeal for reform in details. The very magnitude of such a demand could not but require time to be accomplished. Those who have constituted themselves the guardians of the welfare of so many of their fellow-creatures cannot but hesitate before acceding to a change which, while absolving them from all further liability and responsibility, might not bring the promised improvement in the task. Until Parliament,—or rather the English public,—is convinced that the change desired is both salutary and feasible, it could not abdicate its authority without being false to itself. The clearest and the most conclusive evidence must therefore be laid before Parliament before such an alteration can be expected; and to do that time would have to be allowed.

Perhaps it was thought to be one form of this evidence, that Indians should seek election for a seat in the British Parliament; and from their seat in that house, and by their work in that assembly, convince the people of England of the fitness of the sons of India to govern their own country. So far two successful attempts of this kind have been made,—one by Mr. Dadabhoy Naoroji, and the other by Sir M. Bhownugree. Both these gentlemen were elected by English constituencies; and their presence in the House of Commons served to attract the attention of Parliament to Indian questions. But it would be a mistake to see in this success a solution of India's present aspirations. It is neither possible nor practicable to obtain the real self-government for India by seeking a direct representation in the British Parliament. Even if the Indian members sat as the representatives of Indian constituencies, and not—as these two gentlemen—sitting as representatives of English constituencies, their position in that body can never be so important as to assure a real popular government for Indians in India from Whitehall. For one thing, the experience of the English nation of such members for Ireland is not exactly encouraging enough to induce them to try a second venture in the same direction. Such members, doomed to a perpetual minority, and anxious to achieve a particular object, can only end by becoming mercinaries, selling their votes to whoever promised the speediest accomplishment of their object. They would be in a perpetual minority, because it is hopeless to expect that in an English legislature representation could ever be given to India on the basis of her population. Like the Irish members before them, such members from India, if they ever come into existence, could only hope to achieve their aim by trying to hold the balance between the parties in England. And even then their success is not quite secure; for they must give priority to the business nearer home,–or else they would not get the support of any party in England. If they do so it is just possible that their allies of a while ago might find unexpected difficulties in fulfilling the bargain, not for any want of good faith on their part,—though such infidelities are not unknown in politics,—but because they did not rightly gauge the strength of public opinion in England in favour of such a change. Neither England nor India can expect much from such a makebelieve, mercinary solution of the difficulties of this country.

The expedient of placing the salary of the Secretary of State for India and the charges of his establishment on the revenues of England has often been suggested as the surest means of attracting the attention of the English Parliament to the affairs of India. As to the justice of such an arrangement nothing can be said against it. Not only does the analogy of the colonies suggest it; but the share that India has borne in the defence of the Empire, for a longer period and to a much greater amount than any of the colonies,—makes it but a simple act of justice, all the more graceful on the part of England if by so doing she could assure the people of this country of her sleepless watch on their welfare. Nor would the burden be very great for England. The charges of the India Office do not exceed a quarter of a million sterling, while India has been contributing over 20 million sterling every year for maintaining an army which can be of service,—and has been of service-in any part of the Empire. While the annual revenues of England are nearly 200 million sterling, those of India are much under a hundred. If there be any doubt about the wisdom of such a suggestion, it is due to the apprehension that the actuality may not be the same as the expectation. The mere opportunily to Parliament to discuss, once a year, the expenses of the India office, may, for all we know, be entirely inadequate to afford a permanent solution of all the problems of India. Moreover the inclusion of India on the party programme in England may not prove an unmixed blessing to India. Any desire in the minds of Indians to figure on the party programme in England, any co-operation with any political party in England is due to the belief that by so doing the ultimate goal may be reached the sooner. That goal can **never be anything else but this; that the real Government of India should be in India responsible to the people of India.** And so, though the suggestion under consideration may be an excellent one to realise that goal, it should never be confounded with the aim itself.

If the real object of the agitation in India is not lost sight of there would be no difficulty in understanding at their proper value such other suggestions as that the India Council should be abolished. At best it is a matter of detail. As it stands to-day the India Council is of very little inportance in the administration of India; but its real original object was to serve as brake on the autocracy of the Secretary of State. To abolish it altogether is to remove this one check, however ineffective, on the absolutism of the Secretary of State. On the other hand the proposal that the India Council should be composed of the elected representatives of India would be useless, unless the powers of the Council are increased, and its decisions by majority are made binding upon the Secretary of State on all matters without exception. In the absence of such provisions the Indian members will always have the mortification of being overruled by a man who knows nothing of the questions at issue. A frequent disregard of the wishes of the Council is sure to cause discontent in India if it ever comes to be known. Besides, if the powers of the

Council are increased in this way, the real goal might be lost sight of. The effective powers of no authority in England, however constituted, should be increased at the cost of the authorities in India, if our ultimate goal is self-government in India.

In appraising all these suggestions it must be remembered that the Parliament of England can never interfere, with credit to itself and benefit to India, in the actual details of administration in India. What we want of that body, and what may justly be expected of it, if not as a price of our loyalty as a proof of her appreciation, is to abandon altogether the principles which have so far governed the Empire of India. Time was when the only champion of the Indian people was an independent, private Member of Parliament,—a Burke, a Wilberforce, a Bradlaugh. Time was when the Minister of State for India in England could well be regarded as the real and the only democratic check on the otherwise unlimited autocracy of the Indian Government,—a Canning, a Charles Wood, a Ripon. Time was when the average educated Englishman—of the type of the ordinary Civilian in India,—might be deemed more fit to govern in India than his fellow-subject of Indian birth. His education was more liberal, his experience undoubtedly greater, his neutrality among the religion-divided peoples of India quite probable. But that day has now passed away. The English Parliament, busy with its own immediate problems, cannot play for ever the guardian of the welfare of the Indian people. It has confessed its inability to do so in the case of the colonies planted by Englishmen, and where consequently the problems of Government could not be utterly dissimilar to the local problems of England. It cannot expect us to believe in its competency to go on being the guardian of India, when we are seperated from her by thousands of miles every one of which could give a reason for granting autonomy to India. For with the real problems of India, with our widowed virgins and our untouchable pariah, Parliament is utterly, fundamentally incompetent to deal. And perhaps that is why they never have been approached. The Secretary of State has ceased to be the democratic check that he was meant to be on the absolutism in India, and has ended by becoming the President of the narrowest oligarchy, all the more

3

incompetent to deal with the daily newer and more complex problems of India because the men who compose it have had experience of India as it was 25 years ago. They will maintain themselves to be right with all the dogmatism of out-of-date experts. Even the young English Civilian, actually on the spot in India, and in daily touch with all the complex problems of Indian life, cannot now claim to be a better ruler than his Indian compeer. For his one great claim to superiority is gone or is fast going. As educated India learns the wisdom of religious toleration, his supposed impartiality amidst the warring creeds of India is useless. Education and experience are no longer his monopolies as they used to be. A trial of innate ability shows no unquestioned superiority of the English over the Indian, while his sympathy with his surroundings can never eqaul that of his Indian colleague.

The myriad problems of India must be and can be solved only by the Indians in India. Strangers to Indian life and sentiment, animated with the nobler motives which have governed the best of Englishmen in India, may be efficient rulers, may even be good rulers—so long as the functions of the State are no more than those of a policeman. Change the ideal of the State, and no one people could govern another, especially those utterly dissimilar in their habits and sentiments as the Indians and the English. Indians, when they come to rule in India, may quite conceivably be no better policemen than the English—perhaps no better engineers, financiers, diplomats, lawyers, or soldiers. But they are bound to be,—in spite of themselves, in spite of their history,—immeasurably superior in all those subtle, indescribable attributes which go to make good government as against efficient governmeet, which help to uplift an entire people and make them realise the dignity of a human being, and the mission of human life.

CHAPTER II.

The Secretary of State.

2. (1) Subject to the provisions of this act, the Secretary of State has and performs all such or the like powers and duties relating to the government or revenues of India, and has all such or the like powers over all officers appinted or continued under this act, as, if the Government of India Act, 1858, had not been passed, might or should have been exercised or performed by the East India Company, or by the Court of Directors or Court of Proprietors of that Company, either alone or by the direction or with the sanction or approbation of the Commissioners for the affairs of India, in relation to that government or those revenues and the officers and servants of that Company, and also all such powers as might have been exerised by the said Commissioners alone.

(2) In particular, the Secretary of State may, subject to the provisions of this Act, superintend, direct and control all acts, operations and concerns which relate to the government or revenues of India, and all grants of salaries, gratuities and allowances, and all other payments and charges, out of or on the revenues of India.

(3) There shall be paid out of the revenues of India to the Secretary of State and to his under secretaries respectively the like yearly salaries as may for the time being be paid to any other Secretary of State and his under secretaries respectively.

The Council of India.

3. (1) The Council of India shall consist of such number of members, not less than ten and not more than fourteen, as the Secretary of State may determine.

(2) The right of filling any vacancy in the council shall be vested in the Secretary of State.

(3) Unless at the time of an appointment to fill a vacancy in the council nine of the then existing members of the council are persons who have served or resided in British India for at least ten years, and have not last left British India more than five years before the date of their appointment, the person appointed to fill the vacancy must be so qualified.

(4) Every member of the council shall hold office, except as by this section provided, for a term of seven years.

(5) The Secretary of State may, for special reasons of public advantage, re-appoint for a further term of five years any member of the council whose term of office has expired. In any such case the reasons for the reappointment shall be set forth in a minute signed by the Secretary of State and laid before both Houses of Parliament. Save as aforesaid, a member of the council shall not be capable of re-appointment.

(6) Any member of the council may, by writing signed by him' resign his office. The instrument of resignation shall be recorded in the minutes of the council.

(7) Any member of the council may be removed by His Majesty from his office on an address of both Houses of Parliament.

(8) There shall be paid to each member of the council out of the revenues of India the annual salary of one thousand pounds.

4. No member of the Council of India shall be capaple of sitting or voting in Parliament.

5. The Council of India shall, under the direction of the Secretary of State, and subject to the provisions of this Act, conduct the business transacted in the United Kingdom in relation to the Government of India and the correspondence with India; but every order or communication sent to India, and every order made in the United Kingdom in relation to the Government of India under this Act, shall be signed by the Secretary of State.

6. (1) All powers required to be exercised by the Secretary of State in Council, and all powers of the Council of India, shall be exercised at meetings of the council at which not less than five members are present.

(2) The council may act notwithstanding any vacancy in their number.

7. (1) The Secretary of State shall be the president of the Council of India, with power to vote.

(2) The Secretary of State in Council may appoint any member of the council to be vice-president thereof, and the Secretary of State may at any time remove any person so appointed.

(3) At every meeting of the council the Secretary of State, or in his absence, the vice-president, if present, or, in the absence of both of them, one of the members of the council, chosen by the members present at the meeting, shall preside.

8. Meetings of the Council of India shall be convened and held as and when the Secretary of State directs, but one such meeting at least shall be held in every week.

9. (1) At any meeting of the Council of India at which the Secretary of State is present, if there is a difference of opinion on any question, except a question with respect to which a majority of votes at a meeting is by this Act declared to be necessary, the determination of the Secretary of State shall be final.

(2) In case of an equality of votes at any meeting of the council, the person presiding at the meeting shall have a second or casting vote.

(3) All acts 'done at a meeting of the council in the absence of the Secretary of State shall require the approval in writing of the Secretary of State.

(4) In case of difference of opinion on any question decided at a meeting of the council, the Secretary of State may require that his opinion and the reasons for it be entered in the minutes of the proceedings, and any member of the council, who has been present at the meeting, may require that his opinion, and any reasons for it that he has stated at the meeting, be also entered in like manner.

10. The Secretary of State may constitute committees of the Council of India for the more convenient transaction of business, and direct what departments of business are to be under those committees respectively, and generally direct the manner in which all business of the council or committees thereof is to be transacted.

Orders and Communication.

11. (1) Subject to the provisions of this Act, every order or communication proposed to be sent to India, and every order proposed to be made in the United Kingdom by the Secretary of State under this Act, shall, unless it has been sudmitted to a meeting of the Council of India, be deposited in the council room for the perusal of all members of the council during seven days before the sending or making thereof.

(2) Any member of the council may record, in a minute book kept for that purpose, his opinion with respect to any such order or communication, and a copy of every opinion so recorded shall be sent forthwith to the Secretary of State.

(3) If a majority of the council so recorded their opinions against any act proposed to be done, the Secretary of State shall, unless he defers to the opinion of the majority, record his reasons for acting in opposition thereto.

12. (1) Where it appears to the Secretary of State that the despatch of any communication or the making of any order, not being an order for which a majority of votes at a meeting of the Council of India is by this Act declared to be necessary, is urgently required the communication may be sent or order made, although it has not been submitted to a meeting of the council or deposited for the perusal of the members of the council.

(2) In any such case the Secretary of State shall, except as by this Act provided, record the urgent reasons for sending the communication or making the order, and give notice thereof to every member of the council.

13. (1) Where an order concerns the levying of war or the making of peace, or the treating or negotiating with any prince or state, or the policy to be observed with respect to any prince or state, and is not an order for which a majority of votes at a meeting of the Council of India is by this Act declared to be necessary, and is an order which, in the opinion of the Secretary of State, is of a nature to require secrecy, the Secretary of State may send the order to the Governor General in Council, or to any Governor-in-Council or officer or servant in India without having submitted the order to a meeting of

the council or deposited it for the perusal of the members of the council and without recording or giving notice of the reasons for making the order.

(2) Where any despatch to the Secretary of State from the Governor-General in Council or a Governor in Council conerns the government of India or of any part thereof, or the levying of war, or the making of peace, or negotiations or treaties with any prince or state, and is, in the opinion of the authority sending it, of a nature to require secrecy, it may be marked "Secret" by that authority; and a despatch so marked shall not be communicated to the members of the Council of India unless the Secretary of State so directs.

14. Every despatch to the United Kingdom from the Governor-General in Council or a Governor in Council shall be addressed to the Secretary of State.

15. When any order is sent to India directing the actual commencement of hostilities by His Majesty's forces in India, the fact of the order having been sent shall, unless the order has in the meantime been revoked or suspended, be communicated to both Houses of Parliament within three months after the sending of the order, or, if Parliament is not sitting at the expiration of those three months, then one month after the next sitting of Parliament.

16. It is the duty of the Governor-General in Council to transmit to the Secretary of State constantly and diligently an exact particular of all advices or intelligence, and of all transactions and matters, coming to the knowledge of the Governor General in Council and relating to the government, commerce, revennes or affairs of India.

Establishment of the Secretary of State.

17. (1) No addition may be made to the establishment of the Secretary of State in Council, nor to the salaries of the persons on that establishment, except by an order of His Majesty in Council, to be laid before both Houses of Parliament within fourteen days

after the making thereof, or, if Parliament is not then sitting, then within fourteen days after the next meeting of Parliament.

(2) The rules made by His Majesty for examinations, certificates, probation or other tests of fitness, in relation to appointments to junior situations in the civil service, shall apply to such appointments on the said establishment.

(3) The Secretary of State in Council may, subject to the foregoing provisions of this section, make all appointments to and promotions in the said establishment, and may remove any officer or servant belonging to the establishment.

18. His Majesty may, by warrant under the Royal sign Manual countersigned by the Chanceller of Exchequer, grant to any secretary, officer or servant appointed on the establishment of the Secretary of State in Council, such compensation, superannuation or retiring allowance, or to his legal personal representative such gratuity, as may respectively be granted to persons on the establishment of a Secretary of State, or to the personal representatives of such persons, under the laws for the time being in force concerning superannuations and other allowances to persons having held civil offices in public service or to personal representatives of such perosons.

Indian Appointments.

19. Except as otherwise provided by this Act, all powers of making rules in relation to appointments and admissions to service and other matters connected therewith, and of altering or revoking such rules, which, if the Government of India Act, 1858, had not been passed, might have been exercised by the Court of Directors of the East India Company or the Commissioners for the Affairs of India, may be exercised by the Secretary of State in Council.

Provided that in the appointment of officers to His Majesty's army the same provision as heretofore or equal provision, shall be made for the appointment of sons of persons who have served in India in the military or civil service of the Crown or the East India Company.

COMMENTS.

Ss. 2—19 (both inclusive).

The Secretary of State for India is the direct descendant of the Board of Control, referred to in this Act as the Commsissioners for the Affairs of India, though his powers are much larger. He is the constitutional adviser of the Crown in all questions relating to India. He is appointed, like the other Secretaries of State in England, by the delivery of the seals of office. In passing it may be noticed, as a curiosity of the English constitution, that the office of the Secretary of State is a unit in the theory of the constitutional law of England, though there are really five Secretaries of State. Hence in speaking rather abruptly in s. 2 of the Secretary of State, the Act does not in any way specify him, since any Secretary of State is, theoretically, capable of discharging the duties of any other. Such division of work as there is in the English Secretariat is solely for the sake of administrative convenience, and has no reference to any corresponding distinction in point of law. The Secretary of State for India, however, enjoys power and position, not exactly identical with those of his colleagues. His salary for one thing, is paid not out of the revenues of England, but out of those of India. And in certain matters relating to his department, he is not the absolute master that other Secretaries of State are; he must, by this Act, act in consultation with his council. In all other respects the Secretary for India enjoys the same position. He is assisted by two under secretaries, one permanent, and the other Parliamentary, and both appointed by him. To the Secretary of State is paid an annual salary of £ 5000, to the Permanent Under Secretary an annual salary of £ 2000, and to the Parliamentary Under Secretary an annual salary of £ 1500.

In matters relating to India the Secretary of State has all the powers of the Board of Control, the Court of Directors of the East India Company, their Secret Committee, and the Court of Proprietors.

I. Powers of the Secretary of State.

He has the power of giving orders to every officer in India, including the Governor-General, and of directing all the business relating to the Government of India that is transacted in the United Kingdom. Every order or communication must be signed by him and every despatch from India must likewise be addressed to him.

In considering the position of the Secretary of State for India, it must always be remembered that he is primarily a member of the British Cabinet. As such his interest in his department is like the interest of all the heads of other departments, who are also members of the Cabinet, in England. It is the interest of a politician not that of an expert who knows and loves his work. A long standing convention, never broken since the Government of India was transferred from the Company to the Crown, has laid down that the Secretary of State for India in every Cabinet should be a man who has had previously no experience of or connection with India. He is the democratic chief to control a bureaucratic organization. His position in the Cabinet—of which he is an important member either by his social position or by his political reputation-keeps him in touch with imperial questions. While to the Cabinet he brings the knowledge and experience relating to the local departments of India, to the India Office he brings the wider outlook, the broader policy of an imperial statesman. The convention which keeps India altogether out of party politics may have resulted in modifying the principles of such men as Lord Morley when they went to the India office. But in general it must be admitted that upon the bureaucratic temper of the India Office, the Parliamentary Secretary of State serves a useful brake as he brings in an element of democratic responsibility. This respect for popular opinion—towards which the permanent officials in a department are openly hostile—is all the more emphasised when we remember that the Secretary of State is not only a member of the Cabinet but also a member of the British Parliament, perhaps of the House of Commons. As such, he has to be in constant touch with public opinion. He has always to be on his guard against any criticism from his colleagues in the legislative assembly; and while answering criticism, he must keep himself open to any suggestion or reform that comes from his critics. If the Secretary of State has any ambition to rise still higher in the world of English politics, it would not do for him to ignore altogether popular opinion. The authority, it is true, of Parliament as regards the Government of India is not wide in practice. The salary of the Secretary of State and the expenses of his department never come before Parliament for annual sanction. But yet the very fact of his presence in a democratic legislative assembly, coupled with his close relations with a body of men whose whole career, whose entire reputation, is based upon their successful carrying out of the fundamental principles of English democracy makes him listen to criticism even when he cannot be censured.

II. The Origin of the Council of India.

The Council of India, is, in a certain limited sense, the descendant of the old Court of Directors. When in 1858 the Government of India was brought directly under the Crown, a board of advisers was found to be necessary to aid the minister of the Crown in the Government of India. Under the Act of 1858 it consisted of 15 members, of whom 8 were appointed by the crown, and the remaining 7 were to be elected, in the first instance by the Court of Directors, and afterwards by the council itself. The members were appointed to hold office during good behaviour, *i. e.* during life; and they could only be removed by an address of both the Houses of Parliament to the Sovereign, just like the Judges in England. In 1869 the right of appointing new members as vacancies occurred in the council was vested in the Secretary of State (32 & 33 Vict., c. 97); the tenure of office was also changed from life, or during good behaviour, to a term of ten years, with the power of reappointment for another five years for special reasons. Twenty years later, (52 & 53 Vict., c. 65) the vacancies as they arose need not be filled, but the Secretary of State could only appoint a new member when the number of the Councillors was reduced to ten. The number of the council was still further reduced and the term of office shortened, as well as the qualifications modified, so that at the present time the council consists of:—

> not less than ten and not more than fourteen members, appointed to hold office during a period of seven years, but re-eligible for a further term of five years for special reasons of public advantage which must be recorded in a minute by the Secretary of State and laid before Parliament, not removable from their office during that term except by an address of both Houses of Parliament, the members to be selected from those who have either served or resided in British India for at least ten years, and who must not have left India more than five years before their date of appointment.

The councillors, it may be noted, are not entitled to any pension after their seven or twelve years of service, though by a special Act of Parliament in 1876, an exception was made in the case of Sir Henry Maine, who was given a retiring pension of £ 500 a year; nor are the members of the council entitled to any compensation for the loss of office if Parliament reduces their number or otherwise deals with the constitution of the council.

III. The Composition of the Council.

If we examine critically the qualifications required for the membership of the Council of India, we find that we can divide the members of the India Council roughly speaking into four groups. **First,** and the most important as far as numbers are concerned, is the element of the retired servants of the Crown in India, who, having risen to eminence in their several departments in the service of the Crown in India, retire to their country in the fullness of time, and are there rewarded by this position of an India Councillorship. They furnish the experience gathered during their period of service, and may be taken to represent the expert opinion when questions arise affecting their several departments. The **second** element, important as evidencing the trend of recent developments, is that of the natives of India. Since 1907, it has become possible to appoint two natives of India to this council. Presumably they are there to represent the views of the Indian public on the several questions that may arise relating to Indian administration. The **third**—by no means a negligible—element consists of successful bankers, educationists, merchants etc. who are appointed to the council to furnish it with the light of experience, the maturity of judgment, which is expected to be characteristic of these men. The **last**—and never, numerically speaking, a very important element—is the element of the experts, whom the Secretary of State is at liberty to appoint in connection with some technical departments. At the present day, the council consists of the following gentlemen:—

(1) Sir William Edgerly, Vice President.
(2) Sir Felix O. Schuster, Bart.
(3) Sir Theodore Morrison, K. C. I. E.
(4) General Sir Edumund Barrow.
(5) Abbas Ali Beg, C. S. I., LL. D.
(6) Lawrence Currey.
(7) Sir William Duke, K. C. S. I., K. C. I. E.
(8) Sirdar Daljit Singh.
(9) Sir Charles Arnold White, K. C. S. I.
(10) Sir Murray Hammick, K. C. S. I., C. I. E.
(11) Sir Charles Bailey, G. C. S. I., I. S. O.

Of these, six have been the servants of the Crown in India either in the Civil, Military or Judicial departments. Sir Felix Schuster is an eminent London banker and Sir Theodore Morrison is an eminent educationist of India. Two of these are Indians. Every one of these members is a personage of experience with a good reputation for administrative skill and judgment. They are men, moreover, with a long and personal knowledge of Indian problems.

Their position as councillors or advisers of the Secretary of State is one of peculiar interest. Here is a body of men avowedly qualified to pronounce a good, reasoned opinion—perhaps the best of its kind in London—on questions relating to India. They are set up to advise a man who is as avowedly entirely ignorant of Indian questions. By an unwritten convention of the English constitution, a person appointed to be the Secretary of State is usually a man who has had previously no dealings with India. If we except men who have been reappointed Secretaries of State in two or more administrations, and if we except Sir Charles Wood, there has never been in all these years since the transfer of the Government to the Crown, a Secretary of State who had been previously in any way connected with Indian affairs. And yet the Secretary of State has a sufficient reserve of powers to outvote and overrule, in the most important questions concerning India, the whole of his council if need be.

IV. The Secretary of State and the India Council.

The Secretary of State for India under the present Act is the constitutional adviser of the Crown in all matters relating to India. He has all the powers which were formerly exercised by the Board of Control, the Court of Directors, and the Secret Committee of the Board of Directors in respect of the Government and revenues of India. In particular, he has the power of giving orders to every officer of the Crown in India including the Governor-General, and he directs all business about the Government of India transacted in the United Kingdom whether in borrowing moneys, purchasing stores or getting servants for the Government of India. Now in all these matters, the council is expected to advise him. He is not necessarily bound to accept their views in all matters. For, every order or communication sent to India must be signed by him, and every despatch from India must likewise be addressed to him. This legal recognition of the supremacy of the Secretary of State has more than formal importance. For, the same Act provides that the Secretary of State may act without consulting his council in the following cases:—

(*a*) In advising the Sovereign to make appointments left to his discretion, that is, in all the appointments from the Governors of Presidencies downwards which require the sanction of the Secretary of State, that officer need not consult his council, and if he can thus control the choice of men for the highest appointments in India, his power in the actual administration of India can be readily imagined.

(*b*) He need not also consult his council in sending or receiving communications to India and from India marked "Secret", nor even show such communications to his council. Such communications chiefly relate to the making of war or peace, to negotiations with foreign powers or to relations with the Native States. All these are questions of the highest administrative importance—questions involving some of the fundamental principles of Government, and yet on these questions the Act provides that the Secretary of State need not consult his council. As a rule he transacts business of this description through the Political Committee of his council which takes the place of the old Secret Committee of the Court of Directors.

(*c*) In other cases too, he need not consult his council, provided communications to or from India relating thereto are marked "Urgent", and provided that the Secretary of State has recorded reasons for regarding them urgent.

There are cases no doubt specified in this act, where the Secretary of State is bound to consult his council, and even to have the concurrence of a majority of the members of the council present at a meeting of the council. These are:—

(1) the appropriation of the revenues of India or property, S. 21,

(2) purchase, sale or mortgage of property, S. 28,

(3) the exercising of powers of entering in to contracts, S. 29,

(4) approving rules for making assurances inIndia S. 30,

(5) the alteration of salaries, furlough rules, etc., S. 85,

(6) appointments of natives of India to offices reserved for the Indian Civil Service and the making of provisional appointments to the Council of Governor-General, S. 91 & 99.

But all these are matters on which, normally speaking, there is very little probability of a difference of opinion arising between men of common sense. They involve no question of principle likely to divide such men as the council is generally composed of. And, therefore, the provision that the Secretary of State cannot act without the support of a majority of his council in such cases, has at best but an academic importance.

If we leave aside those cases on the one hand in which the Secretary of State must consult his council and abide by a decision of the majority of his council, and on the other hand those other and by far the most important cases in which he need not consult his council, the rest of the ordinary business of the administration is, it is provided, to be carried on by the Secretary of State in consultation with his council. But it does not mean that in such ordinary cases, even though he has to consult his council, he should abide by the opinion of a majority. Wherever he is not bound by law to have a majority of his council to support him, there is nothing to prevent the Secretary of State from taking a decision against the views of the council-even of the whole council. The utmost that the council can demand is that their views, and the reasons for those views, should be entered on the records of the council, with some faint hope that one day when the public should come to know of their transactions, it should be able to apportion the blame or the merit to the right persons. Hence it follows that the position of the Secretary of State carries with it great powers which practically make him absolute in the government of India. He has an advisory council, but the peculiar position of that body prevents it from being of any effective check upon the powers of the Secretary of State.

V. Control of the Secretary of State over the Council.

The Secretary of State can control the conucil in more than one way.

1. He has the right to fill any vacancy that may be caused in the council by the death or resignation or the expiry of the term of office of a councillor [S.3 (2)]. True, he has not the right to remove a councillor, and he cannot therefore at any given time create his council to suit his views. It is also probable that the security of tenure given to the India councillors makes it impossible that during the tenure of office of the Secretary of State by one individual, the whole council would or could be renovated by that individual to suit his tastes. The fluctuations in English politics, and the continual transfer of the leading politicians from department to department, make the average tenure of office of a Secretary of State by any one individual never longer than the tenure of his councillors. Including reappointments of the same individual, there have been in the fifty-eight years that have elapsed since the transfer of the Government to the Crown, twenty-two Secretaries of State, or an average duration of office of each Secretary of State for slightly over two years and a half, while the normal duration of a councillor's office is now seven years. But still if all allowance is made for this, the fact remains that the power of appointment vested in the Secretary of State gives him a great influence on his council. Apart from the gratitude, the force of which in the cases of such independent men as the councillors of India may be negligible, there is always the possibility of similarity of views influencing a Secretary of State in choosing his concillors. And particularly his power to appoint experts in his council is bound to give him a great influence on his Council.

[*N. B.*—This power to appoint experts to the council is not specifically given by this Act. But it was conferred on the

Secretary of State by 39 & 40 Vict. c. 7; and as this Act has not been repealed by the present Act we may take it that the power remains. The provisions of that Act have been thus summed up by Courtney Ilbert:—

" The Secretary of State may also, if he thinks fit, appoint any person having professional or other peculiar qualification to be a member of the Council of India during good behaviour. (In view of the very general language of S. 3 (4) of this Act it would seem as though such a member also can only be appointed for a period of 7 years, or re-appointed for special reasons for another period of 5 years, or in all twelve years, and not for life.) The special reasons for every such appointment must be stated in a minute signed by the Secretary of State and laid before both Houses of Parliament. Not more than three persons so appointed may be members of the council at the same time. If a member so appointed resigns his office, and has at the date of his resignation been a member of the council for more than ten years the King may, by warrant under his sign manual, countersigned by the Chancellor of the Exchequer, grant to him out of the revenues of India a retiring pension during life of five hundred pounds." He adds in a note, "This exceptional power was exercised in the case of Sir H. S. Maine, and was probably conferred with special reference to his case".]

(2) The mode of conducting the business in the Council also helps to increase the powers of the Secretary of State. As a rule the council is divided into committees as nearly as possible corresponding to the departments of Government. To each committee are appointed four or five councillors with some consideration of their special aptitude for the subjects allotted to each particular committee. It is easier to influence a small body of men, however experienced or obstinate they may be, than to influence a larger body especially if they all agree in a particular opinion, and are men of status. And even if this was not always feasible, the system of working by committees is the surest way of creating difference of opinion and using that for one's own object. Provided the Secretary of State can find either the council as a whole to agree with him, or the committee to adopt his side of the question, he can always have his way; for the support of the council may be represented, if it suits him so to represent it, as the support of common sense against the narrow-minded view of the experts, the committee being regarded as experts of the narrowest views; and if the committee agrees with him and the council as a whole differs from him, he can claim the support of what would now be represented as the sound practical opinion of the men who know their busines. The council meets once a week, and the quorum of five is required. At these meetings the reports of the different committees on different questions are considered in the council. This procedure of transacting business through the committees is of course convenient, but it does weaken the practical utility of the council as a check upon the Secretary of State. The recent proposal in July 1914 to give this procedure, a matter of convenience, the force of law would have perpetuated a system resulting in the practical impotence of the council.

3. Apart from these modes of controlling the council, the Secretary of State has large reserves of powers behind him which would in any case render the council's opposition, even if it makes one, nugatory. In some of the most important questions such as making war or peace, or conducting foreign relations, or cases of urgent emergencies, the Secretary of State need not consult his council. In others again,–by far the largest number of questions though he may consult his council, he is not bound to accept the advice of his council. Such powers cannot but make the Secretary of State the absolute chief of his department even though he has been furnished with constitutional advisers.

4. His position is further strengthened by the monopoly of information. The members of the council have no means of collecting materials for pronouncing an opinion upon any question beyond the information that the Secretary of State places at their disposal, or beyond such information as they can get in common with the ordinary public from the periodical press. Says Sir John Strachey, "Such questions as the Afgan war, negotiations with Russia and the Amir of Kabul regarding the affairs of

Afganistan, or the annexation of Burma do not come before the council. Its members have not only no powers of interference but they have no recognised means of obtaining information in regard to such subjects other than those of the general public". Wanting in information, they can never make up their minds on some of the most important questions. In this respect, the present position of the council differs radically from that of the Court of Directors of the East India Company even after they were superceded by the Board of Control from 1784. The present Council of India can only offer an opinion on matters which the Secretary of State chooses to bring before them, while the Court of Directors received in the first instance all despatches sent from India, and sent in their own name all the despatches from England to India.

5. The Secretary of State, in all matters when he goes counter to the opinion of a majority of his council, can always make a show of independent unbiassed judgment. The fact that the members of the council have all been for a long time connected with India and have all had, in their period of service or residence in India, occasions for crystallising their information on certain matters,—perhaps for becoming partisans on certain questions,—can often be adduced by the Secretary of State as a reason to discredit their judgment. Unlike them he comes to his office with an open mind. A partisan himself in English politics, he claims an entirely unbiassed judgment in Indian affairs. For he comes to his office with no preconceived notions, nor prejudices nor pre-possessions. Such a man, himself of assured status and acknowledged experience in the politics of his own country, may reasonably claim that on questions of fundamental principles, he is a better judge than men who are likely to be partisan, or prejudiced. Besides, his position as the representative of the English democracy at the head of the Indian bureaucracy may well induce him to discount the opinion of a body of men, who could not be in touch with the latest information about Indian questions inspite of their long experience who have perhaps left India some years ago, and whose experience therefore of India is likely to be ten years out of date, while he himself, coming new

to his office, has all the desire to study at first hand all the questions of his department and has every facility to make his knowledge upto date.

6. But the causes which make the Secretary of State supreme in the council are still deeper. His power over appointments, his monopoly of information, the peculiar mode of conducting business, and of using an independent judgment are all but indications of those deeper springs of action, which, because they are seldom brought to light, not the less exist. The Secretary of State is a member of the British Cabinet and also of the British Parliament. To his department, he brings not only an open mind but the long experience and wider outlook of the Imperial Cabinet, and the democratic temperament of the British Parliament. If an occasion should ever arise when the Secretary of State finds himself obliged to disagree with a majority of his council, he can always in the last resource plead in his favour the support of the Cabinet, and also if necessary that of the British Parliament. In questions of policy a man who can speak before his colleagues, who have no other ways of making their opinion known to the public—with the united authority of the Cabinet and the Parliament behind his back, who can refuse to justify or explain a policy, when questioned in Parliament or when criticised by the Government, unless his view of the case is accepted, is bound to create a deep impression upon those colleagues. Hence even in those cases where the Secretary of State is by law bound to have a majority of the council supporting him, his views, should they differ from those of the majority of the council, are bound to command respect, if not from the intrinsic value of those views, at least from the position and the power of the man who maintains them.

VI. The Future of the Council.

The question has been widely debated as to whether it is beneficial to India to leave such vast powers in the absolute control of a man who, however experienced in English politics, is admittedly an amateur in Indian questions. If it was deemed wise by those who were responsible for the act of 1858 transferring the Government of the country to the Crown to provide this responsible officer of the State with some checks, would it not be as well to make those checks effective. At the present day, the council, whenever it disagrees with the Secretary of State, however much its views may be favourable to India, is unable to make its views appreciated or respected by the Secretary of State. And there is no means by which the Council could be so reformed as to be entrusted with wider powers. Even if we suppose that the elective element were to predominate in the Council of India, or to become the sole basis of the constitution of that council, its powers would not be appreciably increased. And if they increased the increase would not necessarily be beneficial to India. For, the questions of Indian politics are so intricate that no body of men—whether the elected representatives of India, or expert or experienced nominees of any other authority, would ever be able to give satisfactory solutions, if they are located at a distance from India. As Mill wrote "The Executive Government of India is and must be seated in India itself. The principal function of the Home Government is not to direct the details of administration, but to criticise or review the past Acts of the Indian Government; to lay down principles and issue general instructions for their future guidance and to give or refuse sanction to great political measures which are referred Home for approval." Citing this opinion with approval, Sir John Strachey adds, "The work of the Secretary of State is mainly confined to answering references made to him by the Government in India; and apart from great political and financial questions, the number and nature of those references mainly depend on the character of the Governor-General for the time being. Some men in that position like to minimise personal responsiblity and to ask for the orders of the Home Government before taking action. Others prefer to act on their own judgment, and on that of their councillors. **The Secretary of State initiates almost nothing.**" It is true Lord Minto said that the last instalment of reforms were initiated in India by the Government of India and not by Lord Morley, but there are instances also on the other side, when the Home Government has initiated and enforced measures upon India, such as the tariff policy of the Government of India. On the whole, however, it is still true that the Secretary of State for India-in Council confines himself ordinarily to reviewing, revising or refusing his sanction to measures or proposals referred to him from India. With this view of the functions of the Home authorities of the Indian Government, every student of political science cannot but agree. It may happen, and it has frequently happened in history, that the governing authorities of one people are situated in another; but if the ideal of government is good government,–government in the interests of the governed,–in whatever form it may be organised, that ideal would never be realised so long as it is hoped to rule a distant dependency from one headquarters in all the details of administration. And especially is this true of a dependency like India which is so utterly dissimilar to England in every respect. The authors of the transfer of the Government of India to the Crown well understood this, and so they left to the Home authorities the power to advise, to criticise, to reject acts and proposals of the Government of India. The idea of providing an advisory council to the chief authority in England was not to strengthen the hands of the Secretary of State at the expense of the local powers, but to enable him to exercise all the better his powers of supervision and control. Another reason, of which the authors of the transfer were barely conscious, was the distrust of every English statesman of the time of all bureaucracies. The Council of India was to be a check, not so much on the Secretary of State, as on the Government of India. The reason for introducing such a deliberate check was obvious. The Government of India was in reality an autocracy; autocracies are bound to go astray,—at any rate to ignore the views of the people; to bring about good Government some popular check,—preferably of the English type, of course,—was indispensable; but the people of India were not in a position to exert that check; hence the establishment of the Council of India consisting of men whom it would be dangerous for any power to thwart. Some such train of reasoning must have guided the men who fixed the first constitution of India under the Crown. The Council of India according to this view does duty for the people of India in checking the otherwise all-powerful Government of India. Any reform in the constitution of that council, any increase in its power can be allowed only if we admit that the people of India are yet unfit, or unable to provide their own effective check on their Government. The need for the Council of India must disappear when the governing authorities in India become amenable to the control of the people of the country.

Accordingly we need say very little of that abortive attempt made a few years ago to amend the constitution of the India Council. The Bill in question tried to reduce the number of the councillors, to make the inclusion of at least two Indian members a statutory requirement, to secure the appointment of the Indian members by a system of indirect election by the non-official members of the Indian legislatures, to increase the salaries of the members to £ 1200 a year together with an additional allowance, in the case of Indian members, of £ 600, to appoint one expert for a period and on conditions to be specially laid down in each case; to simplify the procedure of the council by rules made by the Secretary of State—subject to approval by Parliament, to dispense with the meetings of the council once a week, and to increase the list of "secret" cases with which the Secretary of State may deal without consulting his council. The Bill evoked a strong opposition both in England and in India, for reasons into which we need not go into details, and it was eventually dropped.

The reasoning, however, which leads one to discount the importance of the India Council should not be construed to mean that, the people of India being able to provide their own check, there should be no connection with England in the future. Even when the people of India will be governing themselves in name as well as in fact, there will remain a strong case for keeping up connection with England, and, therefore, maintaining the Secretary of State for India as well as, quite probably, his council. Only in the event of the people of this country being able to impose their will on their Government there will be no occasion for an outside power like the India Council to act their guardian. The Home authorities, under that supposition, would have no need to interfere in the internal affairs of India, their powers of direction and control being ordinarily confined to inter-colonial or foreign questions, in other words in truly Imperial matters.

VII. Indian Appointments.

As regards Indian appointments, under the Company the Court of Directors had the power to make all appointments to every office in the state in India. Since Pitt's India Act of 1784, the Directors were required to obtain the approval of the Crown in making certain appointments to the highest posts in India, though this clause was removed by an Act of 1786. The Crown, however, retained its powers of recalling, by a sign-manual order, any public officer in India; and this power was confirmed by the Charter Act of 1793 and subsequent legislation. The Directors also had a similar power of recall, and they often exercised it, as for instance in the case of Lord Ellenborough. With the transfer of the Government to the Crown, the provision was introduced as regards the power to make rules for the admission of persons to the public service of the country, which is now embodied in s. 19 of the present Act. Two points in that section call for comment. First as regards the provision about appointments in the Indian army. At least one-ten th of the total cadetships in any year are reserved fort he sons of those who had served in India in the military or civil service of the Crown or of the East India Company. This is due to historical resaons. At the time of the transfer the officers for the Indian army were recruited in two ways:–A certain number of cadets was appointed to Addiscombe, from which, according to their success at the college examinations, they went out to India in the engineers, artillery or infantry. Others received direct cadetships and went to India without any previous training. The Indian army was reorganised in 1860. The European army, which till then had been a separate body, was abolished and the abolishing Act (23 & 24 Vict., c. 100) laid down that the same or equal provision for the sons of persons who have served in India shall be maintained in any scheme for the reorganisation of the Indian army. The mode of appointments to the native army was meanwhile also altered, and an order was made in 1862 by which the Secretary of State makes 20 annual appointments, from among the sons of Indian servants to cadetships at Sandhurst. The expenses of these cadets are paid out of the revenues of India if their pecuniary circumstances are such as to require such payment. The cadets, it may be noted, need not join the Indian army after they leave Sandhurst.

Another point requiring comment in this section about appointments is that all the appointments are made during the pleasure of the sovereign, though in practice the Secretary of State enters into a formal contract with persons appointed in England to the various branches of public service in India. Many of these contracts contain a clause by which the men appointed to the service are appointed for a definite term of years. The question whether, during the continuance of the stipulated term of service, the Crown can remove any public officer from his office, on the principles laid down in many cases, "in the present state of the authorities cannot be considered free from doubt", says Sir C. Ilbert. A case in point is *Grant V, the Secretary of State for India in Council.* Grant was an officer in the service of the East India Company since 1840. On the transfer of the Indian army to the Crown, he was continued in the Indian army, and was afterwards placed compulsorily on the Pension List, being thereby obliged to retire from the army. He brought an action for damages against the defendant, but it was held that there was no cause of action as the Crown acting through the defendant had a general power to dismiss a military officer at its will, and no contract could be made in derogation of that power. If this case holds good the Crown can presumably dismiss any public officer at its will. This question of contracts with the Secretary of State on behalf of the Crown is considered more fully below in the comments on ss. 20-32.

PART II.

THE REVENUES OF INDIA.

20. (1) The revenues of India shall be received for and in the name of His Majesty, and shall, subject to the provisions of this Act, be applied for the purposes of the Government of India alone.

(2) There shall be charged on the revenues of India alone

(*a*) all the debts of the East India Company; and

(*b*) all sums of money, costs, charges and expenses which, if the Government of India Act, 1858, had not been passed, would have been payable by the East India Company out of the revenues of India in respect of any treaties, covenants, contracts, grants or liabilities existing at the commencement of that Act; and

(*c*) all expenses, debts and liabilities lawfully contracted and incurred on account of the Government of India; and

(*d*) all payments under this Act.

(3) The expression "the revenues of India" in this Act shall include all the territorial and other revenues of or arising in British India and, in particular,—

(1) all tributes and other payments in respect of any territories which would have been receivable by or in the name of the East India Company if the Government of India Act, 1858, had not been passed; and

(2) all fines and penalties incurred by the sentence or order of any court of justice in British India, and all forfeitures for crimes of any moveable or immoveable property in British India; and

(3) all moveable or immoveable property in British India escheating or lapsing for want of an heir or successor, and all property in British India devolving as bona vacantia for want of a rightful owner.

(4) All property vested in or arising or accruing from property or rights vested in His Majesty under the Government of India Act,

1858, or this Act, or to be received or disposed of by the Secretary of State in Council under this Act, shall be applied in aid of the revenues of India.

21. The expenditure of the revenues of India, both in British India and elsewhere, shall be subject to the control of the Secretary of State in Council; and no grant or appropriation of any part of those revenues, or of any other property coming into the possession of the Secretary of State in Council by virtue of the Government of India Act, 1858, or this Act, shall be made without the concurrence of a majority of votes at a meeting of the Council of India.

22. Except for preventing or repelling actual invasion of His Majesty's Indian possessions, or under other sudden and urgent necessity, the revenues of India shall not, without the consent of both Houses of Parliament, be applicable to defraying the expenses of any military operation carried on beyond the external frontiers of those possessions by His Majesty's forces charged upon these revenues.

23. (1) Such part of the revenues of India as are remitted to the United Kingdom, and all money arising or accruing in the united Kingdom from any property or rights vested in His Majesty for the purposes of the Government of India or from the sale or disposal thereof, shall be paid to the Secretary of State in Council, to be applied for the purposes of this Act.

(2) All such revenues and money shall, except as by this section provided, be paid into the Bank of England to the credit of an account entitled "The account of the Secretary of State in Council of India."

(3) The money placed to the credit of that account shall be paid out on drafts or orders, either signed by two members of the Council of India and countersigned by the Secretary of State or one of his under-secretaries or his assistant under-secretary, or signed by the accountant-general on the establishment of the Secretary of State in Council, or by one of the two senior clerks in the department of that accountant-general and countersigned in such manner as the Secretary of State in Council directs; and any draft or order so signed and countersigned shall effectually discharge the Bank of England for all money paid thereon.

(4) The Secretary of State in Council may, for the payment of current demands, keep at the Bank of England such accounts as he

deems expedient; and every such account shall be kept in such name and be drawn upon by such person and in such manner, as the Secretary of State in Council directs.

(5) There shall be raised in the books of the Bank of England such accounts as may be necessary in respect of stock vested in the Secretary of State in Council; and every such account shall be entitled "the Stock Account of the Secretary of State in Council of India".

(6) Every account referred to in this section shall be a public account.

24. The Secretary of State in Council, by power of attorney executed by two members of the Council of India and counter-signed by the Secretary of State or one of his under-secretaries or his assistant under-secretary, may authorise all or any of the cashiers of the Bank of England:

(*a*) to sell and transfer all or any part of any stock standing in the books of the Bank to the account of the Secretary of State in Council, and

(*b*) to purchase and accept stock for any such account, and

(*c*) to receive dividends on any stock standing to any such account;

and by any writing signed by two members of the Council of India and countersigned as aforesaid, may direct the application of the money to be received in respect of any such sale or dividend.

Provided that stock shall not be purchased or sold and transferred under the authority of any such general power of attorney, except on an order in writing directed to the chief cashier and chief accountant of the Bank of England, and signed and countersigned as aforesaid.

25. All securities held by or lodged with the Bank of England in trust for or in account or on behalf of the Secretary of State in Council may be disposed of, and the proceeds thereof may be applied, as may be authorised by order in writing-signed by two members of the Council of India and countersigned by the Secretary of State or one of his under-secretaries or his assistant under-secretary, and

directed to the chief cashier and chief accountant of the Bank of England.

26. The Secretary of State in Council shall, within the first fourteen days during which Parliament is sitting next after the first day of May in every year, lay before both Houses of Parliament:—

(*a*) an account, for the financial year preceding that last completed, of the annual produce of the revenues of India, distinguishing the same under the respective heads thereof, in each of the several provinces; and of all the annual receipts and disbursements at home and abroad for the purposes of the Government of India, distinguishing the same under the respective heads thereof;

(*b*) the latest estimate of the same for the financial year last completed;

(*c*) account of all stocks, loans, debts and liabilities chargeable on the revenues of India, at home and abroad, at the commencement and close of the financial year preceding that last completed, the loans, debts and liabilities raised or incurred within that year, the amounts paid off or discharged during that year, the rates of interest borne by those loans, debts and liabilities respectively, and the annual amount of that interest;

(*d*) an account of the state of the effects and credits in each province, and in England or elsewhere, applicable to the purposes of the Government of India, according to the latest advices which have been received thereof; and,

(*e*) a list of the establishment of the Secretary of State in Council, and the salaries and allowances payable in respect thereof.

(2) If any new or increased salary or pension of fifty pounds a year or upwards has been granted or credited within any year in respect of the said establishment, the particulars thereof shall be specially stated and explained at the foot of the account for that year,

(3) The account shall be accompanied by a statement, prepared from detailed reports from each province, in such form as best exhibits the moral and material progress and condition of India.

27. (1) His Majesty may, by warrant under His Royal Sign-Manual, countersigned by the Chancellor of the Exchequer, appoint a fit person to be auditor of the accounts of the Secretary of State in Council, and authorise that auditor to appoint and remove such assistants as may be specified in the warrant.

(2) The auditor shall examine and audit the accounts of the receipt, expenditure and disposal in the United Kingdom of all money, stores and property applicable for the purposes of this Act.

(3) The Secretary of State in Council shall, by the officers and servants of his establishment, produce and lay before the auditor all such accounts, accompanied by proper vouchers for their support, and submit to his inspection all books, papers, and writings having relation thereto.

(4) The auditor may examine all such officers and servants of that establishment, being in the United Kingdom, as he thinks fit, in relation to such accounts and the receipt, expenditure or disposal of such money, stores and property, and may for that purpose, by writing signed by him, summon before him any such officer or servant.

(5) The auditor shall report to the Secretary of State in Council his approval or disapproval of the accounts aforesaid, with such remarks and observations in relation thereto, as he thinks fit, specially noting cases (if any) in which it appears to him that any money arising out of the revenues of India has been appropriated to purposes other than those to which they are applicable.

(6) The auditor shall specify in detail in his reports all sums of money, stores and property which ought to be accounted for, and are not brought into account, or have not been appropriated in conformity with the provisions of the law, or which have been expended or disposed of without due authority, and shall also specify any defects, inaccuracies or irregularities which may appear in the accounts, or in the authorities, vouchers, or documents having relation thereto.

(7) The auditor shall lay his reports before both Houses of Parliament, with the accounts of the year to which the reports relate.

(8) The auditor shall hold office during good behaviour.

(9) There shall be paid to the auditor and his assistants, out of the revenues of India, such salaries as His Majesty, by warrant signed and countersigned as aforesaid, may direct.

(10) The auditor and his assistants (notwithstanding that some of them do not hold certificates from the Civil Service Commissioners) shall, for the purposes of superannuation allowance, be in the same position as if they were on the establishment of the Secretary of State in Council.

PART III.

PROPERTY, CONTRACTS AND LIABILITIES.

28. (1) The Secretary of State in Council may, with the concurrence of a majority of votes at a meeting of the Council of India, sell and dispose of any real or personal estate for the time being vested in His Majesty for the purposes of the Government of India, and raise money on any such real estate by way of mortgage, and make the proper assurances for any of those purposes, and purchase and acquire any property.

(2) Any assurance relating to the real estate made by the authority of the Secretary of State in Council, may be made under the hands and seals of three members of the Council of India.

(3) All property acquired in pursuance of this section shall vest in His Majesty for the purposes of the Government of India.

29. (1) The Secretary of State in Council may, with the concurrence of a majority of votes at a meeting of the Council of India, make any contract for the purposes of this Act.

(2) Any contract so made may be expressed to be made by the Secretary of State in Council.

(3) Any contract so made which, if it were made between private persons, would be by law required to be under seal, may be

made, varied or discharged under the hands and seals of two members of the Council of India.

(4) Any contract so made which, if it were made between private persons, would be by law required to be signed by the party to be charged therewith, may be made, varied or discharged under the hands of two members of the Council of India.

(5) Provided that any contract for or relating to the manufacture, sale, purchase, or supply of goods, or for or relating to affreightment or the carriage of goods, or to insurance, may, subject to such rules and restrictions as the Secretary of State in Council prescribes, be made and signed on behalf of the Secretary of State in Council by any person upon the permanent establishment of the Secretary of State in Council who is duly empowered by the Secretary of State in Council in this behalf. Contracts so made and signed shall be as valid and effectual as if made as prescribed by the foregoing provisions of this section. Particulars of all contracts so made and signed shall be laid before the Secretary of State in Council in such manner and form and within such times as the Secretary of State in Council prescribes.

(6) The benefit and liability of every contract made in pursuance of this section shall pass to the Secretary of State in Council for the time being.

30. (1) The Governor-General in Council and any local Government may, on behalf and in the name of the Secretary of State in Council, and subject to such provisions or restrictions as the Secretary of State in Council, with the concurrence of a majority of votes at a meeting of the Council of India, prescribes, sell and dispose of any real or personal estate whatsoever in British India, within the limits of their respective Governments, for the time being vested in His Majesty for the purposes of the Government of India, or raise money on any such real estate by way of mortgage, and make proper assurances for any of those purposes, and purchase or acquire any property in British India within the said respective limits, and make any contract for the purposes of this Act.

(2) Every assurance and contract made for the purposes of this section shall be executed by such person and in such manner as the Governor-General in Council by resolution directs or authorises,

and if so executed may be enforced by or against the Secretary of State in Council for the time being.

(3) All property acquired in pursuance of this section shall vest in His Majesty for the purposes of the Government of India.

31. The Governor-General in Council, and any other person authorised by any Act passed in that behalf by the Governor-General in Legislative Council, may make any grant or disposition of any property in British India accruing to His Majesty by forfeiture, escheat or lapse, or by devolution as bona vacantia, to or in favour of any relative or connection of the person from whom the property has accrued, or to or in favour of any other person.

32. (1) The Secretary of State in Council may sue and be sued by the name of the Secretary of State in Council, as a body corporate.

(2) Every person shall have the same remedies against the Secretary of State in Council as he might have had against the East India Company if the Government of India Act, 1858, and this Act had not been passed.

(3) The property for the time being vested in His Majesty for the purposes of the Government of India shall be liable to the same judgments and executions as it would have been liable to in respect of liabilities lawfully incurred by the East India Company if the Government of India Act, 1858, and this Act had not been passed.

(4) Neither the Secretary of State nor any member of the Council of India shall be personally liable in respect of any assurance or contract made by or on behalf of the Secretary of State in Council, or any other liability incurred by the Secretary of State in Council in his or their official capacity, nor in respect of any contract covenant or engagement of the East India Company; nor shall any person executing any assurance in Council be personally liable in respect thereof, but all such liabilties and all costs and damages in respect thereof, shall be borne by the revenues of India.

COMMENTS.

Ss. 20-32 (inclusive).

The Act speaks throughout of the revenues of India when it would be more accurate to speak of the revenues of British

India, though the third sub-section defines the revenues to include "all tributes and other payments." Against the revenues of India were charged all the debts and liabilities of the East India Company in 1858, and the provision of the Act of 1858 has been repeated in this. The remark is, therefore, often made by the critics of this measure that while the British Crown got the rich patrimony of India, the people of India had to pay the purchase price. Under the East India Company India was conquered for the English traders by Indian soldiers, and when it passed to the Crown by an act of purchase, the price was paid not by England but by India.

Under the Company Parliament had frequently passed laws to restrain what the great Canning described as the irrepressible tendency of our Eastern empire to expand, but they were more frequently ignored than obeyed. The revenues of India were squandered in ceaseless and costly wars, and the Company was almost always in financial difficulties. To safeguard against this irrepressible tendency again asserting itself, it was provided by the Act of 1858 that the expenditure of the revenues of India, in India or outside India, shall be subject to the control of the Secretary of State. The latter was prohibited by the same Act from making any grant of these revenues or appropriating any part thereof, or assigning any property vesting in the Crown, except by the consent of a majority of the India Council. This provision has also been incorporated in the present Act. To make the assurance against a misuse of the revenues of India for military purposes still stronger, it has been further provided that without the consent of Parliament the revenues of India cannot be employed for military operations beyond the frontiers of India, except for preventing or repelling an actual invasion. This is a sufficiently vague provision to leave a margin of discretion to the Government of India and to the Secretary of State. Since the transfer of the Government of India to the Crown there have been numerous occasions on which the spirit of this section, if not the letter, has been infringed upon. In the Afghan war of 1878, in the Burma campaign of 1886, in the Egypt and Soudan campaign, and lastly during the Tibet Campaign of 1904, this section and its effects were discussed in Parliament. It is not yet quite clear whether the consent of Parliament is required before the actual declaration of war. The power to declare war is by the general principle of the British constitution vested in the Crown; and, in the case of the Government of India, is vested in the Crown acting through the Secretary of State by s. 13 of this Act. The consent of Parliament is only needed to appropriate the revenues of India for the purpose of the war already declared. Under the circumstances, it is not unlikely that Parliament would have to give its consent even if it disapproved of the war as such. And all this is apart from the saving clause, " except for preventing or repelling an actual invasion," for which, presumably, the consent of Parliament is not required. Fighting with neighbouring tribes, especially the ever turbulent neighbours of India, may easily be represented as an attempt to prevent a possible, or to repell an actual, invasion.

The revenues of India that are remitted to England or that arise in England are to be paid into the account of the Secretary of State for India in Council at the Bank of England. This account cannot be drawn upon except by a draft or an order signed either by two members of the Council and countersigned by the Secretary of State, or by one of his under-secretaries or by the assistant under-secretary, or signed by the accountant-general of the India Office or by one of the two senior clerks in that department, aud countersigned in the manner prescribed by the Secretary of State. There may also be a seperate account for the stocks and property held by the Secretary of State for India in Council. These accounts, together with a general statement of the moral and material progress of India, must be laid before Parliament at one time or another during the session, and by common practice they are so submitted at the fag end of the session. The accounts are to be audited by an independent officer, who must submit an independent account to both the Houses of Parliament, and whose appointment is during good behaviour.

As regards the contracts by the Secretary of State several points of legal and general importance have to be noted. (i) Contracts, which by English law, if made by private individuals, would have to be made under seal, should be made under the hand and seal of two members of the Council. (2) For making all such contracts the Secreatry of State must have a majority of votes with him in his Council. (3) For contracts so made the Secretary of State for India in Council is regarded as a corporation and may sue and be sued upon these contracts. (4) Neither the Secretary of State nor any member of his Council is personally responsible on these contracts. (5) The Secretary of State is not in the position of a body corporate for the purpose of holding property, though he is in the position of a body corporate for making contracts and for suing or being sued. (6) There is a statutary remedy against the Secretary of State which is not confined to those cases for which a petition of right will lie in England; but it would seem that only such suits,—apart from special statutary provision—may be brought against the Secretary of State as are in respect of acts done in the conduct of undertakings which might be carried on by private individuals without sovereign powers. (7) Hence a suit or action against the Secretary of State may sometimes be met by the plea that the act complained of was an act of state. All these points are illustrated by a few cases given below.

According to a maxim of the constitutional law of England the King can do no wrong, and so the subject in England has no remedy, not even by a petition of right. For a wrong committed in obedience or professed obedience to the Crown the remedy is against the wrong-doer himself, and not his official superior, since the ultimate superior, the Crown, is not responsible. Even for a breach of contract the remedy is not by an ordinary action but by a petition of right, which, since the case of *R. vs. Thomas* in 1874, has been allowed in all cases of breach of contract. In the case of *Frith vs. Regina* in 1872, Frith, representing the creditor of the King of Oudh, whose territory was annexed by the East India Company in 1856, sought to recover the debt by a petition of right from the Queen as the successor of the East India Company. It was held that, assuming the East India Company became liable by reason of the annexation to pay the debt, the remedy of the suppliant was against the Secretary of State for India in Council, who, under the act of 1858, was the successor of the Company, and not the Crown. It was further pointed out that even if a judgment was given for the suppliant it would be barren since the revenues of England could not be liable to pay the claim. In the Tanjore case, (*Secretary of State in Council of India vs. Kamachee Bye Saheba 1856, 13 Moore P. C. 22*) a bill was filed on the equity side of the Supreme Court at Madras to establish a claim as private property to certain property of which the Government had taken possession and for an account. The acts in question were done by a commissioner on behalf of the Government for taking over the administration of the Tanjore State on the death of the Raja without heirs. It was held that the annexation was made by the British Government as a sovereign power, acting through its delegate the East India Company. As such it was an act of state to inquire into the propriety of which no court,—not even the Judicial Committe—ewas competent. Lord Kingsdowne, giving judgment in the Privy Council in that case remarked: "It is sufflcient to say that even if a wrong has been done, it is a wrong for which no municipal court can afford a remedy." The principle of this case was upheld in a quite recent case. The principle was slightly different in *Forester & others vs. the Secretary of State for India in Council*. There the Government of India had resumed the property of Begum Sumroo on her death, and the legality of that act was questioned by her heirs. It appeared that the Begum was not quite an independent sovereign at the time of her death, but a British subject. Hence the annexation of her estate was not the annexation by arbitrary power of the territories of one sovereign power by another, but the resumption, under colour of legal title, oflands previously held from the Government by a subject under a particular tenure, on the alleged determination of that tenure. The questions in that suit, therefore, were regarded as cognisable by a municipal court. The facts in Dhulip Sing's case were very nearly the same as in the Tanjore case and the same principles were upheld. (*Salaman vs. the Secretary of State for India in Council, 1905, 1 K. B. 613*).

Apart from the acts of state the Secretary of State as a corporate body is able to sue and be sued in respect of contracts; but in contracts of service regard must be had also to the principles regulating the tenure of servants under the Crown. In the case of *Jehangir M. Cursetji vs. the Secretary of State for India in Council* (*I. L. R. 27 Bom. 189*) the plaintiff was a Huzur Deputy Collector in Poona, and for certain acts done by him he was censured by a Resolution of the Government of Bombay, dated 6th November 1899. This censure was construed by the plaintiff into a defamation and he sued the Secretary of State for the same. It was held (*a*) that the Governor of Bombay and the members of his Council are exempt by law from the jurisdiction of the High Court of Bombay for acts done in their public capacity. Hence no action lies against the Secretary of State in respect of such acts. (*b*) The Secretary of State could only be sued in respect of those matters for which the East India Company could have been sued, *i. e.* matters for which private individuals and trading corporations could be sued and those matters for which there is express statutary provision. No suit would lie against the East India Company in respect of acts of state, and so no suit lies against the Secretary of State for such matters. (*c*) The plaintiff was a public officer, whose employment was one which could only be given to him by the sovereign or the agents of the sovereign. Such public servants hold their office at the pleasure of the sovereign, being liable to dismissal at his will and pleasure, if that power is not limited by statutary provision as for instance in the case of the members of the Council of India. The power of dismissal includes all other powers of censure or repremand. We may at the cost of some repetition, but for the sake of clearness, sum up once again the position of the Secretary of State in respect of contracts as follows:—

For the purpose of making contracts the Secretary of State is a body corporate–or in the same position as a body corporate, though he is not such for holding property. Such property, as would have formerly vested in the East India Company, now vests in the Crown. [*Kinlock vs. the Secretary of State in Council 1880, L. R. 15 Ch. D.*] The debts due to the Secretary of State in India rank in priority of all other debts. There is a statutary remedy provided against the Secretary of State, and that remedy is not confined to those cases for which a petition of right would lie in England. But, apart from special statutary provisions, the only suits which could have been brought against the East India Company, and which can now be brought against the Secretary of State in Council, are suits in respect of acts done in the conduct of undertakings which might be carried on by private individuals. Hence if an act complained of was an act done by the Secretary of State in the exercise of the sovereign power of the Crown, and on behalf of the Crown, no court of justice would have jurisdiction to try that case. In suits or actions against the Secretary of State for breach of contract of service, regard must also be had to the principles regulating the tenure of servants under the Crown. And the liability of the Secretary of State in Council to be sued does not deprive the Crown of its privileges by virtue of its prerogatives.

Before commencing an action against the Secretary of State notice of 2 months must be given according to S. 80 of the Civil Procedure Code of 1908.

CHAPTER III.

The Governor-General in Council.

PART IV

GENERAL POWERS AND DUTIES OF THE GOVERNOR-GENERAL IN COUNCIL.

The Governor-General in Council.

33. The superintendence, direction and control of the civil and military Government of India is vested in the Governor-General in Council, who is required to pay due obedience to all such orders as he may receive from the Secretary of State.

The Governor-General.

34. The Governor-General of India is appointed by his Majesty by warrant under the Royal Sign Manual.

The Governor-General's Executive Council.

55. The Governor-General's Executive Council consists of the ordinary members and the extra-ordinary members (if any) thereof.

36. (1) The ordinary members of the Governor-General's Executive Council shall be appointed by His Majesty by warrant under the Royal Sign Manual.

(2) The number of the ordinary members of the Council shall be five, or, if His Majesty thinks fit to appoint a sixth member, six.

(3) Three at least of them must be persons who at the time of their appointment have been for at least ten years in the service of the Crown in India, and one must be a barrister of England

or Ireland, or a member of the Faculty of Advocates of Scotland, of not less than five years standing.

(4) If any person appointed an ordinary member of the council is at the time of his appointment in the military service of the Crown, he shall not, during his continuance in office as such member, hold any military command or be employed in actual military duties.

37. (1) The Secretary of State in Council may, if he thinks fit, appoint the commander-in-chief for the time being of His Majesty's forces in India to be an extraordinary member of the Governor-General's Executive Council, and in that case the commander-in-chief shall, subject to the provisions of this Act, have rank and precedence in the council next after the Governor-General.

(2) When and so long as the council assembles in any province having a Governor, he shall be an extraordinary member of the council.

38. The Governor-General shall appoint a member of his Executive Council to be vice-president thereof.

39. (1) The Governor-General's Executive Council shall assemble at such places in India as the Governor-General in Council appoints.

(2) At any meeting of the council the Governor-General or other person presiding and one ordinary member of the council may exercise all the functions of the Governor-General in Council.

40. (1) All orders and other proceedings of the Governor-General in Council shall be expressed to be made by the Governor-General in Council, and shall be signed by a secretary to the Government of India, or otherwise, as the Governor-General in Council may direct.

(2) The Governor-General may make rules and orders for the more convenient transaction of business in his executive council, and every order made, or act done, in accordance with such rules and orders, shall be treated as being the order or the act of the Governor-General in Council.

41. (1) If any difference of opinion arises on any question brought before a meeting of the Governor-General's Executive Council

the Governor-General in Council shall be bound by the opinion and decision of the majority of those present, and, if they are equally divided, the Governor-General or other person presiding shall have a second or casting vote.

(2) Provided that whenever any measure is proposed before the Governor-General in Council whereby the safety, tranquility or interests of British India, or any part thereof, are or may be, in the judgment of the Governor-General, essentially affected, and he is of opinion either that the measure proposed ought to be adopted and carried into execution, or that it ought to be suspended or rejected, and the majority present at a meeting of the council dissent from that opinion, the Governor-General may, on his own authority and responsibility, adopt, suspend or reject the measure, in whole or in part.

(3) In every such case any two members of the dissentient majority may require that the adoption, suspension or rejection of the measure, and the fact of their dissent, be reported to the Secretary of State, and the report shall be accompanied by copies of any minutes which the members of the council have recorded on the subject.

(4) Nothing in this section shall empower the Governor-General to do anything which he could not have lawfully done with the concurrence of his council.

42. If the Governor-General is obliged to absent himself from any meeting of the council, by indisposition or any other cause, and signifies his intended absence to the council, the vice-president, or, if he is absent, the senior ordinary member present at the meeting, shall preside thereat, with the like powers as the Governor-General would have had if present:

Provided that if the Governor-General is at the time resident at the place where the meeting is assembled, and is not prevented by indisposition from signing any act of council made at the meeting, the act shall require his signature; but if he declines or refuses to sign it, the like provisions shall have effect as in cases where the Governor-General, when present, dissents from the majority at a meeting of the council.

43. (1) When the Governor-General in Conucil declares that it is expedient that the Governor-General should visit any part of India

unaccompanied by his executive council, the Governor-General in Council may, by order, authorize the Governor-General alone to exercise, in his discretion, all or any of the powers which might be exercised by the Governor-General in Council at meetings of the council.

(2) The Governor-General during absence from his Executive Council may, if he thinks it necessary, issue, on his own authority and responsibility, any order, which might have been issued by the Governor-General in Council, to any local Government, or to any officers or servants of the Crown acting under the authority of any local Government without previously communicating the order to the local Government; and any such order shall have the same force as if made by the Governor-General in Council; but a copy of the order shall be sent forthwith to the Secretary of State and to the local Government, with the reasons for making the order.

(3) The Secretary of State in Council may, by order, suspend until further order all or any of the powers of the Governor-General under the last foregoing subsection; and those powers shall accordingly be suspended as from the time of the receipt by the Governor-General of the order of the Secretary of State in Council.

War and Treaties.

44. (1) The Governor-General in Council may not, without the express order of the Secretary of State in Council, in any case (except where hostilities have been actually commenced, or preparations for the commencement of hostilities have been actually made against the British Government in India or against any prince or State dependent thereon, or against any prince or state whose territories His Majesty is bound by any subsisting treaty to defend or guarantee), either declare war or commence hostilities or enter into any treaty for making war against any prince or state in India, or enter into any treaty for guaranteeing the possessions of any such prince or state.

(2) In any such excepted case the Governor-General in Council may not declare war, or commence hostilities, or enter into any treaty

for making war, against any other prince or State than such as is actually committing hostilities or making preparations as aforesaid, and may not make any treaty for guaranteeing the possessions of any prince or state except on the consideration of that prince or state actually enagaging to assist His Majesty against such hostilities commenced or preparations made as aforesaid.

(3) When the Governor-General in Council commences any hostilities or makes any treaty, he shall forthwith communicate the same with the reasons therefor, to the Secretary of State.

COMMENTS.

Ss. 33—44 (both inclusive).

The provisions of this consolidating Act do not give an exhaustive statement of the powers of the Governor-General-in-Council. (1) The powers, for instance, of the Government of India, as the paramount power in India, extend beyond the limits of British India. (2) Again the Governor-General-in-Council as representing the Crown in India enjoys all those powers, privileges, prerogatives, and immunities appertaining to the Crown, as are appropriate to the case and consistent with the local legal system. Thus the rule is maintained that the Crown debts rank in priority of all other debts, or that the Crown is not bound by a statute unless expressly mentioned therein. *Ganpat Putaya vs. the Collector of Canara* (*I. L. R. 1, Bom. 7*) West J. said "It is a universal rule that the prerogative and the advantages it affords cannot be taken away except by the consent of the Crown embodied in statute. This rule of interpretation is well established and applies not only to the statutes passed by the British, but also to the Acts of the Indian legislature framed with constant reference to the rules recognised in England." (3) The Governor-General in Council has also by delegation powers of making treaties and arrangements with Asiatic states, of exercising jurisdiction in foreign territory, and of acquiring and ceding territory. It is not quite free from doubt whether the Crown in England can cede territory to foreign powers without the consent of Parliament, though the

Crown has undoubtedly the power to make treaties. It is admitted that a treaty made by the Crown in England, if it imposes any financial obligations upon the British citizens, will not be carried out unless its provisions are given effect to by an Act of Parliament. As regards other treaties involving cession of territory, recent practice has been to seek the approval of Parliament. In India, however, the power of the Governor-General-in-Council to make treaties and to cede or acquire territory thereunder has been long since recognised [*Damodhar Khan vs. Deoram Kanji, I. L. R. 1 Bom. 367*; *The Taluka of Kotda Sangani vs. the State of Gondal, A. C. 1906*] (4) The Government of India, moreover, derive certain of their powers not from the English Crown, but from the native rulers of the country whose place they have taken. Thus the rights of the Government in India in respect of lands and minerals in India are different from the similar rights of the Crown in England. The Governor-General may also be said to have the great Royal prerogative of pardoning criminals, though Ilbert says that power is doubted, since it has not been expressly conferred upon him by his warrant of appointment. This power is possessed by all colonial Governors; and the Viceroy, who is a representative of the King-Emperor par execellence, must be taken to have that power. The Code of Criminal Procedure gives power to remit sentences, and so the question is of little practical importance.

The present authority of the Governor-General-in-Council is, thus, not the result entirely of Parliamentary enactments. No doubt the Government of India have to work under the orders of the Home Government. In such matters as the reduction or increase in taxation, or measures which substantially affect the revenues; changes in the general financial policy regarding currency or debt; matters raising important administrative issues or involving considerable, unusual or novel expenditure the previous sanction of the Secretary of State in Council is required. But when all allowance is made for these, it still remains true that the Governor-General is the immediate ruler of the country. To him in Council are committed the weal and woe of this country. His powers are vast because in all ordinary matters his only superior is too far away from the actual seat of Government to control or overrule him; because to dictate to an authority like the Governor-General-in-Council requires an exceptionally strong personality or an overwhelmingly great principle; because the Viceroy enjoys powers— as the representative of the English Crown, as the successor of the great Moghul, which no Secretary of State can control, no Parliament can alter. And if besides all this, the opinion of the Governor-General-in-Council can be made to appear as the opinion of the people of India, the domination of the Secretary of Stare over the Government of India must be modified.

I. The Governor-General.

The Governor-General is an Imperial Officer appointed on the advice of the Prime Minister and not on the advice of the Secretary of State, by the Crown. He is also called the Viceroy, a title most frequently used in ordinary speech, but yet it has no legal authority, since it has never been employed in any Act of Parliament. The first time that title was used was in the proclamation of 1858 which announced the assumption of the Government of India by the Crown. In the course of the proclamation, Lord Canning was referred to as the first Viceroy and the Governor-General. This title of Viceroy is employed frequently in the statutes of Indian Orders and public notifications; and may be regarded as a title of ceremony used appropriately in connection with the said functions of the representative of His Majesty in India. The Viceroy has a salary of Rs. 256,00c a year.

The Governor-General is usually a man who has already made his reputation in English public life. He is either a diplomatist of experience or one who has served as governor in some of the British colonies. Though no definite qualifications for this office have been laid down, it seems to be generally understood that the highest executive office in India shall be given to a man who ha- already served his apprenticeship in the service of the Crown in one department or another. It is also understood in the same way that the Governor-General shall be a man who has had previously no connection with India. Like the Secretary of State he comes to his task perfectly new and entirely unprejudieed.

Since the transfer of the Government of this country to the Crown, the only permanent Governor-General, who had had previous experience of India, was Sir John Lawrence. But the case of Sir John stands apart. Even at the time of his appointment there was a strong opposition to the idea of an ex-civilian, with all the prejudices and preconceptions of the service, being appointed to the highest executive post under the Crown in India. That the opposition was well-founded is evident from the fact that since the time of Lord Lawrence, the experiment has not been repeated. Among his successors, Lord Curzon seems to be the only man who has had any knowledge of the country and its people, prior to his appointment as Governor-General. Not as a servant of the Crown in India, but as a traveller and a student, a writer and a minister at home, he had gathered information relative to this country long before there was any chance of the greatest ambition of his life being realised. Says his historian, "Lord Curzon embarked with an equipment for his task such as few Viceroys have possessed. He had spent nearly one year at the India Office and three years at the Foreign Office. He had visited India four times and had travelled widely within its borders. He knew at first hand the North-West frontier always an object of deep anxiety" and yet even in his case some critics of his appointment argued that the very greatness of his qualifications disqualified him. The same writer continues, "Reduced to a simple formula, their contention is that the less a Viceroy-elect knows about India, the better ruler he would make, provided he has an open mind and a balanced sense of judgment. The proposition hardly bears serious examination, but it is typical of a certain school of British thought. No one maintains that a man would be a better admiral, or a better general, or a better surgeon if he was entirely without learning or special knowledge; but the task of steering the government of India through the vast and complex issues which constantly beset it, is supposed by these publicists to be best accomplished by an unprepared man with a cross-bench mind. **India cannot be properly governed upon such theories in these stormy days......It is a mistake to think of a Viceroy as a judicial referee,** surrounded by men necessarily far more competent than himself. **A good Viceroy will initiate as well as adjudge.** The Indian Civil Service is the best service in the Empire, but its effect upon its members is to kill initiative in all, save the men of very strong individuality, who rarely rise to the highest place. **The head of the government must not only decide, he should also on occasion lead and direct**; and a Viceroy who realises that his office is something more than a Court of Appeal, therefore, starts with a very long advantage if he has made, as Lord Curzon had made, a serious and detailed study of Indian questions."

This long extract is adduced to show that there are two schools of opinion with regard to the qualifications of a Viceroy. One believes that only such men-selected from among the prominent public men in England-will be a success as Viceroys of India who have had no previous knowledge of the country and its questions. The other regards only those Viceroys likely to be the best rulers for a country, with all its maze of racial and social and political and economic problems, each peculiar to itself—who have had previous experience of the country and who have studied its problems. Between these two views the policy of the Imperial Cabinet has fluctuated, though the weight of opinion is in favour of the former course. Driven to its logical conclusion the ideas of the second school would lead to the appointment only of retired Civil Servants of the Crown in India. It may, however, be safely asserted at this time that this course will never be adopted, notwithstanding the precedent of a very successful Viceroyalty under Sir John Lawrence. And there are good reasons. Thirty years of service in a country like India leaves a man-however strong-minded he may be-with habits of obedience and of dependence upon others for final orders. Besides, the sound principle of the British constitution, whereby the head of even such departments as the Army and the Navy are civilians without technical skill or knowledge, is equally necessary in India; and it is realised only if the Viceroy is unacquainted with India. If the ideal of Ministerial responsibility is ever to be realised in this country, it can only be if the highest officers of the State are neither pedants nor experts. The Viceroy is the only man to-day who brings the democratic atmosphere of English or Colonial public life in the bureaucratic Government of India. A Viceroy who knows too much about India would never know enough to make a good chief of a nascent democracy. It is because the signs of the times have begun to be appreciated by the powers that be, that the Viceroys are chosen from among English diplomats like Lord Hardinge, or the proconsuls of the great English colonies. And the latter class of men are by far the most suitable. The hopes and aspirations of new India can be encouraged and guided only by men who have had some experience of constitutional rule in British democracies over seas.

The idea of the Viceroys for India being selected from the Royal family of England has already been abandoned too long to require a lengthy consideration. The experiment, however, of the Duke of Connaught as the Governor-General of the Dominion of Canada is too great a success, judging from reports, not to give rise to apprehensions for a repetition of the same on the Indian field. The government of this country is a charge vast enough to tempt the ambition or the imagination of a Royal prince. The traditions of constitutional rule of the English Royal family are long enough to reconcile the radical opponents of Royal Viceroys for India merely on constitutional grounds. The days, besides, are long gone by when reasonable fears could be entertained of an ambitious and imaginative Prince of the Blood creating an independent kingdom for himself in India if once appointed a Viceroy. And yet there are strong reasons why a Royal Viceroy might be unacceptable in India under her present circumstances. For one thing the control of the Secretary of State for India would not be so easy over a Royal Viceroy of India as over other English gentlemen—whether peers or commoners. The Government of India is yet an illdisguised autocracy. The only check on that autocracy is that of the Secretary of State. If that check should in any way be weakened, the interests of the people of India might seriously be endangered. Even if a Royal Prince prove successful in colonies like Canada or Australia, that success would be no reason to repeat the experiment, for in the self-governing colonies democracy is an accomplished fact; the Governor or the Governor-General is only a constitutional monarch who can never do wrong, because he never does anything save through his constitutional advisers. In India democracy has still to grow, and the Viceroy can do much more than we are apt to think to promote or retard that growth. Besides, public criticism of Royal personages is bound to be moderate. And the Indian peoples—above all others–are likely to carry their moderation in this respect to extremes. At the time, therefore, when high hopes are entertained in all quarters for a new, healthy democracy in India, it would be most inopportune to appoint Royal Viceroys who quite unconsciously, quite unwillingly, perhaps inspite of themselves, might lend themselves to stifle or repress the growth of a new democracy in this old land.

II. The Duties of the Viceroy.

In one of his last speeches in India, Lord Hardinge said that to his mind the role of the Viceroy consisted in interpreting before the people of India the tradition of self-government of the people of England; and to interpret before the people of Great Britain–the legal and political Sovereign of of India,–the wishes and aspirations of the people of this country. Though by law he is vested with the superintendence, direction and control of the whole government of India under the orders of the Secretary of State, his real functions have well been summarised in this remark of Lord Hardinge's. The Viceroy does no doubt initiate measures whenever he is clever and hard-working as Lord Curzon, or working under special orders from Home as Lord Lytton. But the greater portion of his daily work consists in supervising, with the aid of his council, the work of the various provincial governments; and in directing and controlling those departments for which the Governor-General-in-Council is primarily responsible. It would be impossible for him, even if he was capable of it, to conduct in person the whole administration of this vast Empire. The actual administration is–and must be–left to the various provincial and departmental authorities. He, as the highest executive officer, with his experience of other peoples and other Governments, with his broader outlook and unprejudiced mind, must be ever ready, if not to initiate, at least to advise. He must conciliate and placate and harmonise the discordant elements of this vast machine. He must combine the savoire-faire of the diplomat with the constitutional temperament of the colonial Governor. In a thousand ways a good Viceroy can fulfil his duties—besides those of actual Government. He must discountenance the rapacity and turbulance of some members of the ruling race in India outside the official classes; he must encourage the native princes in improving their administration, appreciate their efforts as well as their difficulties, restrain their waywardness and punish—when necessary—their mis-rule; he must animate the dead routine of departmental work, impress upon the officials their duties as servants of the country where heir position has made them masters; he must eliminate friction and promote good-will among the various races of this tcontinent; and above all, undaunted by temporary ebullition of temper, undismayed by criticism or abuse, uninfluenced by flattery he must ever promote the true interests—social and political—of the new India. All this is outside government, and yet indispensable to make a good Viceroy a great ruler.

III. The Executive Council of the Governor-General.

The History of the Council.

The Governor-General's council dates from 1773 if not from the earliest days of the East India Company's rule in India. Under the Regulating Act the Governor of Fort William in Bengal was made the Governor-General of Bengal, and was given a council of 4 members appointed from England. Each of the members had the same voting power, with the exception of the Governor-General, who, as the President of the council, had a casting vote. The council of the Governor-General, or to speak in technical terms, the Governor-General-in-Council, was made supreme over the other two Presidencies, which also had each their own Governor-in-council from and after 1773. The equal voting power of each member caused embarrassment and dissensions in the council which considerably hampered the task of administration. In an Act passed after the Act of 1784, the Governor-General was given power in certain cases to overrule the majority of his council. The number of the ordinary members of the council was fixed at 3 in 1793, and the Commander-in-chief could be added as an extraordinary member if specially appointed. The act of 1833 added a special member for legislation, who was entitled to sit and vote only when the council of the Governor-General (which from that day becomes the sole legislative authority for the whole of the British India) met for the purpose of passing rules and regulations. In 1853 he was made a full member of the council, *i. e.* he was entitled to sit and vote at every meeting of the council no matter what the question before the council. This feature of the council having special members for certain departments, was further extended in 1859 when the disordered state of the finances of the country required and obtained a trained financier. In 1874, the Governor-General-in-Council obtained the power, under an act of Parliament, to appoint another member for the Public Works Department only if he thought fit. This power was not always exercised, and in 1904 the restriction limiting it to Public Works purposes was removed. In 1905 the Public Works Department was abolished, and a new Department of Commerce and Industry was created, to which was made over the bulk of the Public Works Department, *viz.*, the Railway matters, while Irrigation works were placed under the charge of the Revenue and Agriculture member. The Commander-in-Chief under the present act may be appointed by the Secretary of State in Council as an extraordinary member of the council. In practice, he is always so appointed. Before 1905 the Commander-in-chief had no department under him. In virtue of the changes made in that year, the Military Department of the council was replaced by the Army and Military Supply Departments. The former was placed under the Commander-in-chief who thus for the first time received the charge of a department. The latter was in charge of a separate member who replaced the member in charge of the Military department. In 1909 the Military Supply Department was abolished, and the responsibility for the whole military administration passed to the Commander-in-Chief as member in charge of the Army Department. Finally in November 1910 a sixth ordinary member was again added to take charge of the newly constituted Education Department.

At present, therefore, there are six ordinary and one extraordinary member in the Viceroy's Council. The ordinary members are:--

The Hon. Sir William Vincent, Home Member.
" " Sir William Meyer, Finance Member.
" " Mr. Claude Hill, Revenue & Agriculture Member.
" " Sir Sankar Nair, Education Member.
" " Mr. Lowndes, Law Member.
" " Sir G. Barnes, Commerce & Industry.
" " Sir Charles Munro, the Commander-in-Chief, Extraordinary Member.

Besides this usual extraordinary Member, the Governors of Madras, Bombay and Bengal are also entitled to be extraordinary members of the Viceregal Council whenever it is held within their province.

IV. Qualifications of the Members.

The qualifications of the members according to this Act are:—(1) 3 of them at least must have been in the service of the Crown for at least 10 years at the date of their appointment. (2) One must be a barrister of England or Ireland of at least 5 years standing or a member of the Faculty of Advocates of Scotland. (3) No ordinary member of the council can be a military officer. If, at the time of his appointment, a member is a military officer, he must resign his command; he cannot be employed in military duties during the tenure of his office as member of the Viceregal Council. The qualifications of only 4 members are thus laid down by law, so that there is a discretion in the appointment of the remaining two, who may be chosen for different qualifications.

The presence of an Indian gentleman in the Viceroy's Council is not secured by any legal provision. On the other hand Indians are not by law debarred from holding these offices. Said Lord Morley in 1908, "The absence of an Indian member from the Viceroy's Executive Council can no longer, I think, be defended. **There is no legal obstacle or statutory exclusion.** The Secretary of State can, tomorrow, if he likes, if there be a vacancy on the Viceroy's Council, recommend His Majesty to appoint an Indian member." Lord morley added that he would feel it his duty to advise the King to appoint an Indian, and Lord Minto, the then Viceroy, concurring in, and even suggesting the step himself, an Indian gentleman was appointed for the first time in 1910. It must be noted also that there is nothing in this Act, or any other Act, to prevent the majority or even the entirety of the council being composed of Indians, provided of course, they fulfil the requirements about service etc.

Of the six ordinary members of to-day, Sir W. Vincent, Sir William Meyer and Mr. Claude Hill are distinguished members of the Indian Civil Service. Sir George Barnes is a member of the Home Civil Srevice, who had risen to one of the highest posts in the service of England prior to his appointment to the Governor-General's council in 1915. Sir S. Nair is an Indian gentleman of judicial experience and has been appointed to the Education Department. Mr. Lowndes was a practising barrister in Bombay. He had retired from active practice before his appointment to the council. The Councillors hold their office for 5 years as a matter of custom, though no definite term is laid down by law.

V. Character of the Council.

The council thus consists of a number of men who have distinguished themselves in the task of administration long before their appointment. At least 3 out of the 6 ordinary members must have been connected directly with the task of administration in India; and the other 3 also must in one way or another have long experience of Indian problems. They thus form a body of eminent men of experience and reputation, entrusted with the task of advising and assisting the Governor-General in the administration of India. The Governor-General is, as we have seen already, a novice as regards Indian problems. His councillors on the other hand are admittedly experienced in Indian questions. For those unconnected with the Government it is difficult to say what is the exact influence of the Governor-General and his councillors in the actual administration of India. Arguing on abstract principles, it would seem that in matters of every day routine, it is not probable that the Governor-General would take it upon himself to go against the considered opinion of his experienced advisers, and especially if that opinion is the opinion of the majority of his colleagues. The Governor-General has a right to overrule his Council under certain circumstances. But it is very doubtful if he ever feels the need of exercising this extraordinary power. The last case when this right was exercised was in 1877 or 1878, Lord Lytton, the then Viceroy, having been pledged to carry out the tariff policy of the Home Government at any cost. It may be argued that that incident was of too peculiar a character to form a valid precedent. At any rate the mere fact that the right was exercised but once in the course of nearly sixty years is enough to show that, though the provision is incorporated in the present act, the power it gives will not be lightly resorted to. In cases like this, mere disuse of a legal power does not amount to its abolition, though it shows its abeyance. The prerogative of the King in England to veto Bills sent up by Parliament has not been specifically abolished by any Act of Parliament, and yet almost every writer on the English constitution takes it for granted that the royal veto is dead. The prerogative has been in abeyance—as far as England is concerned—for more than 2 centuries. It must be admitted that the presence of such a clause shows, more than anything else, the absolute, autocratic nature of the Government of India. In proportion, however, as the principles of representative Government are extended, bringing in their train the ideas of responsible government, such powers in the supreme head of the Government, however closely circumscribed, would be found to be incompatible if not altogether useless.

VI. The Council at Work.

By subclause (2), Sec. 40, power is given to the Governor-General to make rules and orders for the more convenient transaction of business in his executive council. This power, first given by the Indian Councils Act 1861, was utilised by Lord Canning to introduce some division of work in the Council. Before 1861 every question of administration had to go through the whole council, no matter what the department in which it had originated, because the council worked as a collective board, and left no power to individual members to work each for a separate department. Under the Indian Councils Act of 1861, the provisions of which have been incorporated in Sec. 40 (2) of this act, the Governor-Generel can, for the more convenient transaction of business, parcel out the work of administration amongst his colleagues. By that method can be secured

19

more convenient as well as expeditious transaction of business. Each member of the council is thus also the head of a Department. At the present time, the business of the Government of India, it may be said, is conducted in a manner analogous to the Cabinet administration prevalent in England. The papers regarding any subject which comes up for consideration are prepared by the department concerned, and are first submitted to the member in charge of that department. The member passes his own orders in all minor cases; but in important cases, and especially in cases where two departments differ in opinion, or when it is proposed to overrule a Provincial Government, the member cannot pass final orders by himself. Such cases are, therefore, referred to the Governor-General. He may pass final orders in consultation only with the member in whose department the question originally arose. If he concurs with the member in charge, and the question is relatively a minor one, the usual practice would be for the Governor-General to pass the final orders. Questions involving large issues of general policy, or questions which cannot be decided without legislation of the Government of India are referred to the whole council, and are decided by a mojority in case of a difference of opinion. The council usually meets once a week but it may meet more frequently. The meetings are private and the decisions arrived at are always represented as the decisions of the Governor-General-in-Council.

The council is divided into 8 departments. They are: (1) the Foreign Department, usually in charge of the Governor-General himself, (2) the Army Department in charge of the Commander-in-Chief since 1909, (3) the Home Department, (4) the Revenue and Agricultural Department, (5) the Commerce and Industry Department, (6) the Education Department, (7) the Finance Department and (8) the Legislative Department.

VII. The Work of each Department.

The Foreign Department transacts all business relating to the foreign policy of the Governmet of India, to the frontier tribes, and to the Native States in India. It also controls the general administration of such provinces as Ajmer-Merwara, Coorg, the North-West Frontier Province, and British Baluchistan. The Government of India have really speaking very little control over their external relations; and such control as they have is confined to the relations with the frontier powers in the North-West, such as Afghanistan and Persia, and in the North-East such as Tibet, China and Siam. The Foreign Department also deals with questions of ceremonial, and those relating to the Indian orders, the Imperial Service Troops, the Cadet Corps, and the Chiefs' colleges.

The **Home Department** is concerned with the work of general administration, and deals with internal politics, law and justice, police, hospitals, public houses, Municipalities, Local Boards and a number of other subjects. Matters ecclesiastical are also under this department. As all these matters fall primarily within the jurisdiction of Local Governments, the work of the Home Department consists chiefly in controlling and supervising the Provincial Governments. Its share of actual administration is confined to the Government of the penal settlement of Port Blair.

The department of Revenue and Agriculture, created in 1871 and abolished in 1879, and reconstituted in 1881, is concerned with the administration of land revenue and agricultural enquiry, agricultural means and famine relief. The organisation of economic and scientific investigation and of measures of agricultural improvement is also in the charge of this department. The mere enunciation of its branches *e. g.* the Metereological Department, the Survey Department, the Civil Veterinary Department, the Forest Department, will suffice to show its multifarious activities. As in the case of the Home Department the functions here again are primarily falling within the jurisdiction of Local Governments, and the functions of the Revenue and Agricultural Department are mainly of a supervising and controlling character. Since 1905, it has also received charge of the Irrigation branch of the Public Works Department.

The Commerce and Industry Department, formed in 1905, has taken over some portion of the work from other departments, and is concerned with the questions relating to the trade and manufactures of the country. It is also the department which represents the railways in the council of the Governor-General. It is concerned with the administration of the Factories, Petroleum, and Explosives acts. Postal business, customs, statistics, printing and stationary; and everything relating to ports, shipping, and trade generally have been transferred to this from the finance department. Other functions directly connected with the trade and under this department are the Merchandise Marks Act. It controls the Post-office—an Imperial Department under a Director General under whom are the Provincial Post-Masters—and also the Telegraph Department. It considers all labour questions including emigration to foreign countries, as also to Assam. The control of expert mining staff, including inspection of all mines, and the matters relating to geological enquiries are made over to that department.

The Legislative Department is responsible for all matters connected with the conduct of the Legislative Council of the Governor-General. It is also entrusted with drafting of enactments and of publishing and revising the Statute book. It also supervises the legislation of the provincial councils, and it assists the other departments of the Government of India with advice on legal questions and principles.

The Army Department is under the sole charge, since 1909, of the Commander-in-Chief. It deals with all questions relating to enlistment, pay and promotion of soldiers, volunteers, and the Royal Indian Marine, and the Indian Medical Service, ordnance and stores.

The Education Department, created in 1909, deals with all educational matters such as the control and establishment of universities and technical institutions, the grants-in-aid, the establishment of schools and their equipment, the extension of education etc. As all these matters fall within the jurisdiction of the various provincial governments, the work of the Department is chiefly of a supervising and controlling nature, besides the main question of formulating the educational policy of the Government of India.

The Finance Department deals with the general administration of Imperial and Provincial Finance, with questions relating to the salaries, leave and pensions of public officers, and with currency and banking. It supervises and controls such sources of revenue as opium, excise, stamps, salt and assessed taxes. It also administers the mint, and the Gevernment Treasuries. One single department manages the civil accounts of both the supreme and the provincial governments. At the head of this department is the Comptroller and Auditor General who is also the Head Commissioner of paper currency. A separate branch, called the Military Finance Department, is entrusted with all questions relating to the financial administration of the Army.

VIII. The Indian Council and the English Cabinet.

Is the Council a Cabinet ? Says Sir J. Strachey, "Although the separation of departments is less complete than in England, and the authority of the member of Council much less extensive and exclusive than that of an English Secretary of State, **the members of Council are now virtually cabinet ministers,** each of whom has charge of one of the great departments of Government. Their ordinary duties are rather those of administrators than of Councillors." In spite of the writer's intimate experience of the system of the Government of India, it is difficult to accept the opinion that the Indian Council is a Cabinet in miniature. Apart from the delegation to each member of a specific department, there is no resemblance between the Council of the Governor-General and the Cabinet of Western democratic countries. On the other hand, the differences between the two are many and striking. (1) The authority of a Cabinet Minister in England or France is much wider–as Sir John himself admits than–that of a Councillor of the Viceroy of India. (2) The public actions of a Cabinet Minister in those countries, moreover, are taken by each Minister by himself, while the similar actions of the Councillors in India are invariably expressed as being the acts of the collective entity, the Governor-General-in-Council. (3) It is true that these Councillors like the Cabinet Ministers in European countries are members of the Legislature, apparently pursuing a uniform, pre-concerted policy, but there the resemblance ends. The councillors in India by no means hold their position in the Council, as do the Cabinet Ministers in democratic countries, because they are the acknowledged leaders of the dominant party in the legislature. There are no parties in politics in this country. There is also no duty imposed upon the Councillors to hold themselves answerable to the legislature for their :acts, and to resign in the event of their acts or policies not finding favour with the legislative assembly. (4) There is also no Prime Minister in India—unless, indeed, we take the Viceroy to be his own Prime Minister--as is usual in all cabinets; And even if we take the Viceroy to be his own premier, there is not that bond of union between him and his colleagues as is always found between the prime minister and his cabinet colleagues in England or France,:the bond of identical opinions on leading political questions of the day and of sympathetic changes of political fortune. The Viceroy is a new comer, while his colleagues are all veterans in the service of India. The Viceroy is immeasurably their superior in social position and theoretical powers, and they are his superiors in local knowledge. They do not, by any means, come to their work at the same moment, and leave it also at the same. Beyond the fact that the Viceroy usually takes charge of a department of State, and that he regulates the distribution of work among his colleagues, there is really no similarity between an English Prime Minister and the Viceroy of India. (5) The English Cabinet is a body quite unknown to the constitutional law of England. In other countries they have legal existence; but no where has constitutional law invested them with that corporate capacity which we find in the case of the Executive Council of the Viceroy. (6) The fancied resemblance to a Cabinet breaks down even when we look to points merely of detail. Thus the position of the Secretary in an Indian Department has been compared to that of the permanent Under Secretary in England. But there are important differences between the Indian Secretary to the Government and the English permanent (of course he cannot be compared to the Parliamentary) Under Secretary of State. The report of the Royal Commission on Decentralisation says:- "The Secretary, as above stated, is present at Council meetings. He attends on the Viceroy, usually once a week, and discusses with him all matters arising in his department, and he has the right of bringing to the Viceroy's special notice any case in which he considers that His Excellency's concurrence should be obtained to action proposed by the departmental member of council. His tenure of office is usually limited to three years." In all these respects, the position of the English permanent Under-Secretary is radically different. He cannot be present at Cabinet meetings; he has no direct excess to the Prime Minister nor the right to appeal against his departmental chief; and his tenure of office is in no way limited.

Under these circumstance, it would be impossible to regard the Government of India in the same light as the Cabinet Government in England. The principles which guide the working of the Indian Council have been well summarised by J. S. Mill. "The Councils" he says in his representative government, "should be consultative merely in this sense, that the ultimate decision should rest undividedly with the Minister himself; but neither ought they to be looked upon, or to look upon themselves, as ciphers, or as capable of being reduced to such at his pleasure. The advisers attached to a powerful and perhaps self-willed man ought to be placed under conditions which make it impossible for them, without discredit, not to express an opinion; and impossible for him not to listen to and consider their recommendations, whether he adopts them or not. The relation which ought to exist between a chief and this description of advisers is very acurately hit by the councils of the Governor-General and those of the different presidencies in India. As a rule every member is expected to give an opinion, which is, of course, very often a simple acquiescence;

but if there is difference of opinion, it is at the option of every member, and is the invariable practice, to record the reasons of his opinion; the Governor-General or Governor doing the same. In ordinary cases the decision is according to the sense of the majority. The Council, therefore, has a substantial part in the government, but if the Governor-General or Governor thinks fit, he may set aside even their unanimous opinion, recording his reasons. **The result is that the chief is, individually and effectually, responsible for every act of the government.** " No apology is needed to record at length the opinion of one of the most eminent political thinkers of the last century, who was himself for a long time in the service of the East India Company. At the time when Mill was writing this, however, the council was working as a collective board, each member in which shared equally in every act of administration. The distribution of the work of the council in different departments, each in the charge of one member, was introduced subsequently. But the principles he has laid down still hold good. It is even now recognised as a fundamental principle of the Government of India that while the Governor-General of India possesses in the last resort power to act upon his own judgment, even against the unanimous opinion of his colleagues, he is also obliged to hear the opinion of his experienced councillors. And those counsellors have the right to make known their opinion, not merely as regards their particular departments, but on all questions coming before the council. On account, however, of the cumbrousness of the system of collective working, the practice which prevailed under the Company was abandoned in 1861, though in form the acts of the Government of India are even now the acts of the Governor-General-in-Council.

It is impossible, therefore, to accept the opinion that the Indian Council is for all practical purposes a Cabinet like that of England. Those who are entitled to as much deference as Sir John Strachey have declared that the Government of India is even now conducted by a collective board or committee, in which every member—even the Viceroy—has the same powers. Says Lord Curzon, "Never let it be forgotten that the Government of India is conducted not by an individual but by a committee. No important act can be taken without the assent of a majority of that committee. In practice this cuts both ways. The Viceroy is constantly spoken of as though he and he alone were the Government. This is, of course, unjust to his colleagues, who are equally responsible with himself, and very often deserve the credit which he unfairly obtains. On the other hand, it is sometimes unfair to him, for he may have to bear the entire responsibility for administrative acts or policies which were participated in or originated by them. **The Viceroy has no more weight in his council than any individual member of it.**" If such a strong willed ruler as Lord Curzon could publicly utter such sentiments, there is every reason to believe that the growth of departmentalism has by no means diminished the importance of the council, or displaced old theories of Government.

IX. The Councils of the Governor-General and of the Secretary of State compared.

A comparison of the powers of these two great bodies shows that while in theory the council of the superior authority, the Secretary of State, appears to have wider powers, in practice, the Conncil of the Governor-General, the man on the spot, must of necessity have the more effective powers. (1) It is true the councillors of the Governor-General may be overruled by him in any case whenever the tranquillity, safety and interests of British India, in his opinion, require him to do so, while the India Council cannot be overruled by the Secretary of State in certain specified matters. (2) At the same time, it must be remembered that the council of the Governor-General is not excluded from any matters whether secret or urgent. (3) Again, though the tenure of office of an India councillor is definite, and though he is not removeable from office except by a joint address of both the Houses of Parliament, thus apparently enjoying a more indepedent position, he does not in reality enjoy the same position as the viceregal councillor whose tenure of office is less secure, because the latter is never confronted by the opposition of a man, with the influence and importance of the Secretary of State, whenever he differs from his chief. (4) The Secretary of State, moreover, in most matters, is not bound to accept the opinion of the majority of his council, even when he consults them, while the Viceroy must in most cases abide by the decision of a majority of his council.

In considering the wider question as to the relations between the Government of India and the Secretary of State, it is difficult to say exactly what is the principle governing these relations. Sir Courtney Ilbert says that the relations are governed by well known constitutional usages. When we think only of the past the opinion of Ilbert seems to contain a considerable degree of truth. In every case that has arisen in the last 60 years or so, the Secretary of State has always been acknowledged as the final authority; and the Governor-General, in cases where he differs from the Secretary of State, has no alternative but to submit or to resign. Lord Northbrook in 1875, and again Lord Curzon in 1905, chose to resign when they could not accept and carry out the policy determined upon by the Secretary of State. The action of Lord Lytton in 1878 seems to be conclusive on the point that in all matters the Government of India have in the last recourse to obey the orders of the Secretary of State. At the same time Sir John Strachey, who was intimately connected with the Government of India for nearly half a century, takes a different view. Much depends, according to him, upon the character of the individuals for the time being holding the two offices of the Governor-General and the Secretary of State. It must be confessed that in the administration of any progressive country no amount of petrified usuage, however sanctified by precedent, can hold its ground before the daily expanding needs of the Government. A critic so shrewd and penetrating as Sir Valentine Chirol has declared that the effect of the constitutional reforms of Lord Morley, giving some share in the Government of the country to the representatives of the people, is bound to result in developments, which must inevitably enhance the importance of the Government of India in the eyes of the home authorities.

In proportion as the ideas of responsibility to the people of India is recognised and accepted by the Government of the country, they will ever carry that weight due to the offic ia spokesmen of three hundred million human beings, which could never be attributed to a committee of bureaucrats however experienced they might be. As the control of the Indian people grows, the control of the Secretary of State and his council must diminish and eventually disappear. This does not necessarily mean that the sovereignty of the Imperial Parliament would in any way be impaired.

The legal liability of the Governor-General and his councillors—and of all Governors and their councillors—is very different from those of the colonial Governor. For acts done in their official capacity the Indian Governors and their councillors are immune from any liability. They can in no way be proceeded against, or arrested or imprisoned before the Indian High Courts. For certain specified offences, however, such as engaging in trade on their own account or receiving presents, they may be prosecuted before the King's Bench division of the High Court in London.

CHAPTER IV.

Local Government.

PART V

GENERAL.

General.

45. (1) Every local Government shall obey the of orders the Governor-General-in-Council, and keep him constantly and diligently informed of its proceedings and of all matters, which ought, in its opinion, to be reported to him, or as to which he requires information, and is under his superintendence, direction and control in all matters relating to the government of its province.

(2) No local Government may make or issue any order for commencing hostilities or levying war, or negotiate or conclude any treaty of peace or other treaty with any Indian prince or state (except in cases of sudden emergency or imminent danger when it appears dangerous to postpone such hostilities or treaty), unless in pursuance of express orders from the Governor-General-in-Council or from the Secretary of State; and every such treaty shall, if possible, contain a clause subjecting the same to the ratification or rejection of the Governor-General-in-Council. If any governor, lieutenant-governor or chief commissioner, or any member of a governor's or lieutenant-governor's executive council, wilfully disobeys any order received from the Governor-General-in-Council under this subsection, he may be suspended or removed and sent to England by the Governor-General-in-Council, and shall be subject to such further pains and penalties as are provided by law in that behalf.

(3) The authority of a local Government is not superseded by the presence in its province of the governor-general.

Governorships.

46. (1) The presidencies of Fort William in Bengal, Fort St. George and Bombay are, subject to the provisions of this Act governed by the Governors in Council of those presidencies respectively, and the two former presidencies are in this Act referred to as the presidencies of Bengal and of Madras.

(2) The Governors of Bengal, Madras and Bombay are appointed by His Majesty by warrant under the Royal Sign Manual.

(3) The Secretary of State may, if he thinks fit, by order, revoke or suspend, for such period as he may direct, the appointment of a council for any or all of those presidencies; and whilst any such order is in force the Governor of the presidency to which the order refers shall have all the powers of the Governor thereof in Council.

47. (1) The members of a Governor's Executive council shall be appointed by His Majesty by warrant under the Royal Sign Manual, and shall be of such number, not exceeding four, as the Secretary of State in Council directs.

(2) Two at leat of them must be persons who at the time of their appointment have been for at least twelve years in the service of the Crown in India.

(3) Provided that, if the Commander-in-chief of His Majesty's forces in India (not being likewise Governor-General) happens to be resident at Calcutta, Madras or Bombay, he shall, during his continuance there, be a member of the Governor's council.

48. Every Governor of a presidency shall appoint a member of his Executive council to be vice-president thereof.

49. (1) All orders and other proceedings of the Governor in Council of any presidency shall be expressed to be made by the Governor in Council, and shall be signed by a secretary to the Government of the presidency, or otherwise, as the Governor in Council may direct.

(2) A Governor may make rules and orders for the more convenient transaction of business in his Executive council, and every order made or act done in accordance with those rules and orders shall be treated as being the order or the act of the Governor in Council.

50. (1) If any difference of opinion arises on any question brought before a meeting of a Governor's Executive council, the Governor in Council shall be bound by the opinion and decision of the majority of those present, and if they are equally divided the Governor or other person presiding shall have a second or casting vote.

(2) Provided that, whenever any measure is proposed before a Governor in Council whereby the safety, tranquillity, or interests of his presidency, or of any part thereof, are or may be, in the judgment of the Governor, essentially affected, and he is of opinion either that the measure proposed ought to be adopted and carried into execution, or that it ought to be suspended or rejected, and the majority present at a meeting of the council dissent from that opinion, the Governor may, on his own authority and responsibility, by order in writing, adopt, suspend, or reject the measure, in whole or in part.

(3) In every such case the Governor, and the members of the council present at the meeting shall mutually exchange written communications (to be recorded at large in their secret proceedings) stating the grounds of their respective opinions, and the order of the Governor shall be signed by the Governor and by those members.

(4) Nothing in this section shall empower a Governor to do anything which he could not lawfully have done with the concurrence of his council.

51. If a Governor is obliged to absent himself from any meeting of his Executive council, by indisposition or any other cause, and signifies his intended absence to the council, the vice-president, or, if he is absent, the senior civil member present at the meeting, shall preside thereat, with the like powers as the Governor would have had if present.

Provided that if the governor is at the time resident at the place where the meeting is assembled, and is not prevented by indiposition from signing any act of council made at the meeting, the act shall require his signature; but, if he declines or refuses to sign it, the like provisions shall have effect as in cases where the governor, when present, dissents from the majority at a meeting of the council.

52. The Secretary of State in Council may, if he thinks fit, direct that the province of Agra be constituted a presidency under a Governor in Council, and, if that direction is given, the presidency shall be constituted on the terms and under the conditions mentioned

in section nineteen of the Government of India Act, 1858, and section four of the Government of India Act, 1854.

Lieutenant-Governorships and other Provinces.

53. (1) Each of the following provinces, namely, those known as Bihar and Orissa, the United Provinces of Agra and Oudh, the Punjab, and Burma, is, subject to the provisions of this Act, governed by a Lieutenant-Governor, with or without an executive council.

(2) The Governor-General-in-Council may, by notification with the sanction of His Majesty previously signified by the Secretary of State in Council, constitute a new province under a Lieutenant-Governor.

54. (1) A Lieutenant-Governor is appointed by the Governor-General with the approval of His Majesty.

(2) A Lieutenant-Governor must have been, at the time of his appointment, at least ten years in the service of the Crown in India.

(3) The Governor-General-in-Council may, with the sanction of His Majesty previously signified by the Secretary of State in Council, declare and limit the extent of the authority of any lieutenant-governor.

55. (1) The Governor-General-in-Council, with the approval of the Secretary of State in Council, may, by notification, create a council in any province under a lieutenant-governor, for the purpose of assisting the lieutenant-governor in the executive government of the province, and by such notification

(*a*) make provision for determining what shall be the number (not exceeding four) and qualifications of the members of the council; and

(*b*) make provision for the appointment of temporary or acting members of the council during the absence of any member from illness or otherwise, and for the procedure to be adopted in case of a difference of opinion between a lieutenant-governor and his council, and in the case of equality of votes, and in the case of a lieutenant-governor being obliged to absent himself from his council by indisposition or any other cause:

Provided that, before any such notification is published, a draft thereof shall be laid before each House of Parliament for not less than sixty days during the session of Parliament, and if, before the expiration of that time, and address is presented to His Majesty by either House of Parliament against the draft or any part thereof, no further proceedings shall be taken thereon, without prejudice to the making of any new draft.

(2) Every notification under this section shall be laid before both Houses of Parliament as soon as may be after it is made.

(3) Every member of a lieutenant-governor's executive council shall be appointed by the governor-general, with the approval of His Majesty.

56. A Lieutenant-Governor who has an executive council shall appoint a member of the council to be vice-president thereof, and that vice-president shall preside at meetings of the council in the absence of the lieutenant-governor.

57. A Lieutenant-Governor who has an executive council may, with the consent of the Govornor-General-in-Council, make rules and orders for more convenient transaction of business in the council, and every order made, or act done, in accordance with such rules and orders, shall be treated as being the order or the act of the Lieutenant-Governor in council.

58. Each of the following provinces, namely, those known as Assam, the Central Provinces, the North-West Frontier Province, British Baluchistan, Delhi, Ajmer-Merwara, Coorg, and the Andaman and Nicobar Islands, is, subject to the provisions of this Act, administered by a chief commissioner.

59. The Governor-General in Conucil may, with the approval of the Secretary of State, and by notification, take any part of British India under the immediate authority and management of the Governor-General in Council, and thereupon give all necessary orders and directions respecting the administration of that part, by placing it under a chief commissioner, or by otherwise providing for its administration.

Boundaries.

60. The Governor-General-in-Council may, by notification, declare, appoint or alter the boundaries of any of the provinces into which British India is for the time being divided, and distribute the territories of British India among the several provinces thereof in such manner as may seem expedient, subject to these qualifications, namely:—

(1) an entire district may not be transferred from one province to another without the previous sanction of the Crown, signified by the Secretary of State in Council; and

(2) any notification under this section may be disallowed by the Secretary of State in Council.

61. An alteration in pursuance of the foregoing provisions of the mode of administration of any part of British India, or of the boundaries of any part of British India, shall not affect the law for the time being in force in that part.

62. The Governor of Bengal in Council, the Governor of Madras in Council, and the Governor of Bombay in Council may, with the approval of the Secretary of State in Council, and by notification, extend the limits of the towns of Calcutta, Madras and Bombay, respectively; and any Act of Parliament, letters, patent, charter, law or usage conferring jurisdiction, power or authority within the limits of those towns respectively, shall have effect within the limits as so extended.

COMMENTS.

I. The Development of the Provincial Governments in India.

British India is divided into 8 large provinces and 7 lesser charges each of which is termed a Local Government. The provinces are the two old Presidencies of Madras and Bombay, to which, since 1912, has been added the Presidency of

Bengal; the four Lieutenant-Governorships of the United Provinces, the Punjab, Burma, and Bihar and Orissa; the Chief Commissionerships of the Central Provinces, Assam, North—West Frontier province; British Baluchistan, Ajmere-Merwara, Coorg and the Penal Settlement of Andaman Island. To these was added in 1912 the Commissionership of Delhi, when that city was made the capital of the Government of India. The new Chief Commissionership was a charge created by separating the district of Delhi and the enclave of territory around it from the Punjab, and placing it under a Commissioner directly under the Government of India. Originally, the three Presidencies of Fort St. George or Madras, of Fort William or Bengal, and Bombay were centres of the East India Company, politically independent of one another. Though in point of history, Madras was the oldest of the East India Company's possessions in India, the acquisition by Clive in 1765 of the Diwani of Bengal, Bihar and Orissa from the Mogul Emperor made the Presidency of Fort William the premier Presidency in India. From 1773 this practical importance was recognised also in theory, the Governor of Fort William being made the Governor-General of Bengal, and being given supremacy over other provinces and over the Governors of Bombay and Madras. This supremacy of the Governor-General of Bengal was carried a step further in 1785, and was made permanent in 1833, when the Governor-General of Bengal was declared to be the Governor-General of India, though the same officer was also the Governor of Bengal.

The year 1833 is also remarkable in the history of the provinces in India, because in that year Parliament permitted the East India Company to erect a fourth Presidency out of territories acquired by the Company on the north-west frontiers of Bengal, and comprising a great portion of the modern provinces of Agra and Oudh. This permissive clause of the Charter Act of 1833 was not carried into execution till 3 years later; and even then in a modified form. The territories on the north-west frontier of Bengal were erected into a Lieutenant-Governorship by notification in the gazette of February 21, 1836. They were styled the North-West Provinces upto 1901, when, in order to distinguish them from the North-West Frontier Province, formed in that year, they came to be known as the United Provinces of Agra and Oudh. By section 53 of the present Act these provinces may be erected into a Presidency by the Secretary of State in Council.

Another change came 20 years later in 1853, when the Governor-General of India was relieved from the immediate administration of the Presidency of Bengal, and a new Lieutenant Governorship was created to administer that province. Here also s. 16 of the Government of India Act gave power to the Court of Directors, subject to the sanction of the Board of Control, to appoint a Governor for the Presidency of Fort William. Until, however, a separate Governor was appointed under that Act, the Governor-General was given power to appoint a Lieutenant-Governor. The Governor-General exercised this alternative power and Bengal remained a Lieutenant-Governorship till 1912. The Governor General becomes from that date, both in name as well as in fact, the Governor-General of India and not immediately of any particular province.

The Punjab, annexed in 1849, was governed first by a board, afterwards by a Chief Commissioner, and was made a Lieutenant-Governorship in 1859. Oudh, which was annexed in 1856, was first placed in charge of a Chief Commissioner; but was later on merged in the Lieutenant-Governorship of the then North Western Province, and the modern United Provinces of Agra and Oudh. Burma was the next Lieutenant Governorship. In 1862 the Burma provinces were known as British Burma and were administered by a Chief Commissioner. After the war of 1886 the whole province was styled Burma and was raised to the status of a Lieutenant-Governorship in 1897. On their annexation in 1853 the territories of the Raja of Nagpur were made a separate administration, and placed under the charge of a Chief Commissioner in 1861. To them was added the district of Berar ceded by the Nizam in 1903. Assam was at first added to Bengal on its annexation in 1876; but in the same year it was detached and placed under the charge of a Chief Commissioner. In 1905 it was combined with the short-lived province of Eastern Bengal and Assam,

Seven years later, however, by the decree of the King Emperor the partition of Bengal of 1905 was rescinded. Bengal became once more the Presidency that it was before 1833. The provinces of Behar and Orissa became a new Lieutenant-Governorship; and Assam was once more made a separate Chief Commissionership. The North-West Frontier province was created in 1901, and consisted of the districts detached from the Punjab, partly to allow the Government of India to exercise more direct control over frontier questions, and partly to relieve the Government of the Punjab. To them also were added a number of adjoining border tracts over which direct influence had been exercised by the Government of India since 1892. British Baluchistan was formed into a Chief Commissionership in 1877. Coorg, conquered and annexed in 1829, is administered by the Resident of Mysore who is also the Chief Commissioner of Coorg. So also the small British territory of Ajmere-Merwara in Rajputana, which is administered by the Agent to the Governor-General in Rajputana, being also Chief Commissioner of Ajmere. Finally, in 1912, the district of Delhi, with a territory round about it, was detached from the Punjab (to which it had been annexed after the mutiny) and was made into a Commissionership under the immediate charge of the Government of India, who since that date have made it their capital.

II. Procedure to create new Provinces.

The power of the Governor-General, by notification in the Gazette, and subject to the approval of the Secretary of State for India in Council, to take any part of British India under the direct authority of the Government of India, was questioned by Sir Barnes Peacock in 1852. It was therefore expressly granted by s. 3 of the Act of 1853; and has been embodied in s. 59 of the present Act. This power has been frequently used, *e. g.* in the case of Arracan, originally annexed to Lower Burma, taken under this authority directly under the Government of India, and annexed to British Burma in 1862, by notification. So also the Province of Assam. On the other haud in creating the Chief Commissionerships of Oudh, Central Provinces, and British Burma the procedure followed was the issue of a resolution reciting the reasons for such a creation, defining the territories included in it, and specifying the staff appointed, without making any reference to any Statute. The reason for this difference in procedure is that the Government of India do not consider the section of the Act of 1858 to apply to territories already included in a Chief Commissionership, for a Chief Commissionership is already under the direct management of the Government of India. A Chief Commissioner merely administers the territory under his charge on behalf of the Governor-General in Council, and the latter does not divest himself of any of his powers in making over the administration to a Chief Commissioner. The Chief Commissioner, however, is, according to Act X of 1897, s. 3 (29), a local Government and is so considered by the present Act.

The power to alter the boundaries of the existing provinces, by notification in the Gazette, was given by the Charter Act of 1833, s. 38. It is subject to the reservation that (*a*) an entire district may not be transferred from one to another province, without the previous consent of the Crown through the Secretary of State in Council; and (*b*) that any such notification may be disallowed by the Secretary of State. In 1878 the Government of India were advised that the Act of 1865, by which this power was first modified, enabled the Governor-General in Council to transfer territory from a Chief Commissionership to a Presidency or a Lieutenant-Governorship but not vice versa.

Both these powers are subject to the proviso that no law or regulation in force at the time of the transfer shall be altered or repealed except by law made by a the Governor-General in Council.

III. The relative Status of the Provincial Governments.

The provinces, as we have seen, are divided into Governorships, Lieutenant-Governorships and Chief Commissionerships,

This division does not by any means suggest a great difference in the powers and position enjoyed by each of these classes of provinces. For all practical purposes within his own jurisdiction each head of a Provincial Government, whether a Governor, a Lieutenant-Governor, or a Chief Commissioner enjoys very nearly the same independence and authority. In fact one might even say that the more dignified position of the Governor carries with it less actual powers,—the powers of government being shared by the Governor with his council, while the Lieutenant-Governorship gives more substantial powers. Nevertheless there is some difference in the relative rank and position of each of these provinces. The difference is important because it points to the old historic distinction, because it has some practical importance even to-day, and because it throws some curious light on the question of Provincial autonomy.

IV. The Presidency Governors.

The three governorships of Madras, Bombay and Bengal have a certain superiority over all the other provinces. Not only that they are historically the oldest provinces, existing even before the Central Government itself came into existence; but this prior existence of theirs and the independent position they enjoyed at the time, is reflected even to-day in the position of their chief authorities in their relations with the Government of India. Each of these provinces is governed by a Governor in Council on the model of the Government of India. The Governor, like the Viceroy, is appointed directly from England by the Crown. He is usually a person of some importance in the social or political life of England. Like the Viceroy, the Governor is styled His Excellency; and is, virtute officii, an extraordinary member of the Viceregal Executive Council whenever that Council assembles within the jurisdiction of his Presidency. His Council, like the Council of the Governor-General, is appointed to advise and assist him in the task of administration. He has the same powers of overruling the council as the Governor-General has, in cases of emergency. The Governors have still the right of communicating directly with the Secretary of State (cp.S. 14 of this Act); and also to appeal to the Secretary of State against the Government of India in cases where they differ from the Government of India, provided the appeal is transmitted to and communicated through the Government of India. They are more independent, besides, than the other governments in such matters as their revenue settlement, or the choice of persons to certain important posts, like the nominated members of the Legislative Council for instance. Altogether their position, even to-day, contains many traces of their original equality with, and independence of, one another.

V. Lieutenant-Governors.

Next in authority to the three Presidency Governments, there are four Lieutenant-Governorships of the United Provinces, the Punjab, Burma, Bihar and Orissa. Of these the last alone is governed by a Lieutenant-Governor, with an executive council of three members one of whom is an Indian, and it therefore falls in a special class by itself. The present Act contains provisions enabling the Governor-General to establish executive councils in any of the Lieutenant-Governorships by a proclamation, provided the draft proclamation is submitted to both the Houses of Parliament 60 days before coming into operation, and provided that neither of the Houses of Parliament moves an address to the King against such a proclamation. Lord Hardinge attempted to utilise this power in 1915 for establishing an executive council in the United Provinces. But the House of Lords addressed the King against such a proclamation and the reform has been postponed, if not dropped altogether. The presence of a council in a Local Government may be taken to mean a restraint on the powers of the executive head of the Government. If so, the Lieutenant-Governors, who do not have a council, concentrate in their own person the whole authority of the Government in their provinces.

And in so far as the ideal of Government is promptness in action and uniformity in policy, the ideal may, indeed, be said to be fully realised in the case of the Lieutenant-Governors of India. On the other hand it must not be forgotten that there are also disadvantages inseparable from such an eminent position. The Lieutenant-Governor of a province like the United Provinces rule over a larger population, and therefore is under a much heavier burden of work, than the Governor of a Presidency like Bombay. Not only is the work too great for a single officer; it throws on him an entirely disproportionate share of responsibility. Nor is it quite certain that the ideal of bureaucratic government—efficiency—is best realised under a Lieutenant-Governor. A single executive officer has neither the time nor the equipment to consider fully each one of the scores of administrative questions coming before him from every department, which an officer, of perhaps the same standing, assisting him, by looking after one or two specific departments, could devote. Government by such means loses inefficiency and in the close personal attention to each important question what it might conceivably gain in theory by the possibility of prompt action and expeditious transaction of business.

All this is apart from the other advantage of council government in important provinces, that the insitution of a council in a Lieutenant Governorship would almost certainly involve the appointment of at least one more Indian gentleman to an executive office of the highest importance. The presence of an Indian in an executive council is claimed to be an advantage to the Government, not because it means more employment for Indians; men who are appointed to such a position are almost always in a position to dispense with their official emoluments; and to get these emoluments they have to make much greater sacrifices. It is an advantage because the presence of an Indian gentleman in the executive council brings the Government into touch with the sentiments of the people, which, presumably, they otherwise would not have appreciated at their proper value.

The position of a Lieutenant-Governor with all its load of business and responsibility is not in any way indemnified by the possession of more extensive and independent powers as might appear at first sight. Says Sir John Stratchey "The checks against the wrongful exercise by the Lieutenant Governor of the arbitrary power are, however, complete. There is no branch of the administration in which he is not bound either by positive law, by the standing orders of the supreme Government, or by the system which has gradually grown up under his respective predecessors." Any great changes which he may desire to introduce must first receive the approval of the Governor-General-in-Council. He can impose no dues or taxation. He has no control over the military forces. His power, in fine, large in appearance, is carefully restricted in practice.

For many years after the transfer of the Government of India to the British Crown, the Lieutenant-Governors were also the legislative authority for their provinces. Since the establishment of the Legislative Councils in their provinces, the legislative authority has been separated from the executive. This process has more than ever intensified the necessity of an Executive Council. The letter of the Government of India, dated 1st October 1908, says, *inter alia*, "We recognise that the effect of our propcsals will be to throw a greater burden on the heads of the Local Governments, not only by reason of the actual increase of the work caused by the long sittings of the Legislative Councils, and in dealing with the recommendations of those councils. It may be that experience will show the desirability of strengthening the hands of the Lieutenant-Governors in the larger provinces by the creation of Executive Councils. The Executive Councils, by allowing a distribution of administrative work among the different members of the council, would relieve the Lieutenant-Governor from attending personally to the every day routine of all the departments of the administration; and leave him more free to attend to the general principles of administration."

We may, then, sum up the points in which a Lieutenant-Governor differs from a Governor; (1) he is styled only "His Honour" while a Governor is described as "His Excellency." (2) He is appointed by the Viceroy from among the members of the

Indian Civil Service, while a Governor, often of the same or even of a superior social position than the Viceroy, is appointed by the Home authorities. (3) Excepti n Bihar and Orissa, a Lientenant-Governor has no executive Council. (4) The powers of a Lientenant-Governor are more narrowly circumscribed, and the interference of the Viceroy in their domestic concerns is greater, than in the case of the Presidencies. (5) A Lieutenant-Governor has no right to communicate directly with the Secretary of State.

VI. Chief Commissioners.

Next in authority to the Lieutenant-Governors are the Chief Commissioners. The title of the Chief Commissioner was adoped to distinguish the head of the administration in a minor province from the financial and judicial commissioners. The title was first introduced in 1853, when John Lawrence was appointed Chief Commissioner in the Punjab and Baluchistan. The Chief Commissioners stand on a lower footing than the Lieutenant-Governors. There are 8 Chief Commissionerships, those of the Central Provinces, Assam (in which there are legislative coun cils also), the North-West Frontier Province, British Baluchistan, the new province of Delhi, Ajmere-Merwara, Coorg, and Andaman and Nicobar Islands. The appointment of the Chief Commissioners is not, unlike that of the Lieutenant-Governors, specifically provided for by a special Act of Parliament. The territories under their charge are, under the theory of the law, under the immediate authority and management of the Governor-General-in-Council, who appoints Chief Commissioners at his discretion, and delegates to them such powers as are necessary for the purpose of administration. In practice, however there is very little difference between the powers of the Chief Commissioners of the Central Provinces and Assam and those of the Lieutenant-Governors of other provinces. The Chief Commissioners of the North-West Frontier Province and of British Baluchistan are officers administering territories of less magnitude.

They are at the same time agents to the Governor-General for dealing with the tribes and territories outside British India. The chief commissionership of Delhi has a special importance of its own on account of Delhi city being made the capital of India. British territories in Ajmere-Merwara and Coorg are governed by the agent to the Governor-General-in Rajputana and the resident in Mysore respectively.

A general survey of Provincial Government shows the following **Principles of Provincial administration in India.**

The Governor-General in Council is responsible for the entire administration of British India, and for the control exercised in varying degrees over the Native States. The Local Governments must obey the orders received from the Governor-General-in-Council, and they must communicate to him their own proceedings. This subordination is derived partly from Acts of Parliament, partly from the terms of the delegation of authority by the Governor-General to Lieutenant-Governors and Chief Commissioners. Every local government, including a Chief Commissioner, is the executive head of the administration within the province; and, though there are minor differences in the relative status of the different local governments *inter se*, they are all alike in this: that they are all the delegates, or at least the subordinates, of the Supreme Government of India represented by the Governor-General-in-Council.

The actual work of administration is divided between the Government of India and thelocal Governments on the following principles. All matters of Imperial importance, or matters which concern more than one province, are controlled by the Government of India exclusively, as also matters having relation to concerns outside British-India. On the other hand matters requiring local knowledge and experience for efficient administration are left to the Provincial Governments. Thus the Supreme Government retains in its own hands all matters relating to (1) foreign relations, (2) the defence of the country, (3) general taxation, (4) currency, (5) public debt, (6) tariffs, (7) post office and telegraphs, and (8) railways. On the other hand ordinary internal administration, assessment and collection of revenue from land, education, medical and sanitary arrangements, irrigation and public buildings, fall to the share of the Provincial Governments. But **in all these matters the Government of India exercises a general and constant control in different ways.** (1) The most important method of supervising and controlling the working of every provincial administration is the financial power of the Government of India. Not only do they habitually receive, and, if necessary, modify, the annual budgets of all local governments, not only are they the common banker for every province; but every new appointment of importance, every large addition, even to minor establishments, must receive their specific sanction, so that no new departure in administration could be undertaken without its previous approval. (2) The Government of India also lays down lines of general policy for carrying on the work of different departments under the the control of the Provincial Governments; and it finds out how far these principles have been carried out by the annual administration reports of the main departments under the local governments submitted to the Supreme Government. (3) In the departments for which it is itself directly responsible, the Government of India has controlling officers for those departments in the different provinces. (4) In the departments which are primarily left to the local Governments, such as agriculture, irrigation, medical, education, and archeology the Government of India employs a number of inspecting or advising officers. Those Inspectors-General frequently examine the working of the department to which they are attached in the different provinces and report to the Government of India the result of their inspection. Should the Government discover any shortcoming or complaints in any of these reports it would take action to remedy the particular question. (5) Besides all these a wide field of appeal to the Government of India is given to officials and private individuals who may have any cause of complaint against any particular local Government. (6) Outside the major provinces of Madras, Bombay, and probably Bengal, appointments made to the most important posts under the provincial Governments are subject to the approval of the

Governor-General. (7) In matters of legislation every proposed provincial legislation is subject to the preliminary scrutiny of the Government of India; and, when passed by the local Government, it must also receive the assent of the Governoar-General before it could become valid. (8) Specific instructions may also be issued to particular local Governments in regard to matters which may have attracted the attention of the Government of India, whether the from departmental administration reports, or the from reports of the proceedings of a local Government submitted to the Imperial Government.

VII. Regulation and Non-Regulation Provinces.

In the present Act the old distinction between the Regulation and Non-regulation Provinces is almost ignored. For administrative purposes, however, the distinction still exists. Upto 1834 the common mode of legislation was by Regulations issued by the Councils of Fort William, Fort St. George and Bombay. The intricacy and complexity of these early Regulations made them unsuitable to newer conquests of the East India Company; and so, on their annexation, simple codes were passed on the principles of the regulations, but modified to suit the circumstances of each case. The provinces in India came to be distinguished into Regulation and Non-regulation provinces according as they were originally administered under regulations or less formal codes. The only Regulation provinces are Bengal, Madras, Bombay and Agra. On account of the development in material progress and legislative activity, the distinction between the more advanced Regulation provinces and their non-Regulation compeers has practically disappeared, except in certain differences in administrative arrangements explained below. So far as legislation is concerned the contrast now is not between the Regulation and Non-Regulation areas, but rather between the territories for which the Government of India can still legislate by the Executive Council alone, and the rest of British India where the machinery of a local Legislative Council is required. Among the provinces to which this method of legislation has been made applicable may be mentioned Aden, Perim, Hill tracts of Chitagong, the Sonthal Parganas, parts of the Punjab and the North-West Frontier Province, Ajmere-Merwara, Coorg, and the Andaman and Nicobar Islands.

VIII. A Sketch of a Provincial Administration.

At the head of the Government in a Regulation Province is the Governor in Council, or the Lieutenant-Governor, as the case may be. The Executive Councils of Madras, Bombay and Bengal carry on the business of the administration in much the same way as the larger council of the the Governor-General. The departments of the administration are divided between the members of the council. All important questions are dealt with by the council collectively, the decisions being arrived at by majority. The Governor, however, has a right to over-rule his Council in special cases [c. s. 50 (2)]. For the province of Agra the Lieutenant-Governor is solely responsible for the administration, his powers being limited only by law, and the standing orders of the Supreme Government. The Secretariats of the Provincial Governments are divided into departments, each under a Secretary with subordinate officers as in the case of the Supreme Government. Thus in Bombay the secretariat is divided into five main departments. 1. Revenue and Financial; 2. Political, Judicial and Special; 3. General, Marine and Eclesiastical; 4. Ordinary public works; 5. Irrigation. The senior of the three Civilian Secretaries is called the Chief Secretary. In addition to the secretariat there are special departments such as Inspectors-General of Police, Jails and Registration, Director of Public Institution, the Inspector-General of Civil Hospitals, the Sanitary Commissioner, and the Superintendent of the Civil Veterinary Departments. There are also the Chief Engineers for Public Works who are likewise Secretaries to the Governments in the Public Works Department. Each of the principal department of the civil service is under the charge of an officer who is attached to and advises the local Government. He himself is brought in touch with local works by making frequent tours of Inspection. Except in Bombay, the Revenue Department is administered under the Governor by a Board of Revenue, consisting of two or three members who are the highest officers in the administrative branch of the service. The work of this board may be divided into departments of Land Revenue and the departments of Excise, Opium, Income Tax, etc. The members of the Board may act separately or collectively according to the practice prevailing in each province. In Madras the Board consists of four members, two of whom are Land Revenue Commissioners, one a Settlement Commissioner, and one a Commissioner for Salt, Excise, Income Tax and Customs. The similar departments are controlled in Bombay by the Director of Land Records and Agriculture, and the Commissioner of Stamps, Excise, and Opium. These officers are immediately subordinate to a local Government. Besides these officers each Government has its own law officer, called the Advocate General, to advise it on legal questions, and to conduct important cases in which the Government is interested.

In both Regulation and Non-regualtion provinces the actual system of administration is based on the repeated division of territories. Each unit of administration is in the responsible charge of an officer who is subordinate to the officer next in rank above him. The most important of this administrative units is the District, and the most accurate impression of the system of Indian administration is gained by regarding a Province as consisting of a collection of districts, which may themselves be spilt up into sub-districts and smaller areas still. There are 250 districts in British India, each of an average size of 4432 square miles, and the average population of close upon a million. Several districts are combined in a Division. There are four such Divisions in the Presidency of Bombay namely Sind, the Northern Division, the Central Division and the Southern Division. Each Division is in the charge of a Divisional Commissioner. In Madras there are no such Divisions, the

Districts being immediately under the Provincial Government there.

IX. District Administration.

"The District Officer," says Sir William Hunter in the Indian Empire, "whether known as the Collector-Magistrate or Deputy Commissioner, is the responsible head of his jurisdiction. Upon his energy and personal character depends ultimately the efficiency of our Indian Government. His own special duties are so numerous and various as to bewilder the outsider; and the work of his subordinates, European and Native, largely depends upon the stimulus of his personal example. The Indian Collector is a strongly individualised worker in every department of rural wellbeing, with a large measure of local independence and of individual initiative. As the name of the Collector-Magistrate implies, his main functions are two-fold. He is a fiscal officer charged with the collection of the revenue from land and other sources; he is also a Revenue, and Criminal Judge, both in first instance and in appeal. But his title by no means exhausts his multifarious duties. He does in his smaller sphere all that the Home Secretary superintends in England, and a great deal more, for he is the representative of a paternal, and not of a constitutional, Government. Police, jails, education, municipalities, roads, sanitation, dispensaries, the local taxation and the Imperial revenues of his district are to him matters of daily concern. He is expected to make himself acquainted with every phase of the social life of the natives, and with each natural aspect of the country. He should be a lawyer, an accountant, a financier and a ready writer of state-papers. He ought also to possess no mean knowledge of agriculture, political economy and engineering."

This sketch of his duties is substantially true, though the independent initiative which the District Officers formerly enjoyed has been of late considerably restricted. Even to-day a Collector is the principal officer in his district. He is a local representative of the Government. His duties as Collector differ in different provinces according to the system on which the Land Revenue is assessed. Though he is not the only officer in the district, he is the supreme officer; and nothing can pass in the district of which it is not his duty to keep himself informed and to watch the operation. He must watch the vicissitudes of trade, the state of the weather, the administration of the civil justice. He must avoid undue interference in matters which are not primarily within his control, but must offer his remonstrance against anything which he believes to be wrong in the interests of the people. He is also a Magistrate of the First Class, though in practice he does not try in person many criminal cases. But he supervises the work of all other magistrates in his district. He is responsible for the peace of the district and suppression of crime.

The District Officer is assisted by a staff of officers both English and Indian. The most important officer under his command is the assistant Magistrate who is also called the senior Assistant Collector. He must be a man of some length of service and experience; the extent of his authority mainly depends on the amount of confidence reposed in him by the District Officer. The District Superintendent of Police is another Officer on the staff of the District Officer to whom he is responsible for the internal peace and order of the district, for the detection and suppression of crimes, and for the prosecution of criminals. For the internal management of the Police affairs, he is, however, responsible only to his immediate superior at the headquarters.

In consequence of the formation of special departments, such as those of public works, sanitation and education, the functions of the District Officers are now-a-days less important than before. But even in these special departments the active co-operation and the advice of the District Officer are always needed. So also in the new self-governing institutions, such as the municipalities within his districts, which are all guided and controlled in their working by the District Officer. He is also generally the chairman of the District Board which, with the aid of subsidiary Boards, maintains roads, schools and dispensaries and carries sanitary improvements in rural areas.

In fine the District Officer rules and guides the people, informs the Government of every thing that takes place in his district, suggests improvements, and protests against innovations which he considers detrimental to the interests of the people within his jurisdiction, and maintains peace and order and good feeling among the various races in his charge.

The District is divided into a number of small units each in the charge of a responsible officer. In general the districts are split up into sub-divisions under the charge of officers of the Imperial Civil Service, or the members of the provincial service; and these sub-divisions are in their turn further divided into minor charges each under officers of the subordinate service. Each sub-divisional officer usually resides at the headquarters of his jurisdiction and has a court house, office, sub-treasury, and sub-jail at his headquarters. In Bombay and in the United Provinces the sub-divisional officers generally live at the head office of the district when not on tour. In these two provinces, as well as in Madras, sub-district units are styled Talukas or Tahsils, and are administered by Tahasildars, or Mamlatdars as they are called in Bombay. These officers belong to the subordinate service. The area of an ordinary Tahsil is from 400 to 600 spuare miles. The Tahsildar is assisted by his subordinate officers, styled revenue inspectors, or Kanungos and the village officers. The latter are mostly hereditary. The most important of them are: the Patel or the headman who collects the revenue, and, in Madras, also acts as a petty Magistrate and Civil Judge, the Kulkarni or Patvari who keeps the village accounts, register of holdings, and in general all records connected with the land revenue; and the Chokidar or village watchman who is the rural policeman. The Indian village organization is very ancient and endures even now, though with modifications required by the peculiar character of the present system of government.

Such is the organization of a Provincial Government in the Regulation provinces. The Non-Regulation provinces differ in their organization in accordance with the importance and the progress which they have made. The head of the administration in those provinces is either a Lieutenant-Governor, or a Chief Commissioner, who governs with the aid of a Secretariat and departmental chiefs. The superior officers of the administration were formerly drawn from a variety of sources; but at the present day they are chiefly drawn from the Indian Civil Service and from the Indian army. Since 1903 the appointment of Military officers has been discontinued in the Punjab, and since 1906 in Assam. Burma is the only major province in which important posts are still given to Military as well as to Civilian officers. The District Officer in the Non-Regulation province is called a Deputy Commissioner and not Collector-Magistrate; and his sudordinates are similarly called the Assistant Commissioners or Extra Assistant Commissioners. With the exception of Oudh, which may be, and is now practically regarded as one of the United Provinces, Non-Regulation provinces have no Board of Revenue, the functions of the Board being discharged either by a Financial Commissioner—as in the Punjab and Burma—or by the Commissioners of divisions and Revenue Officers at the head quarters, as in the Central Provinces. The district administration is pretty nearly the same as in the Regulation provinces, but the District Magistrates and his First Class Subordinates have more extensive criminal jurisdiction. Thus they may be invested with powers to try all criminal cases not involving capital punishment, and can inflict sentences upto seven years' imprisonment or transportation. Moreover administrative and judicial functions are, in the less advanced provinces, frequently combined. But the system in the Punjab, and to some extent in the Central Provinces, approximates very closely to the system in the Regulation provinces, except that the judicial functions of a District Judge are divided between a Divisional Judge and a local District Judge entrusted with less important functions.

The Presidencies as well as the United Provinces, and, since 1915, Bihar and Orissa have each a High Court, while the highest

Judicial Tribunal in the Punjab and Burma is called a Chief Court; and authority similar to the Chief Courts is exercised in the Central Provinces and Assam by one or more Judicial Commissioners.

Of the minor Provinces, two—the North-West Frontier Province and British Baluchistan—are administered on nearly the same lines. As the more important Non-Regulation provinces, they are divided into districts and administered by Deputy Commissioners. In the former the Chief Commissioner is also agent to the Governor General for frontier tribes. He is aided by the principal officers who are: the Revenue and Judicial Commissioners, corresponding to the financial Commissioners and the Chief Court of the present province of the Punjab. So also British Baluchistan which is made up of three British Districts, the agency territories held on lease, and the native states of Kalat and Lasbela. Ajmere-Merwara and Coorg are governed by the agent to the Governor General in Rajputana and the resident in Mysore respectively, while the Superintendent of the penal settlement of Port Blair is also the Chief Commissioner of Aandman and Nicobar Islands.

X. Relations between the Government of India and the Heads of Provinces.

It would be as interesting to know as it is difficult to say, what exactly are the relations between the supreme Government and its various subordinate chiefs. On paper, of course, every thing seems to be so well ordered as to leave hardly any room for friction. But in reality there is not always found that smooth and noiselsas working of the wheels of government as an uniniated outsider would be inclined to believe in. We know for a fact that Sir Bartle Frere, as the Governor of Bombay, in the days when Sir John Lawrence was the Viceroy of India, caused more than one sleepless night to the Viceroy on the question of the failure of the Bank of Bombay as well as on questions of Frontier policy. It is also recorded that the Duke of Buckingham, as Governor of Madras under Lord Lytton, caused a serious obstructrion to that Viceroy's famine policy; so much so that the Home Government had to interfere, and to recall, almost peremptorily, the refractory Duke. Perhaps it was to such cases as these that Lord Curzon alluded in one of his farewell speeches: "In old volumes of our proceedings which it has been my duty to study at midnight hours, I have sometimes come across peppery letters or indignant remonstrances, and have seen the spectacle of infuriated proconsuls strutting up and down the stage." For himself, he added, notwithstanding the fact that during his seven years' tenure of the Viceroyalty nearly thirty Governors, Lieutenant-Governors and Chief Commissioners had come and gone, there never had been a time when the relations between the Supreme Government and the heads of the local Government had been so free from friction or so harmonious. No one except those intimately connected with the Government of India can say how often such friction arises even to-day. It would seem, however, that the prevalance of the more liberal views as regards the extent of the authority of local Governments, the great expansion of their Legislative Councils and the greater harmony between the rulers and the ruled resulting therefrom, the large concessions in matters of finance, the definite demarcation of the other spheres of public activity, the growth of precedent, the improved means of rapid communications, and above all the characters of the men chosen for such posts have all combined to minimise, if not entirely to destroy, all causes of friction. The right to be obeyed is so firmly established in the Government of India, that the privilege of subordinate proconsuls to tender their resignation by way of a protest against the undue encroachments or interference of the supreme authority has ceased to be a censure upon the Viceregal powers, and is rather a means of affording a speedy solution of an unpleasant problem. The resignation of Sir Bamfylde Fuller afforded the last instance of this nature, vindicating the right of the Supreme Government to be obeyed, as well as the right of its lieutenant to be relieved of an untenable situation.

XI. The Structure of Indian Government.

The question of provincial autonomy, which has been exercising the minds of the public for some time past, and which is discussed more in detail hereafter, will best be solved by trying to understand whether our present constitution is unitary or federal in form. In a Unitary Government, like that of England or France, all sovereign power is concentrated in the hands of the Central Government. There may, indeed, be a division of functions between the central and local governing bodies. But this division in no case amounts to a distribution of sovereign powers. The local governing bodies are the creatures, the delegates and the dependents of the central power, which is the sole, supreme, sovereign authority in the state; and between which and the local bodies no other sovereign or semi-sovereign authority is interposed. On the other hand the chief characteristic of a Federal Government is the distribution of sovereignty between the Federal power and its constituent states. A federation is a combination of several independent states into one single state. The combining state may have desired, or been compelled, to unite in order to promote their economic development, or to secure their political integrity or safety. But even when combined they do not lose all trace of their original independence. Hence the new central state, made by the union of the old independent states, is entrusted only with such sovereign powers as the combining state might decide to vest in a central authority. Consequently even in cases where the necessity of unification is enforced by the considerations of self-preservation, the central authority, though allowed a liberal share of sovereign powers, is never quite the undisputed sovereign which the similar authority in a unitary state is. There is always a difference between powers allotted to the central power and those reserved for individual state.

The Government of India resembles, as well as differs from, both these kinds of states. The dominant position of the Supreme Government in India. and its unquestioned powers of control, and even of creation, suggest a great affinity to a unitary state. But the presence of Provincial Governments, which are an intermediary between the Supreme Government and the local governing bodies, and which are essentially deputies of the Supreme Government, serves to distinguish the Government of India from a unitary state. Nor can we quite describe it as a federal state. The mere presence of a number of provinces, with each its own separate Government, is not enough to constitute a federation. With the exception of the three Presidencies, all the other provinces in India have been created by the central authority in order to relieve the latter of some portion of its heavy administrative work. In stead, therefore, of the provinces combining to create a united central Government, as is the case in federations, it was rather the central Government which deputed its minor functions of government in order to strengthen its main hold. Even the originally independent Presidencies were forced to submit to the central authority. Besides, the supremacy of the central Government once established, it is unquestioned in every province. In so far as the Government of India can themselves be called a sovereign power, there is really no distribution of sovereignty between them and the various provincial Governments. It must, however, be remembered that the Government of India themselves are not sovereign in the sense that the King in Parliament is the sovereign of the whole British Empire. They are, in fact, more under the control of the Secretary of State for India, than the self-governing colonies are under the control of the Secretary of State for the colonies. Such decentralisation, therefore, as already exists in this country, notably in financial matters, is hardly large enough to amount to a distribution of sovereignty, and yet not insignificant enough to be described as a mere delegation of powers which can be resumed by the Central Government whenever the latter choose to do so.

The case of the Government of India, therefore, must be classed by itself. There is no doubt a division of work between the Supreme and the Provincial Governments; but the division is brought about for the sake of administrative convenience, and not out of any deliberate desire to create independent, semi-sovereign authorities. The view, however, is gaining ground that even if in the past, there was no such deliberate intention to establish semi-sovereign states in the provinces, it is high time that they were so regarded now—a view which will be examined hereafter. This tendency, more than any actual organization of Government, precludes us from regarding ours as a unitary state.

XII. Provincial Autonomy.

The question of giving wider powers to the provinces is at least as old as the Government by the Crown directly. In his speeches on India about the time that the government of the country was transferred to the Crown, Mr. Bright repeatedly insisted upon the necessity of a greater decentralisation. Says he in one of his most famous speeches, "What you want is to decentralise the Government. You will not make a single step towards the improvement of India unless you change your whole system of Government, unless you give to each Presidency more independent powers than are now possessed by them......How long does England propose to govern India? Nobody answers that question, and nobody can answer it. Be it 50, or 100, or 500 years, does any man, with the smallest glimmering of common sense, believe that so great a country, with its 20 different nations and its 20 different languages, can be bound up and consolidated into one compact and enduring Empire? We must fail in the attempt if we ever make it, and we are bound to look in the future with reference to that point."

Commenting on this subject, Sir John Strachey remarks that the suggestion of Bright for a separate, independent government for each of the Presidencies of India, subject only to the British Crown, and for the abolition of the Central Government is impracticable. "There is clearly nothing more essential to the maintenance of our empire in India," says he "than a strong central authority: but Mr. Bright's belief was undoubtedly true that there could be no successful government in India, unless the fundamental fact of the immense diversity of the Indian peoples and countries be recognised, and each great province be administered with a minimum of interference from outside."

On the other hand Lord Curzon remarked in his speech already quoted, "I am not one of those who hold the view that local Governments are hampered in their administration by excessive centralisation or that any great measures of devolution would produce better results. × × × × I believe that with due allowance for the astonishing diversities of local conditions, it is essential that there should be certain uniform principles running through our entire administration, and that nothing could be worse either for India or for the British dominion in India than that the country should be split up into a number of separate and rival units, very much like the Austro-Hungarian Empire in Europe where the independent factors are only held together by the nexus of a single Crown. × × × × × I believe, therefore, in a strong Government of India gathering into its own hands and controlling all the reins. But I would ride local Governments on the shaffle and not on the curb: and I would do all in our power to consult their feelings, to enhance their dignity, and to stimulate their sense of responsibility and power."

This presents in the strongest possible light the case for centralisation. But the views of the Government of India underwent an almost radical change six years later. The famous Delhi despatch of Lord Hardinge's Government says, "The maintenance of British rule in India depends on the ultimate supremacy of the Governor-General-in-Council; and the Indian Concils Act of 1909 itself bears testimony to the impossibility of allowing matters of vital concern to be decided by a majority of non-official votes in the Imperial Legislative Council. Nevertheless it is certain that, in the course of time, the just demands of Indians for a larger share in the Government of the country will have to be satisfied, and the question will be how this devolution of power can be conceded without impairing the Supreme authority of the Governor-General-in-Council. The only possible solution of the difficulty would appear to be gradually to give the provinces a larger measure of self Government, until at last India would consist of a number of administrations, autonomous in all provincial affairs, with the Government of India above them all, and possessing powers to interfere in cases of mis-government, but ordinarily restricting themselves to matters of Imperial concern. In order that this consummation may be attained, it is essential that the Supreme Government should not be associated with any particular provincial Government."

These long extracts from the speeches or writings of great statesmen have been adduced to show how easy it is even for trained and experienced public men, to take different views of such a complex problem, and how difficult it is to offer a simple and satisfactory solution by men relatively inexperienced and ignorant of the actual difficulties of the problem. As early as 1833 an attempt was made to confine the interference of the Supreme Government in a local concern to the requirements of a just control, indispensable to the maintenance of the Imperial unity and avoid all "petty, vexatious and meddling interference." But in practice it is very difficult to determine exactly where the just control of general principles ends, and the petty, vexatious, meddlesome interference in details begins. It may quite conceivably happen that what is normally a detail, which had best be left to the local Government, might, in exceptional circumstances, assume the dignity of a great principle. Take for instance the Cawnpore Mosque case, where the Viceroy interfered in apparently only a local riot; or the still later case of the United Provinces Municipalities Act, where the interference of the Supreme Government was invoked by the people, though strictly speaking, it is only a matter of detail. Under such circumstances the Government of India, and even the Secretary of State, must assert themselves. It is, therefore, not quite a thing to be wished for that the relations, between the Supreme Government and its local subordinates should acquire the rigidity of a federal constitution; rather should they be capable of being readily adaptable to new or changing conditions.

The various requirements of the maintenance of Imperial supremacy and local autonomy, and constitutional elasticity, and national solidarity which are all desired at the same time make the question still more difficult. India is, at the present moment, under the simultaneous operation of what Brice calls the centrifugal as well as centripedal tendencies. On the one hand there is the development of rapid means of postal and telegraphic communications, which preclude the possibility for the Provincial Governments of the old excuse for acting without orders—the exigency of the moment requiring prompt action without delay. The ease and rapidity with which the advice of the Supreme Government can be always procured, the obviously superior information of the Supreme Government in all important questions and their wider outlook, the elimination from the Provincial Governments of all those spheres of activity in which promptness of action is more valuable than sound deliberation,—all combine to make references to the Central Government more frequent and the dependence of the Provincial Governments much closer. The spread of English language, which creates and intensifies a consciousness of national solidarity among the educate classes of the peoples themselves, has also worked—though perhaps unconsciously,—towards the same goal. The recognition of the economic needs of the country, and the consequent efforts towards its material development make it inevitable that the control of the Central Government be constant and universal, and the welding of the country into a single solid block, not only desirable, but absolutely indispensable. The increasing attention paid in Parliament to the details of Indian administration makes the control of Home authorities more effective even on the Government of India itself. The edifice of the Indian Emprie, moreover, includes not only British provinces, but also the Native States. They are in India, and yet, for many purposes, not of it. No scheme of reorganisation can be formulated without taking account of them; and yet to attempt to include them in a new structure, without radically altering the principles which now govern their existence and determine their powers and position, is to invite inevitable failure. Above all the character of the present provinces makes any scheme of complete provincial independence and autonomy almost unthinkable. Our provinces are no homogenous units whether by race or religion, by language or geography, by traditional unity or sentimental or economic identity of interests. They are mere administrative charges, with the possible exception of Bengal, created merely to afford relief to the Central Government. The only uniting factor throughout India is the common obedience to a single Government. And the idea of provincial autonomy is inimical in its nature to this one single uniting principle.

On the other hand there are grave forces working in the opposite direction. The difficulty in administering a vast continent like India from a single headquarters, and the consequent failure in statesmanship and inefficiency in Government are too obvious to need :a detailed consideration. The very divergence in the social and economic conditions of the different provinces is a strong reason for decentralization. For the principles which a Central Governmant like that of India can lay down must, of necessity, be uniform, and therefore hardly suitable to every province alike. There is, moreover, great political wisdom in the desire to make local authorities feel their responsibility more vividly, which can only be done if they were made independent in some measure. And, above all, the aspirations of the people towards self-government are easier to be realised on the narrower field of a Provincial Government, than on the wider stage of the Supreme Government. The decentralisation commission recorded its opinion that "both the Government of India and the Provincial Governments have hitherto been too much dominated by considerations .of administrative efficiency. They have, we think, paid too little regard to the importance of developing a strong sense of responsibility among their subordinate agents, and of giving sufficient weight to local sentiments and traditions."

In the face of these opposing tendencies it is almost impossible to say whether the present situation needs a change. The ideal of provincial autonomy has been too definitely accepted by the leaders of native opinion to allow a criticism of that ideal without a charge of want of sympathy with the noble ideal of self-government. And yet it must be said that the history of the last century or so all over the world shows the struggle of imperialism—if one may so describe the centralising tendencies—against provincialism, resulting in the indisputable victory of the former. Prussia helps to form the German Empire, and Sardinia Italy. The provinces of Canada unite to form a Dominion and the States of Australia–admittedly the most democratic of the self-governing colonies of England–voluntarily combine to form the Commonwealth. Even in the United States the power and prestige of the central federal Government have grown immensely at the expense of local independence. And territorial acquisitions, or political influence, beyond the frontiers of the United States are not rigidly excluded. Hence a centralised government is not necessarily hostile to the development of democracy, or to its maintenance. It is doubtful, moreover, if a complete provincial autonomy in India would be quite to the advantage of the people. No doubt provincial autonomy would secure better representation of the people in the councils of the Government, and facilitate the advent of responsible government on the model of the Governments in England or the colonies. But if this increased representation in the Provincial Councils and greater responsibility are obtained without any change in the powers of Supreme Government, the self-government so obtained would be perfectly illusory. Real self-government for India can only be realised when the Supreme Government becomes perfectly amenable to public opinion in India. If that is accomplished provincial autonomy would have very little value beyond sentiment; and if that remains unachieved provincial autonomy would be only one more agency to raise hopes which might never be realised. The necessity a real self-government as thus defined is emphasised by the economic conditions of India. If our industrial development is to be pushed on as repidly as possible, if our citizens in other parts of the British Empire are to be considered and treated much better than slaves, we need a Central Government which is national in its composition as well as in its tone; and which can protect and promote the interests of its citizens both at home and abroad more than any Provincial Government possibly can do,

If we stretch our imagination and look a little in the future the problem of decentralisation,–of Provincial Autonomy,–would be seen to wear an entirely different aspect. The people of India disunited by centuries of misunderstandings have at last been united, or are beginning to be united in a single nationality. If they would be left to themselves they would soon forget that they are Hindus or Mahomedans in trying to learn that they are Indians, and that they have to accomplish the herculian task of restoring India to the position that she once occupied as the centre of the civilised world. This task can never be accomplished by another people than the Indians themselves, however sincere and sympathetic that other people might be. To achieve this self-government would be indispensable. But it does not need, it would indeed be gravely prejudiced by, any separation in different provinces. The most serious problem before a united self-governing India in the near future would be, not how to give the greatest play to local sentiment, but how to wrest the economic supremacy from Japan or Germany. To solve that we shall need the undivided strength of every one who thinks of India before thinking of Bengal or Gujerat; we shall have to organise and co-ordinate the resources of the entire peninsula with a view to bring them to bear on one single issue. If therefore, the ideal of provincial autonomy means the weakening of the central government, we may confidently say that a self-governing India, ten years after the realisation of self-government, will have no need for it, whatever be the vogue for it to-day.

The problem of decentralisation no doubt exists, and the foregoing remarks should not be construed to mean that the present arrangements, whether as between the Imperial and the Provincial Governments, or as between the Provincial Governments and the local-governing institutions, are the best possible arrangements. But perhaps the best solution of the problem is not so much in the creation of almost independant provincial Governments with no bonds *ninter se*, but rather by basing our local self-governing institutions on a broader, more liberal, more genuinely democratic principle. India has arrived at a stage when the municipalities and the District Boards may safely be given the powers and the position of the County Council in England. If democracy is fully realised at the base in this way, and also at the top, we shall have no great need for Provincial Autonomy.

CHAPTER V.

Indian Legislature.

PART VI.

INDIAN LEGISLATION.

The Governor-General in Legislative Counci.

63. (1) For purposes of legislation the Governor-General's Council shall consist of the members of his Executive Council with the addition of members nominated or elected in accordance with rules made under this Act. The council so constituted is in this Act referred to as the Indian Legislative Council.

(2) The number of additional members so nominated or elected, the number of such members required to constitute a quorum, the term of office of such members, and the manner of filling casual vacancies occurring by reason of absence from India, inability to attend to duty, death, acceptance of office, or resignation duly accepted, or otherwise, shall be such as may be prescribed by rules made under this Act.

Provided that the aggregate number of members so nominated or elected shall not exceed the number specified in that behalf in the second column of the first schedule to this Act.

(3) At least one-half of the additional members of the council must be persons not in the civil or military service of the Crown in India; and, if any additional member accepts office under the Crown in India, his seat as an additional member shall thereupon become vacant.

(4) When and so long as the Indian Legislative Council assembles in a province having a Lieutenant-Governor or Chief Commissioner he shall be an additional member of the council, in excess, if

necessary, of the aggregate number of nominated or elected additional members prescribed by this section.

(5) The additional members of the council are not entitled to be present at meetings of the Governor-General's Executive Council.

(6) The Governor-General-in-Council may, with the approval of the Secretary of State in Council, make rules as to the conditions under which and manner in which persons resident in India may be nominated or elected as additional members of the Indian Legislative Council, and as to the qualifications for being, and for being nominated or elected, an additional member of that council, and as to any other matter for which rules are authorised to be made under this section, and also as to the manner in which those rules are to be carried into effect.

(7) All rules made under this section shall be laid before both Houses of Parliament as soon as may be after they are made, and those rules shall not be subject to repeal or alteration by the Governor-General in Legislative Council.

64. (1) The Indian Legislative Council shall assemble at such times and places as the Goveronor-General-in-Council appoints.

(2) Any meeting of the council may be adjourned, under the authority of the Governor-General in Council, by the Governor-General or other person presiding.

(3) In the absence of the Governor-General from any meeting of the council the person to preside thereat shall be the vice-president of the council, or, in his absence, the senior ordinary member of the council present at the meeting, or, during the discussion of the annual financial statement or of any matter of general public interest, the vice-president or the member appointed to preside in accordance with rules made under this Act.

(4) If any difference of opinion arises on any question brought before a meeting of the council, the person presiding shall have a second or casting vote.

65. (1) The Governor-General in Legislative Council has power to make laws—

16

(a) for all persons, for all courts, and for all places and things, within British India; and

(b) for all subjects of His Majesty and servants of the Crown within other parts of India; and

(c) for all native Indian subjects of His Majesty, without and beyond as well as within British India; and

(d) for the government officers, soldiers and followers in His Majesty's Indian forces, wherever they are serving, in so far as they are not subject to the Army Act;

(e) and for all persons employed or serving in or belonging to the Royal Indian Marine Service; and

(f) for repealing or altering any laws which for the time being are in force in any part of British India or apply to persons for whom the Governor-General in Legislative Council has power to make laws.

(2) provided that the Governor-General in Legislative Council has not, unless (expressly so authorised by Act of Parliament,) power to make any law repealing or affecting

(1) any Act of Parliament passed after the year one thousand eight hundred and sixty and extending to British India (including the Army Act and any Act amending the same), or

(2) any Act of Parliament enabling the Secretary of State in Council to raise money in the United Kingdom for the Government of India;

and has not power to make any law affecting the authority of Parliament, or any part of the unwritten laws or constitution of the United Kngdom of Great Britain and Ireland whereon may depend in any degree the allegiance of any person to the Crown of the United Kingdom, or affecting the sovereignty or dominion of the Crown over any part of British India.

(3) The Governor-General in Legislative Council has not power, without the previous approval of the Secretary of State in Council, to make any law empowering any court, other than a High Court, to

sentence to the punishment of death any of His Majesty's subjects born in Europe, or the children of such subjects, or abolishing any High Court.

66. (1) A law made under this Act for the Royal Indian Marine Service shall not apply to any offence unless the vessel to which the offender belongs is at the time of the commission of the offence within the limits of Indian waters, that is to say, the high seas between the Cape of Good Hope on the West and the Straits of Magellan on the East and any territorial waters between those limits.

(2) The punishments imposed by any such law for offences shall be similar in character to, and not in excess of, the punishments which may, at the time of making the law, be imposed for similar offences under the Acts relating to His Majesty's Navy, except that in case of persons other than Europeans or Americans, imprisonment for any term not exceeding fourteen years, or transportation for life or any less term, may be substituted for penal servitude.

67. (1) At a meeting of the Indian Legislative Council no motion shall be entertained other than a motion for leave to introduce a measure into the council for the purpose of enactment, or having reference to a measure introduced or proposed to be introduced into the council for that purpose, or having reference to some rule for the conduct of business in the council, and no business shall be transacted other than the consideration of those motions or the alteration of those rules.

(2) It shall not be lawful, without the previous sanction of the Governor-General, to introduce at any meeting of the council any measure affecting:—

(*a*) the public debt or public revenues of India, or imposing any charge on the revenues of India; or

(*b*) the religion or religious rites and usuages of any class of British subjects in India; or

(*c*) the discipline or maintenance of any part of His Majesty's military or naval forces; or

(*d*) the relations of the Government with foreign princes or states.

(3) Notwithstanding anything in the foregoing provisions of this section, the Governor-General-in-Council may, with the sanction of the Secretary of State in Council, make rules authorising at any meeting of the Indian Legislative Council the discussion of the annual financial statement of the Governor-General in Council and of any matter of general public interest and the asking of questions, under such conditions and restrictions as may be prescribed in the rules. Rules made under this sub-section may provide for the appointment of a member of the council to preside at any such discussion in the place of the Governor-General and of the vice-president, and shall be laid before both Houses of Parliament as soon as may be after they are made, and shall not be subject to repeal or alteration by the Governor-General in Legislative Council.

68. (1) When an act has been passed at a meeting of the Indian Legislative Council, the Governor-General, whether he was or was not present in council at the passing thereof, may declare that he assents to the Act, or that he withholds assent to the Act, or that he reserves the Act for the signification of His Majesty's pleasure thereon.

(2) An Act of the Governor-General in Legislative Council has no validity until the Governor-General has declared his assent thereto, or, in the case of an Act reserved for the signification of His Majesty's pleasure, until His Majesty has signified his assent to the Governor-General through the Secretary of State in Council, and that assent has been notified by the Governor-General.

69 (1) When an Act of the Governor-General in Legislative Council has been assented to by the Governor-General, he shall send to the Secretary of State an authentic copy thereof, and it shall be lawful for His Majesty to signify, through the Secretary of State in Council, his disallowance of any such Act.

(2) Where the disallowance of any such Act has been so signified, the Governor-General shall forthwith notify the disallowance, and thereupon the Act, as from the date of the notification, shall become void accordingly.

70. The Governor-General in Legislative Council may, subject to the assent of the Governor-General, alter the rules for the conduct of legislative business in the Indian Legislative Council (including

rules prescribing the mode of promulgation and authentication of Acts passed by that Council); but any alteration so made may be disallowed by the Secretary of State in Council, and if so disallowed shall have no effect.

Regulations and Ordinances.

71. (1) The Local Government of any part of British India to which this section for the time being applies may propose to the Governor-General in Council the draft of any regulation for the peace and good Government of that part with the reasons for proposing the regulation.

(2) Thereupon the Governor-General in Council may take any such draft and reasons into consideration; and, when any such draft has been approved by the Governor-General in Council, and assented to by the Governor-General, it shall be published in the Gazette of India and in the local official gazette, if any, and shall thereupon have the like force of law and be subject to the like disallowance as if it were an Act of the Governor-General in Legislative Council.

(3) The Governor-General shall send to the Secretary of State in Council an authentic copy of every regulation to which he has assented under this section.

(4) The Secretary of State may, by resolution in council, apply this section to any part of British India, as from a date to be fixed in the resolution, and withdraw the application of this section from any part to which it has been applied.

72. The Governor-General may, in cases of emergency, make and promulgate ordinances for the peace and good Government of British India or any part thereof, and any ordinance so made, shall, for the space of not more than six months from its promulgation, have the like force of law as an Act passed by the Governor-General in Legislative Council; but the power of making ordinances under this section is subject to the like restrictions as the power of the Governor-General in Legislative Council to make laws; and any ordinance made under this section is subject to the like disallowance

as an Act passed by the Governor-General in Legislative Council, and may be controlled or superseded by any such Act.

Local Legislatures.

72. (1) For purposes of legislation, the Council of a Governor or of a Lieutenant-Governor having an Executive Council, shall consist of the members of his Executive Council with the addition of members nominated or elected in accordance with rules made under this Act.

(2) In the case of the Councils of the Governors of Madras and Bombay (and, if so ordered by the Governor of Bengal, in the case of his Council), the Advocate-General or acting Advocate-General for the time being of the presidency shall be one of the members so nominated.

(3) The Legislative Council of a Lieutenant-Governor, not having an executive Council, or of a Chief Commissioner, shall consist of members nominated or elected in accordance with rules made under this Act.

(4) Councils constituted as provided by this section are in this Act referred to as Local Legislative Councils, and Governors, Lieutenant-Governors and Chief Commissioners in Legislative Council are in this Act referred to as local legislatures.

74. (1) The number of additional members nominated or elected to the Legislative Council of the Governor of Bengal, Madras or Bombay, the number of such members required to constitute a quorum, the term of office of such members, and the manner of filling casual vacancies occurring by reason of absence from India, inability to attend to duty, death, acceptance of office, or resignation duly accepted, or otherwise, shall, in the case of each such Council, be such as may be prescribed by rules made under this Act.

Provided that the aggregate number of members so nominated or elected shall not exceed the number specified in that behalf in the second column of the First Schedule to this Act.

(2) At least one-half of the additional members so nominated or elected to any of those councils must be persons not in the civil or

military service of the crown in India; and if any such person accepts office under the crown in India his seat as a member shall thereupon become vacant.

(3) An additional member of any of those councils is not entitled to be present at meetings of the Governor's Executive Council.

(4) The Governor-General-in-Council may, with the approval of the Secretary of State in Council, make rules as to the conditions under which and manner in which persons resident in India may be nominated or elected additional members of any of those Councils, and as to the qualifications for being, and for being nominated or elected, an additional member of any of those councils, and as to any other matter for which rules are authorised to be made under this section, and also as to the manner in which those rules are to be carried into effect.

(5) All rules made under this section shall be laid before both Houses of Parliament as soon as may be after they are made, and those rules shall not be subject to repeal or alteration by the Governor-General in Legislative Council.

75. (1) The Legislative Council of the Governor of Bengal, Madras or Bombay shall assemble at such times and places as the Governor appoints.

(2) Any meeting of the council may be adjourned by the Governor, or, under his authority, by the other person presiding.

(3) If the absence of the governor from any meeting of the council the person to preside thereat shall be the vice-president of the council, or, in his absence, the senior civil member of the Executive Council present at the meeting, or during the discussion of the annual financial statement, or of any matter of general public interest, the vice-president or the member appointed to preside in accordance with rules made under this Act.

(4) If any difference of opinion arises on any question brought before a meeting of the council, the person presiding shall have a second or casting vote.

76. (1) The number of members nominated or elected to the legislative council of a Lieutenant-Governor or Chief Commissioner,

the number of such members required to constitute a quorum, the term of office of such members, and the manner of filling casual vacancies, occurring by reason of absence from India, inability to attend to duty, death, acceptance of office, or resignation duly accepted, or otherwise, shall, in the case of each such council, be such as may be prescribed, by rules made under this Act.

Provided that the aggregate number of members so nominated or elected shall not, in the case of any Legislative Council mentioned in the first column of the First Schedule to this Act, exceed the number specified in that behalf in the second column of that schedule.

(2) At least one-third of the persons so nominated or elected to the Legislative Council of a Lieutenant-Governor or Chief Commissioner must be persons not in the civil or military service of the Crown in India.

(3) The Governor-General in Council may, with the approval of the Secretary of State in Council, make rules as to conditions under which persons resident in India may be nominated or elected members of any of those Legislative Councils, and as to the qualifications for being, and for being nominated or elected, a member of any of those councils, and as to any other matter for which rules are authorised to be made under this section, and as to the manner in which those rules are to be carried into effect.

(4) All rules made under this section shall be laid before both Houses of Parliament as soon as may be after they are made, and those rules shall not be subject to repeal or alteration by the Governor-General in Legislative Council.

77. (1) When a new Lieutenant-Governorship is constituted under this Act, the Governor-General-in-Council may, by notification, with the sanction of His Majesty previously signified by the Secretary of State in Council, constitute the Lieutenant-Governor in Legislative Council of the province, as from a date specified in the notification a local legislature for that province, and define the limits of the province for which the Lieutenant-Governor in Legislative Council is to exercise legislative powers.

(2) The Governor-General-in-Council may, by notification, extend the provisions of this Act relating to Legislative Councils of

Lieutenant-Governors, subject to such modifications and adaptations as he may consider necessary, to any province for the time being a chief commissioner.

78. (1) Every Lieutenant-Governor who has no Executive Council, and every chief commissioner who has a Legistative Council, shall appoint a member of his Legislative Council to be vice president.

(2) In the absence of the Lieutenant-Governor or chief commissioner from any meeting of his Legislative Council the person to preside thereat shall be the vice-president of the council, or in his absence, the member of the council who is highest in official rank, among those holding office under the Crown who are present at the meeting, or, during the discussion of the annual financial statement, or of any matter of general public interest, the vice-president or the member appointed to preside in accordance with rules made under this Act.

(3) If any difference of opinion arises on any question brought before a meeting of the council, the person presiding shall have a second or casting vote.

79. (1) The local legislature of any province has power, subject to the provisions of this Act, to make laws for the peace and good Government of the territories for the time being constituting that province.

(2) The local legislature of any province may, with the previous sanction of the Governor-General, but not otherwise, repeal or alter as to that province any law made either before or after the commencement of this Act by any authority in British India other than that local legislature.

(3) The local legislature of any province may not, without the previous sanction of the Governor-General, make or take into consideration any law

(a) affecting the public debt of India, or the customs duties, or any other tax or duty for the time being in force, and imposed by the authority of the Governor-General in Council for the general purposes of the Government of India; or (*b*) regulating any of the current coin, or the issue of any bills, notes or other paper currency; or

(*c*) regulating the conveyance of letters by the post office or messages by the electric telegraph; or

(*d*) altering in any way the Indian Penal Code; or

(*e*) affecting the religion or religious rites and usages of any class of British subjects in India; or

(*f*) affecting the discipline or maintenance of any part of His Majesty's naval or military forces; or

(*g*) regulating patents or copyright; or

(*h*) affecting the relations of the Government with foreign princes or states.

(4) The local legislature of any province has not power to make any law affecting any Act of Parliament.

(5) Provided that an Act or a provision of an Act made by a local legislature, and subsequently assented to by the Governor-General in pursuance of this Act, shall not be deemed invalid by reason only of its requiring the previous sanction of the Governor-General under this Act.

80. (1) At a meeting of a local Legislative Council no motion shall be entertained other than a motion for leave to introduce a measure into the council for the purpose of enactment, or having reference to a measure introduced or proposed to be introduced into the council for that purpose, or having reference to some rule for the conduct of business in the council, and no business shall be transacted other than the consideration of those motions or the alteration of those rules.

(2) It shall not be lawful for any member of any local Legislative Council to introduce, without the previous sanction of the Governor, Lieutenant-Governor or chief commissioner, any measure affecting the public revenues of the province or imposing any charge on those revenues.

(3) Notwithstanding anything in the foregoing provisions of this section, the local Government may, with the sanction of the Governor-

General in Council, make rules authorising, at any meeting of the local Legislative Council, the discussion of the annual financial statement of the local Government, and of any matter of general public interest, and the asking of questions, under such conditions and restrictions as may be prescribed in the rules. Rules made under this sub-section for any council may provide for the appointment of a member of the council to preside at any such discussion in place of the Governor, Lieutenant-Governor or chief commissioner, as the case may be, and of the vice-president, and shall be laid before both Houses of Parliament as soon as may be after they are made, and shall not be subject to repeal or alteration by the Governor-General in Legislative Council or the local legislature.

81. (1) When an Act has been passed at a meeting of a local Legislative Council, the Governor, Lieutenant-Governor, or chief commissioner, whether he was or was not present in council at the passing of the Act, may declare that he assents to or withholds his assent from the Act.

(2) If the Governor, Lieutenant-Governor, or chief commissioner, withholds his assent from any such Act, the Act has no effect.

(3) If the Governor, Lieutenant–Governor or chief commissioner assents to any such Act, he shall forthwith send an authentic copy of the Act to the Governor-General, and the Act shall not have validity until the Governor-General has assented thereto, and that assent has been signified by the Governor-General to, and published by, the Governor, Lieutenant-Governor, or chief commissioner.

(4) Where the Governor-General withholds his assent from any such Act, he shall signify to the Governor, Lieutenant-Governor or chief commissioner in writing his reason for so with-holding his assent.

82. (1) When any such Act has been assented to by the Governor-General, he shall send to the Secretary of State an authentic copy thereof, and it shall be lawful for His Majesty to signify through the Secretary of State in Council, his disallowance of any such Act.

(2) Where the disallowance of any such Act has been so signified, the Governor, Lieutenant-Governor or chief commissioner shall forthwith notify the disallowance, and thereupon the Act, as from the date of the notification, shall become void accordingly.

83. (1) The local Government of any province, for which a local Legislative Council is hereafter constituted under this Act, shall, before the first meeting of that Council, and with the sanction of the Governor-General-in-Council, make rules for the conduct of legislative business in that council (including rules for prescribing the mode of promulgation and authentication of laws passed by that council.)

(2) A local legislature may, subject to the assent of the Governor, Lieutenant-Governor or chief commissioner, alter the rules for the conduct of legislative business in the local Legislative Council (including rules prescribing the mode of promulgation and authentication of laws passed by the council); but any alteration so made may be disallowed by the Governor-General-in-Council, and if so disallowed shall have no effect.

Validity of Indian Laws.

84. A law made by any authority in British India shall not be deemed invalid solely on account of any one or more of the following reasons:—

(*a*) in the case of a law made by the Governor-General in Legislative Council, because it affects the prerogative of the Crown; or

(*b*) in the case of any law, because the requisite proportion of members not holding office under the Crown in India was not complete at the date of its introduction into the council or its enactment; or

(*c*) in the case of a law made by a local legislature, because it confers on magistrates, being justices of the peace, the same jurisdiction over European British subjects as that legislature, by Acts duly made, could lawfully confer on magistrates in the exercise of authority over other British subjects in the like cases.

COMMENTS.

Ss. 63–84 (both inclusive).

Below is given a general description and criticism of the constitution and powers of the Indian Legislatures, both Imperial and Provincial. Here we append some remarks on the extent of the law-making powers of the India Legislative Councils.

The law-making powers of the Indian legislatures, as laid down in s. 65 of the present Act (and s. 79 for the local councils) are not exhaustive. Under various Acts of Parliament the Indian Councils, like other British legislatures with limited powers, have power to make laws on specified subjects with more extensive operation than laws made under its ordinary power. Thus the Extradition Act of 1870, the Slave Trade Act of 1876, the Fugitive Offenders Act of 1881, the Colonial Courts of Admiralty Act of 1890, the Colonial Probates Act of 1892, and the Merchant Shipping Act of 1894 have each given wider powers than are contained in the provisions of this Act.

As regards the general powers of the Indian legislatures, the leading case is that of *Queen vs. Burah* (*1878, L. R. 3, App. Cas. 889*). In that case an act of the Indian legislature, (XII of 1869) was questioned. By that act the Garo Hills were removed from the jurisdiction of the ordinary civil and criminal courts, and the administration of civil and criminal justice in those territories was vested in officers appointed by the Lieutenant-Governor of Bengal. By s. 9 of that Act the Lieutenant-Governor was authorised to extend the operation of the Act to any of the adjoining mountains. The Privy Council maintained the validity of the Act as well as that of the ninth section. It was held that (1) the Act was not inconsistent with the Indian High Courts Act of 1861 or with the Charter of the Calcutta High Court; (2) it was in its general scope within the powers of the Governor-General in Council; (3) s. 9 was conditional legislation and not a delegation of legislative authority; and (4) where plenary powers of legislation exist as to particular objects, they may be well exercised either absolutely or conditionally. In delivering the judgment of the Privy Council in this case Lord Selborne said, "The Indian Legislature has powers expressly limited by the Act of the Imperial Parliament which created it, and it can, of course, do nothing beyond the limits which circumscribe these powers. *But, when acting within these limits, it is not in any sense an agent or delegate of the Imperial Parliament, but has, and was intended to have, plenary powers of legislation, as large, and of the same nature, as those of Parliament itself.* The established courts of justice, when a question arises whether the prescribed limits have been exceeded, must of necessity determine that question; and the only way in which they can do so is by looking to the terms of the instrument, by which affirmatively the legislative powers were created, and by which negatively they were restricted. If what has been done is legislation within the general scope of the affirmative words which give the power, and if it violates no express condition or restriction by which that power is limited, (in which catagory would of course be included any Act of the Imperial Parliament at variance with it), it is not for any court of justice to inquire further, or to enlarge constructively those conditions or restrictions."

Ilbert, commenting on s. 63, (2) (d) of his digest, which corresponds to s. 65 (2) (ii) of the present Act, asks, "Are the words, 'or the sovereignty &c, to be connected with' 'whereon may depend,' or with 'affecting?' probably the latter." The present act has removed that doubt by making "affecting" govern "sovereignty". Hence Indian legislatures cannot pass laws to authorise or confirm the cession of territory. According to the decision in *Damodhar Khan vs. Deoram Kanji*,—the Bhavnagar case,—the Governor-General as the representative of the Crown in India has the power to cede territory.

As regards provincial legislation, local legislation cannot affect the Indian High Courts Act; hence questions have arisen as to the validity of laws affecting the jurisdiction of the High Courts. In *Premshankar Ragunathji us. The Government of Bombay* (*8 Bom. H. C. Rep. A. C. I. 195*) it was held that the Governor of Bombay in Council has power to pass laws affecting the jurisdiction of the courts established by the local legislature; and that such acts are not void merely because the indirect effect is to affect the appellate jurisdiction of the High Court. The Bombay legislative Council may make laws affecting the rights and obligations of the subjects of that presidency, but not the power of the High Court to deal with those rights and obligations. (*Collector of Thana vs. Bhaskar Mahadev Reth I. L. R. 8 Bombay 264*).

The liability of the Secretary of State to be sued for certain matters being given by an Act of Parliament, the Government of India cannot pass any act which would prevent a subject from suing him in a civil court, in any case in which he could have sued the East India Company. In *Secretary of State vs. Moment* (*15 Bom. 27*) s. 41 (b) of Act iv of 1898, Burma, which debarred a civil court from entertaining any claim against the Government to any rights over land, was held to be *ultra vires*. By s. 2 (2) of the Government of India Amenment Act of 1916 it has been provided "A law made by any authority in British India, and repugnant to any provision of this or any other Act of Parliament, shall, to the extent of that repugnancy, but not otherwise, be void."

I. The Chief Characteristics of Indian Legislatures.

I. The Indian legislatures are not sovereign law making bodies. They are not sovereign because (1) they cannot make laws like a sovereign legislative authority on any topic whatsoever and touching any person or place within their jurisdiction. Thus they cannot pass laws affecting (*a*) Acts of British Parliament passed after 1860 and extending to British India including therein the Army Act. They cannot touch (*b*) Acts of Parliament enabling the Secretary of State to raise money in England on behalf of the Government of India, (*c*) and in general, affecting any part of the written or unwritten constitutions of the United Kingdom or affecting the authority of Parliament, (*d*) nor can they pass any laws on which may depend the allegiance of the subjects of the Crown of Great Britain or the sovereignty or dominion of the King Emperor over any part of British India. Of course they cannot alter or amend in any way this main Act, the Government of India Act of 1915, on which now their own existence and authority depend. Besides these kinds of laws which they can in no way touch, there are other subjects on which, though competent to pass laws, they cannot undertake legislation without the previous sanction of the Governor-General. Such subjects are the public debt and public revenues of India, the religion and religious rites and usages of the British subjects in India, the relations of the Government with foreign princes or states, and the descipline and maintenance of any part of His Majesty's Military and Naval forces. (2) Besides being precluded from passing any laws of the classes enumerated above there is a furthur limitation upon their authority which make them non-sovereign. All laws passed by them may be declared *ultra vires* by the courts of law, should any such law be involved in a case coming before them in the ordinary course of their work.

Further, even as far as British India is concerned the whole legislative authority is not centred in them. Apart from the omnipotent British Parliament, power is vested in the Governor-General to pass ordinances independent of his council which ordinances have all the force of laws duly passed by the council at least for six months.

The legislatures in India are derived from and dependent upon the executive. In theory they are even to-day merely an extension of the executive councils of the Governor-General and of the Presidency Governors. In the case of the Lieutenant Governors and Chief Commissioners without executive councils, the Legislative Councils are, it would seem, in point of law, a body convened by the executive authority to pass laws. The supreme Legislative Council consists of the ordinary members plus a varying number of additional members. That they are dependent upon the executive is evident from the fact that the executive guides and controls them at every stage whether it is in making laws, in discussing the finances or in critising the administration of the country. They are also derived from the executive. The fact, however, that the Indian legislatures are derived from the executive, would, by itself, in no way constitute a peculiarity of the Indian system. The legislative authority in every modern civilised state all the world over is derived from the executive. It may seem strange but is yet true that in the political development of every modern nation the executive had the precedence of the legislative. In fact the whole legislative authority was once centered in the executive. But while in the democratic countries the trend of political development has been towards a gradual separation, resulting either in a complete independence of the executive and legislative authorities, as in the case of the United States, or at least the control of the executive by the legislative authority as in England and France. In India on the other hand the legislative is merely an extension of the executive, the creature, and therefore a dependent, that at every stage is conscious of its dependence. We find that even in England the cabinet *i. e.* the executive collectively, proposes, frames, initiates and carries through all legislative measures; and the legislative assembly *i. e.* Parliament, has merely the power, under the present circumstances, of critising, amending, and, in the last instance rejecting the measures proposed by the executive. In the last instance, of course, the legislative body, bringing about the rejection of the measures of the executive, does so, not so much perhaps because it objects to the measures, as because it objects to the executive which had charge of those measures; and in that way, by destroying their off-spring, they help to destroy the parent also. In India on the other hand the executive hold their position entirely independent of the legislative. They are appointed to their posts for a term of years which cannot be determined, by the desires of the Legislative Councils. Their membership of the Legislative Councils arises from their office *i. e.* they are members of the legislature because they are officers, and not that they are officers because they are members and leaders of the legislature.

The principal business of the Indian legislatures—the business sanctioned definitely by the present Act, is to discuss and pass measures placed before them by the executive. In other countries, the activity of the legislative assemblies is not confined merely to legislation. By far the greater part of the work of the British Parliament, and of all such assemblies which have copied the British model, consists of checking and controlling the executive authorities whether by questions, by motions for discussion of public business, or by direct votes of censure. The power of the purse enjoyed by them enables them, by refusing supplies, to bring the executive to book. In all these respects the Indian legislatures are in a class by themselves. They have no power of the purse. They cannot refuse the annual supplies to the executive, and thus cannot bring home to the highest servants of the country the responsibility of their high office. The utmost they can do is to make suggestions which the executive need not accept. Lastly, even in the domain of legislation, they can only legislate on certain subjects, and on most of these it is usual with the executive to frame the proposed legislation. It only remains for the legislation to assent to these proposals, or offer a hardly effective protest.

II. Official Majority.

The maintenance of the standing official majority by the rules of the councils is another peculiarity of the Supreme Legislative Council in India. The composition of the Indian legislature, allowing as it does great powers to the executive to nominate a certain number of the members of the Legislative Council, always affords a guarantee to the executive that their proposals will never be formally out-voted by the legislatures of the country, whatever may be the trend of public opinion on a given measure. Not satisfied, however, by this safe-guard which was considered quite ample even by the bureaucratic chiefs of the Government of India under Lord

Minto, Lord Morley, the professedly liberal Secretary of State, who had won his political renown by his active sympathy for the Nationalist cause in Ireland, insisted upon an official majority in the Viceregal Legislative Council. Says Lord Morley,

"While I desire to liberalise as far as possible the Provincial Councils, I recognise that it is an essential condition of this policy that the Imperial supremacy shall be in no degree compromised. I must, therefore, regard as essential that Your Excellency's Council, in its legislative as well as its executive character, should continue to be so constituted as to ensure its constant and uninterrupted power to fulfil the constitutional obligations that it owes, and must always owe, to His Majesty's Government and to the Imperial Parliament. I see formidable drawbacks, that have certainly not escaped Your Excellency, to the expedient which you propose, and I cannot regard with favour the power of calling into play an official majority while seeming to dispense with it. I am unable to persuade myself that to import a number of gentlemen, to vote down something upon which they may or may not have heard the arguments, will prove satisfactory. To secure the required relations, **I am convinced that a permanent official majority in the Imperial Legislative Council is** absolutely necessary." And so the present Imperial Legislative Council has a majority, though a bare majority, of nominated official members, who are bound to vote with the Government in every case irrespective of their individual opinions on a subject.

The considerations which led Lord Morley to accept the discontinuance of an official majority in the Provincial Councils were various and all powerful. (1) The field for legislation left to the Provincial Councils is so limited that it is almost inconceivable that even the most radical and irresponsible council could pass legislation which might endanger or embarrass the Imperial Government. (2) The composition of the Provincial Councils, representing a variety of interests seldom likely to be unanimous, and to offer a concerted opposition to the Government, was in itself a sufficient guarantee against hasty, ill-considered or dangerous legislation–quite apart from the fact that with the increase in their numbers would come an increased sense of responsibility, making it psychologically impossible for them to undertake and carry through revolutionary legislation. (3) The presence in the councils of nominated members, who, though not officials, and therefore, not bound to vote with the Government in all cases regardless of their own private judgment on the subject before them, may, however, be quite reasonably presumed to be anxious not to offer a constant and meaningless opposition to Government measures, would be another safeguard against provincial legislation of a radical description. Membership of Legislative Councils in India is yet regarded as a distinction much greater than the similar position in England. We in India cannot yet say that a man is likely to be more famous by writing a score of flippant essays or a realistic play about high life than by a whole session of dutiful and steady attendance in the councils. Being prized as a distinction, which men of average ability cannot hope to obtain at the hands of their fellow-countrymen, the membership of the council will not be lightly hazarded by nominated members through an unreasonable opposition to Government schemes. (4) In addition to all this is the power of the Local Government in the first instance, and of the Viceroy afterwards, to veto bills passed by the councils, if they do not approve of those measures. The power of vetoing bills duly passed by councils is indeed one which should not be lightly resorted to. Frequent or hasty vetoing of measures passed by the representatives of the people is dangerous for every Government; and particularly so for the Government in India, which are, from their very nature, supposed to be out of touch with public sentiment, and which cannot therefore offer their own alternatives–likely to be acceptable to the people–for measures vetoed by them. But when all is said, when we have appreciated fully the danger of the veto to the Government, it must be said that exercised properly–or rather properly not exercised–the power of veto constitutes a handsome reserve in the hands of the executive to repress the possible excesses of an inconsiderate legislature. (5) Finally, in the words of Lord Morley, " If, however, the combination of all these non-official members against the Government were to occur, that might be a very good reason for thinking that the proposed measure was really open to objection, and should not be proceeded with."

These very reasons could also be adduced for a similar course in the Imperial Legislative Council. The field for legislation, though wide, is not all-embracing. The presence of the nominated element is even more prominent in the Imperial than in the Provincial Councils, and its composition not less diverse. The Viceroy, and, above him, the Secretary of State have the power of refusing assent while the almost inconceivable combination of the divergent elements in the non-official membership of the Viceregal Council would be a more emphatic condemnation of a measure in the Imperial Council, than any such combination could offer in the Provincial Councils. In the six or seven years during which the councils have been working, the Governmeut of India have hardly ever had an occasion to make good their proposals by the use of their official majority. And yet Lord Morley thought fit absolutely to insist upon it. His only reason was the necessity he alleged that the supreme council, both Legislative and Executive, should be so composed as to allow of a smooth fulfilment of the obligations of the Government of India towards the Home Government and the Imperial Parliament. The maintenance of a permanent official majority is not always so great a palladium as is implied by Lord Morley's statements. Even in the old state of things—before the reforms of 1909—when the Government of India was an unadulterated bureaucracy, the spectacle of the Government of India differing from their constitutional superior in Whitehall was not entirely unknown. And if an exclusive bureaucracy could occasionally prove restive, the presumption of a purely democratic assembly proving altogether unamenable to the autocracy of Charles Street cannot be said to be altogether unreasonable. But just as the old unmitigated bureaucracy used to be brought to reason where it showed a refractory tendency, by the salutary power reserved to the Viceroy to overrule his Council, so there is no reason to believe, that the same expedient would not succeed with a democratic legislature in India. Examples of the like nature are not wanting in the short, but already instructive, history of the self-governing colonies. The Governor or the Governor-General in these colonies frequently exercises this power; and everybody, even those against whom this power is exercised, is agreed that such a power is reasonable in theory and useful in practice. It is less offensive without being less effective. It maintains unimpaired imperial supremacy, and yet permits a full and free scope to local ambitions.

The truth is that there seems to be a total, absence of agreement as to what constitutes the maintenance of imperial supremacy. If it be meant by that phrase that the wishes of the King's Government should prevail in all concerns affecting equally the various parts of the Empire, or that the Imperial Parliament should be the sovereign legislative body in all those subjects for legislation, such as Extradition or Copy-right Acts, no one would deny that, under the existing circumstances, such an idea is eminently just and reasonable. But if it be meant—and public opinion in Inda is more than faintly suspicious on this point—that the maintenance of Imperial supremacy in the case of India is only an euphemism for making her accept a policy, in her own internal concerns, which is all but universally repudiated in India, and the only justification for which is that the position of the Secretary of State and his colleagues in the British Cabinet is dependent on the acceptance of that policy in India. Because such instances have occurred in the past, however rarely, when the supremacy of the Imperial Government has resulted in the compulsion of our Government, in the teeth of the almost unanimous opposition of officials and non-officials, to accept the policy on which depended the prestige—the political future of the British Cabinet, Indian opinion quite naturally assumes that it is intended to avoid a repetition of a definite opposition to the unmistakable sentiments of the people by this thin disguise of a permanent official majority in the Imperial Council. If this were true it would be a very unpleasant reflection. It may well be asked, if Imperial supremacy can only be maintained by the purchased votes of a few officials, is it worth the trouble ? or, to put the same thing differently, if Imperial supremacy is likely to be endangered by the extension of democratic institutions in India, should such institutions be expanded?

III. The Composition of the Legislative Council of the Governor-General.

The composition of the council, apart from the official majority, is also peculiar. The maximum number of the additional members of the Governor-General's Legislative Council is fixed at 60. Of these some members are nominated by the Governor-General, not exceeding 33; and out of these 33 not more than 28 can be officials. Out of the remaining 5, three should be selected, one from the Indian Commercial community in general, one from the Mahomedan community in the Punjab, and one from the landholders of the Punjab; and the remaining two may be nominated by the Governor-General as experts. The 28 additional official members, together with the 6 ordinary members of the Governor-General's council and the Commander-in-Chief make up a total strength of 35 official members, as against 32 non-officials, not including the Governor-General.

Out of the 32 non-officials, 27 are elected as follows:—Two each by the non-official elected members of the Legislative Councils of Madras, Bombay, Bengal, and the United Provinces; (8), and one each by the non-official members of the Legislative Councils of the Punjab, Burma, Bihar & Orissa, and Assam (4), One member could be elected by the District Councils and Municipal Committees in the Central Provinces while the Province had no Legislative Council; (1) one each, by the landholders in each of the following provinces, Madras, Bombay, Bengal, United Provinces, Bihar and Orissa, and the Central Provinces; (6) One each by the Mahomedan community of Madras, Bombay, Bengal, United Provinces, Bihar and Orissa. (5). One each by the Bengal and Bombay Chambers of Commerce (2). In addition to these the Mahomedans of the United Provinces may elect an additional member at alternate elections as also the Mahomedans of Bengal (1). (8+4+1+

6+5+2+1)=27. This composition has been criticised seriously ever since the intentions of the Government of India became known. We have already discussed at length the presence of the official element. Coming to the non-official elected element, it is clear that the electoral system in this country has been divised so as to secure adequate representation to all classes and interests of the community. The problem of securing adequate representation to all important interests in the councils is not peculiar to India. But the solution which we have found for the problem is peculiar in the extreme. The Government of India were impressed very much with what was taken to be the partial representation of the whole Indian people by the non-official members of the Legislative Councils before 1909. Those members were nearly all professional men, and the preponderant majority of them was Hindus. The landed interest and the commercial interests all escaped any representation, at all proportional to their importance in the country. It was deemed necessary to give " Substantial representation to the great landholders, who not only constitute the aristocratic and stable elements in the Indian society, but also represent the interests of landlords great and small. And as regards the Muslim community it was admitted that "neither on the Provincial nor in the Imperial Legislative Councils has the Mahomedan community hitherto received a measure of representation commensurate with its numbers and political and historical importance." In their despatch on the subject the Government of India declared " this electorate, (since 1892), while it has worked advantageously in the case of one class, can hardly be said to have afforded proportionate representation to the other interests concerned. Of the non-official members elected to the Imperial Council since 1893, 45 per cent have belonged to this professional middle class; the landholders have obtained 21 per: cent of the seats and the Mahomedans only 12 per cent; while the Indian mercantile community, a large and increasingly important body, have had no representative at all."

In their proposals, therefore, the Government of Lord Minto, while accepting and slightly enlarging the existing territorial electorates, sought to introduce special electorates on the basis of economic or religious distinction. Of these the special electorates for the Mahomedans—based as they are on distinctions of race and religion—have provoked the greatest criticism. This emphasis on the division of races suggests a divergence of political interest which does not in reality exist. The enlightened leaders of either of these two great communities rejoice in the development of a feeling of nationality and of community of interests, that has been silently effected under the fostering care of British Rule. But this process of bringing about a strong, united nationality cannot be accomplished if racial differences and the old historical antagonism of the past are rejuvenated by such means. While it must be admitted that the relative backwardness of the Mahomedan community and their peculiar psychology cannot simply be ignored, their adequate representation could have been secured in other ways than by creating a special electorate for them. And even if the special representation of the Mahomedans can be justified on grounds of Justice, not the same reasons would support the special treatment given to the landholders and the commercial community. The divergence of interest is by no means so great as to render it impossible for a member of the one community to represent the interest of any other in the common councils of the nation. In the case of the special Mahomedan electorate there is this further argument that all those subjects, on which the Hindu legislators might take a view different from, and repugnant to, the Mahomedans, are studiously kept outside the cognisance even of the supreme legislature in India. Without the specific consent of the Viceroy, legislation concerning the religious rites and usages of any class of His Majesty's subjects in India cannot be introduced in the Imperial Council, while it is altogether outside the scope of the Provincial Councils. It is not too much to assume, that the Viceroy, an impartial English gentleman with a truly imperial outlook, will not lightly accord his approval to measures to be introduced in a council without adequate Mahomedan representation, if such measures are at all likely to wound the religious susceptibilities

19

of that great community. In the case of the landed interest, the problems concerning land coming up before the Legislative Councils are more likely to affect the small cultivator, who does not get any representation in the enlarged councils unless it were from the official members. For the representation given to the landed class is almost exclusively enjoyed by the large landowners whose interests, if anything, are likely to be divergent from those of the cultivators. The creation of a landed aristocracy, and the recognition of that aristocracy by such special representation, is justified on the ground that it is the only stable element in Indian society. Even if it were—and it is doubtful how far it is more permanent than the other elements in our society—its claim to special representation is bereft of all justice, when we find that the introduction of that element has only served to exclude that vast interest–the actual cultivators of the soil, who need, if any class or community in India does need it, a special attention.

The representation of the Universities in the provincial councils, though a fitting tribute to learning, is but an imitation of the English system in this connection. The Indian Universities are by no means so important as to raise special problems of their own very frequently, and such problems as do rise can very well be discussed by the ordinary educated members. And if on occasions special aid was necessary it could always be obtained by the privilege of the executive to nominate experts.

IV. The Indian Electorates and Franchise.

Not only is the principle of election in a permanent minority in the Supreme Council; not only is it extremely complicated in its working; there is also the extemely limited franchise which makes it useless for getting into actual touch with the sentiments of the people. It must of course be admitted that, in a country where barely three per cent of the population is literate even in their own languages, where the system of representative government is still in its infancy, it would be futile to urge a completely democratic franchise on the model prevailing in England or her chief colonies. But though the time has not yet come when we might reasonably assume every Indian to be capable of pronouncing an opinion on concerns that affect him vitally, it is certainly not too much to say that the attempt to popularise the Western ideas of government in India would meet with a larger measure of success if the franchise were more liberal and the electorates a little wider. To take but a few examples, the only territorial electorate for election to the Supreme Council is composed of non-official members of the various Provincial Councils. These number 32 in Bengal, 26 in Madras, 28 in Bombay, 25 in Bihar, and 27 in the United Provinces, 14 in the Punjab, 15 in Assam and 9 in Burma. And as regards franchise, in the case of the Imperial Council the landholders entitled to elect an additional member in (a) Madras must have an annual income of not less than Rs. 15,000 or be receiving a similar allowance from the Government; in Bombay they must be Sardars or Jagirdars; in Bengal they must be paying an annual land revenue of not less than Rs. 10,000, or have a title of Raja or Nawab and so on. Or, in the case of the Mahomedans, the electors must be either land owners with a cetrain annual income or be paying income-tax on an income of 6000, or be in possession of certain honours and distinctions, or the non-official members of the local councils, or be fellows of the local Universities, or be pensioned officers of the Government. Such regulations show that the electorates are narrow and the franchise high, because, after all, these are only experiments in India.

Single Chamber.

In all these respects the Indian legislatures compare unfavourably with democratic legislatures in other countries. In one respect, however, Indian legislatures are more advanced even than those of the most democratic countries. India has been spared the dangers or difficulties of a double-chamber legislature. Proposals were, indeed, made when the reforms were being discussed, to create a sort of a second chamber. But the idea of an advisory council of the ruling Princes and Chiefs did not find favour with the Secretary of State. On this project Lord Morley writes "I confess that, while entirely appreciating. and sympathising with your object, I judge the practical difficulties in the way of such a council assembling under satisfactory conditions to be considerable, expense, precedence, housing, for instance, even if there were no others. Yet if not definitely constituted with a view to assembly it could possess little or no reality." Though not definitely rejected the project was suffered to drop. And in all subsequent schemes for further reform it is a noteworthy fact that no one has made any suggestion for a second chamber–elected, nominated or hereditary–in India.

V. The Qualifications and Disqualifications of Elected Members.

The elected members must be duly elected. After election, but before taking their seat in the council, they must, at a meeting of the council, take an oath or make an affirmation of allegiance to the Crown in a prescribed form. The Governor-General has the power to declare seats vacant, and to order new elections, in cases where the election was not properly carried out. Candidates elected by more than one constituency may, by notice signed by them, declare for which of these constituencies they would serve. A candidate offering himself for election, must be a male British subject of 25 years of age and of sound mind. Officials, uncertificated bankrupts, undischarged insolvents, men dismissed from Government service, or sentenced by a criminal court to imprisonment for an offence punishable with imprisonment for more than 6 months or transportation, or men ordered to find security for good behaviour, or men debarred by a competent authority from practising as lawyers, or men "Declared by the Governor-General-in-Council to be of such reputation and antecedents that their election would, in the opinion of the Governor-General-in-Council, be contrary to the public interest." The last 4 disqualifications, however, may be removed by an order of the Governor-General-in-Council. Members are all elected for three years, unless a member is elected in the middle of the term, in which case he is to be a councillor only for the unexpired period.

VI. Voters and Voting.

The qualifications for voters are much wider than those for the candidates. Only aliens, women, minors and persons duly declared to be of unsound mind are excluded. As regards the positive qualifications, the principal qualifications, almost in all provinces, are: the payment of a certain amount of land-revenue or income-tax varying in different provinces (in the case of the Mahomedans and the land owners), the membership of certain associations like the Chamber of Commerce, or of Municipalities.

The different kinds of electoral machinery may be broadly classified under two main heads: one under which the electors vote direct for the members, as in the case of the non-official members of the provincial councils voting for one or two members for the Imperial Council; and the other under which they select delegates by whom the members are elected, as in the case of Municipalities or District Boards. There is a further subsidiary distinction. In some cases the electors or delegates vote at a single centre before a Returning Officer, or vote at different places before an Attesting Officer who despatches the voting papers to the Returning Officer. These are general rules. More particularly in Bengal the delegates have each a varying number of votes, the number depending, in the case of District Boards and Municipalities, upon the income of those bodies, and in the case of the Mahomedans upon the strength or importance of the population of the community in the district or group of districts. In other provinces the same object has been attained by varying the number of delegates for similar reasons, each delegate then having only one vote. A particular case of voting by delegates is that of the election of a member of the Governor-General's Council for the Mahomedan Community of Bombay. The delegates in this case are not appointed *ad hoc*, but consist of the Mahomedan members of the provincial council.

The procedure for voting is generally similar to that prescribed by the Ballot Act in England, though of course, there are not the same safeguards for securing secrecy.

The process of election is begun in India upon a notification of the Governor or Governor-General-in-Council, just as in England it begins upon a Writ from the Crown. This notification is issued on the termination of three years, or on the death or resignation of a member, or any other cause leading to vacancy. As the term of office of almost all members now expires at the same time the notifications in India bear a great resemblance to the Writs in England, at a general election. Before the election can take place the electoral roll—whenever one is kept—must be revised. This revision is now done annually, and is begun by the publication of draft electoral rolls in July every year. On this draft publication claims and objections may be urged before the Collector of each District; and these being all decided, the electoral roll is finally published before the 1st of October every year. This roll is conclusive evidence of the right to vote. The actual election proceedings begin by the nomination of candidates made in writing by at least two voters in due form. If only one person is nominated for a seat, or two where there are two seats, the candidates are forthwith declared elected; but if more candidates are nominated the voters have then to proceed to an election on the date fixed for recording their votes.

On the declaration of the results on an appointed date, elections may be contested on the grounds of;—

(*a*) Improper rejection or reception of a nomination.

(*b*) Improper rejection or reception of a vote.

(*c*) Corrupt practices *i. e.*, bribery, undue influence, and false personation.

The contest is decided by the Chief Executive authority for each province, and not by the Courts of Justice as in England.

A comparision on this subject alone of the difference between England and India is enough to show that the one is a democratic, the other a bureaucratic, if not an autocratic, country. There is not the same interest taken by the public at large in India in a general election as in England, because in India the electorates are small and the electors almost all men of wealth and standing. In India moreover the executive at every stage dominates the elections. It orders the elections, it lays down and decides upon the claims of the voters, it receives, records, and declares the result of their votes, and, finally, it decides upon the questions of disputed elections. For India to be a truly democratic country many of these duties will have to be made over to Judicial officers, or at least officers who are unlikely to be influenced by the Executive authority.

VII. Sketch of the Bombay Legislative Council.

Within the limits of this work it would be impossible to describe the constitution of all the provincial councils. A sketch, however, of one provincial council is attempted in order to give the reader a general idea of the composition of the local legislatures in India. The same general principles of nomination of officials and others and election are to be found in the provincial councils as in the Imperial Council; with this difference, however, that while in the Imperial Council there is a permanent official majority, in the local councils the official majority has been dispensed with. This does not mean, however, that the strength of the Government is in any way reduced. For the officials together with the nominated non-officials are always and everywhere in a majority, apart from the fact that the elected members are so secured that there is hardly any chance of their all acting together against the Government in any case. Besides the general territorial electorate of the Municipalities and District Boards, seats have also been provided for the elected representatives of land-holders and Mahomedans, Chambers of Commerce and the Universities, Presidency Municipalities and Port Trusts, and other special local interests like the Trades Association or Planters' Association. Thus in Bombay 4 members are elected by the Municipalities of the 4 divisions of the Presidency, and 4 by the District Boards of the 4 Divisions. Four more are elected by the Mahomedan Community, one by that community in Bombay, and one each by the community in the Northern, Central, and Southern Divisions. Three others are elected by the land owning interest, one by the Sardars of Gujarat and one by those of the Deccan; while one more is added by the Jagirdars and Zamindars in Sind. The Chambers of Commerce of Bombay and Karachi, the Municipal Corporation of Bombay, the Mill Owners' Association of Ahmedabad, the University of Bombay, and the Indian Commercial community elect one each. That makes 21 elected members. Against these there are 23 nominated by the Governor, of whom not more than 14 may be officials. Besides these there are the four ex-officio members. Hence the Bombay legislative council consists of:—

The Governor		
Members of the Council	3	Ex-Officio.
Advocate General	1	Ex-Officio.
Nominated officials	14	
Nominated non-officials	9	
Elected	21	
Total	49	

Against the elected members the Government have practically a majority of six not including the Governor; whilst against the Government the non-officials—if they could all combine on a measure—have a majority of 12 not including the Governor.

It may be added that on each provincial council two members (experts) may be added whenever the lagislation in hand is of a peculiar nature requiring expert advice.

VIII. The Work of the Councils.

The functions of the councils under the Act of 1909 have also been considerably enlarged. Under the Statute of 1861 the only business that could be transacted at any meeting of the Legislative Council was the consideration and passing of bills. The amending Act of 1892 permitted the asking of questions and also the discussion of the actual budget, provided that no member used either of the privileges to propose a resolution or to divide the council. Under the present Act the legislative functions and powers of the councils remain almost unaltered; but in the place of the section of the Act of 1892, which allowed the discussion of the annual financial statement and the asking of questions, there is now inserted the following provision.

'Notwithstanding anything in the Indian Councils Act, 1861, the Governor-General in Council, the Governors in Council of Fort St. George and Bombay respectively, and the Lieutenant-Governor or the Lieutenant-Governor in Council of every province shall make rules authorising at any meeting of their respective legislative councils the discussion of the annual financial statement of the Governor-General-in-Council or of their respective local Governments, as the case may be, and of any matter of general public interest, and the asking of questions under such conditions and restrictions as may be prescribed in the rules applicable to the several councils.'

Hence the most important changes made under the Act of 1909 are in relation to the asking of questions, (the rules permit also the asking of supplementary questions), the discussion of the financial statement and the moving of resolutions. As regards the discussion of the financial statement the changes may be thus summarised. The discussion now extends over several days instead of one or two, and it takes place before, instead of after, the budget is finally adopted. Members, moreover, have the right to propose the resolutions and to divide the council on them.

IX. The Financial Procedure in the Imperial Council.

Early in each calendar year the Finance Minister, in the case of the Government of India, presents his preliminary estimates with an explanatory memorandum. On a subsequent day he makes such further explanation as he thinks necessary. Members can thereupon move resolutions regarding (*a*) any proposed alteration in taxation, (*b*) any proposed loan, or (*c*) any additional grant to a local Government. When these resolutions have been voted upon the first stage in the discussion of the budget of the Government of India is over. The second stage commences when the estimates are taken by groups. At this stage also resolutions may be moved on any heads of revenue and expenditure that are opened to the council for discussion.

Heads of Revenue and Expenditure open to the Council for discussion.

REVENUE.		EXPENDITURE.	
Heads open.	Heads not open	Heads open.	Heads not open.
Land Revenue.	Stamps.	Refunds & drawbacks	Assignments and compensation.
Opium.	Customs.	Land Revenue.	Interest on debt.
Salt.	Assessed Taxes.	Opium.	Ecclesiastical.
Excise.	Tribute from native states.	Salt.	Political.
Provincial rates.	Court fees.	Stamps.	Territorial and political pensions.
Forest.	Army.	Excise.	State Railways. (interest, annuities etc.)
Registration.	Marine.	Provincial rates.	Major Works. (interest on debt.)
Post office.	Military works.	Customs.	Army.
Telegraphs.	All purely provincial revenue and revenue accruing from divided heads in provinces possessing Legislatvie Councils.	Assessed Taxes.	Marine.
Mint.		Forests.	Military works.
Jails.		Registration.	Special defence.
Police.		Interest on other obligations.	Statutory charges.
Education.		Post office.	Provincial expenditure and expenditure arising from divided heads in provinces possessing Legislative Councils.
Medical.		Telegraphs.	
Scientific and other departments.		Mint.	
Receipts in aid of superannuation etc.		General Administration.	
Stationery and printing.		Courts of Law.	
Exchange.		Jails.	
Miscellaneous.		Police.	
State Railways.		Education.	
Subsidised Companies.		Medical.	
Irrigation major works.		Scientific and other minor departments	
Minor works and navigation.		Civil.	
Civil works.		Furlough, and absence allowance.	
		Superannuation charges.	
		Stationery and printing.	
		Exchange.	
		Miscellaneous.	
		Famine relief.	
		Protective Railways	
		Protective irrigation works.	
		Reduction of debt.	
		Subsidised Companies	
		Miscellaneous Railway expenses.	
		Irrigation, major and minor.	
		Civil works.	
		Capital expenditure on State Railways and on irrigation works.	

This policy of excluding important heads of revenue and expenditure considerably mitigates the value of this great concession in financial matters. From the point of view of the Government each head excluded from discussion has, no doubt, its own special justification for such exclusion, whether the want of fiscal autonomy for the Government of India, or the political expediency in particular matters.

When all these resolutions have been moved and voted upon, the Finance Minister takes the discussion into consideration, makes such changes as have been suggested and found practicable, and then presents his final Budget. At this, the 3rd stage, the Finance Minister describes the changes made and explains why other suggestions have not been accepted. A general discussion of the Budget as a whole then follows: but in this stage no resolution may be moved or votes taken.

The right of discussing the Budget and making specific recommendations upon it was regarded as a great concession. Certainly it was a great concession when we think of the state of things before the reforms. Nevertheless if the ideal of political evolution for India be self-government on colonial lines, the present practice is hardly adequate to promote that ideal. In the 1st place India—even the Supreme Government of India—is really not independent in financial matters. Whatever the control of the Secretary of State may be in other departments, there is reason to believe that in matters of Finance the Home Authorities exert all their legal powers over the Government of India. And as, unfortunately, the impression is generally prevalent that the fiscal policy which is in the best interest of this country, would quite conceivably be prejudicial to the interest of a considerable section of the British electorate, the public in India feel that the Government of India—even if their own opinions are in sympathy with those of the Indian public—are kept in very tight leading strings by the Home Government for hardly veiled selfish reasons. One must remember, however, that there are other reasons, besides this which disincline English Statesmen to favour fiscal autonomy for India. (A). India is a habitual borrower on a large scale in the London money market. That these borrowings may be effected at the best possible terms for the Government of India, it is essential that their credit be kept up at a very high level, and, therefore, their revenue and expenditure be under a close and constant supervision by English statesmen, who are, in the last resource amenable to the English Parliament. (B). Moreover, so far the Government of India was exclusively composed of men, who were not the children of the soil. In the interests of the people of India, the control of a democratic chief, such as the English Secretary of State, over our bureaucracy was as necessary as it was desirable. Hence the necessity for the Secretary of State to have a majority of his Council voting with him in some financial matters. Hence also the provisions of the Acts of Parliament as regards the necessity of and the previous sanction of Parliament for the employment of Indian troops and Indian Revenue outside the frontiers of India. These reasons are no doubt not so strong to-day as they were fifty or even twenty years ago. The Government of India is too well managed to give grounds for any reasonable anxiety about its credit. And the people of India are not so utterly excluded from the councils of their country as to make it necessary for us to claim and maintain the financial supremacy of the English Secretary of State for India. Even in matters where there is a suspicion that the fiscal policy, likely to be popular in India, is bound to be prejudicial to England, opinion is by no means so dogmatically unanimous in England herself to-day as it was in the days of Lord Lytton. The absence of fiscal autonomy, therefore, modifies considerably the value of this concession.

Secondly, the exclusion of important heads from discussion operates in the same direction. Reasons of political expediency have an unpleasant tendency to be interpreted, or rather misinterpreted, as a want of confidence in the judgment or the loyalty of the Council. These reasons have been thus summarised. "The grounds for exclusion are various. Some items both of Revenue and expenditure are fixed by law, and the proper method of proposing any variation of them is the introduction of a bill. Most of the Political heads are governed by treaties and engagements with which the Councils have no concern; the debt heads depend upon contracts which cannot be altered; and military and ecclesiastical charges raise far reaching questions of policy which it would be inexpedient to discuss, and impossible to put to the vote. Finally it is obvious that the Imperial Council can only discuss with advantage the revenue and expenditure which is under the administration of the Government of India, while a provincial council must equally be restricted to items subject to the control of the local Government." To these reasons must be added the fact of the analogy between the practice in India and in England. There, too, some heads are excluded from discussion—the so-called consolidated fund services. But the motives for such an exclusion there are shown too clearly in each case by the history of the country to be at all misinterpreted. Moreover the unquestioned sovereignty of Parliament can always be relied upon to annul or modify an exclusion whenever it becomes unreasonable or inexpedient. Laws imposing taxes can be altered, contracts of debt can be varied, treaties and engagements can be given effect to by Acts of the same Legislature. Not so in India. It is desirable, therefore, that this list of excluded topics should be curtailed as far as possible. And this curtailment would in no way be embarrassing to the Government–even in the absence of financial autonomy–if it be remembered that the Council has the power only to discuss, not to initiate, or negative any financial proposal.

This is the third reason which makes the concession almost valueless. The Council may discuss, but it has no right to vote or veto a Budget. The initiation of the Budget by the Executive is apparently modelled on the English practice, where supplies can be demanded only by a minister of the Crown; while new expenditure may be suggested by the Commons by an address to the Crown. But the copy has belied the original. In England, under the thin disguise of outward forms remaining unchanged, the real matter has altered altogether. The sovereignty of the people is in no instance so complete as in the department of finance. The King may demand, but the Commons are not bound to grant all his demands. In India the Council is bound to pass the Budget even when it is widely criticised by the members themselves. It can only make recommendations which the Government need not accept. This indication of absolutism is all the more unreasonable when one sees that the Government of India is amply secured against resolutions being carried in the council if they are distasteful to the Government. If, inspite of the official majority, which would make it impossible to carry any adverse vote in the council, the Government of India still found it desirable to insist upon the character of the resolutions as mere recommendations, it can only mean that the Government desired to emphasise–to make clear beyond the possibility of a doubt–the absolute nature of their power.

X. Provincial Finance:

Constitutional Practice.

At this stage a description of the provincial Budgets may well be added. The main principles governing the constitutional practice in respect of Provincial Finance are that the Councils should be afforded facilities for expressing their views upon the Budget. These facilities are given at a sufficiently early stage to enable the Government to profit by the advice of the Council by adopting and carrying out such suggestions as may be found practicable. The ultimate control in this case, as in the case of the Government of India, rests with the Government. To suggest is the privilege of the Council. To carry out is in the discretion of Government. On these lines the Budget procedure in the provincial councils has been drawn up in four stages. The 1st stage commences by a rough draft of the provincial estimates, including in it all projects involving an expenditure of over 5,000 rupees. All these projects are given in a schedule, which is divided into two parts, the first containing all those items which must be carried out because they have already been taken in hand, or because they are ordered by the Government of India or the Secretary of State to be completed, and the 2nd containing items not so earmarked. This draft

Budget is submitted to the Government of India. The latter correct the estimate of the revenue, and determine, in consultation with the provincial Government, the aggregate expenditure for which the provincial Governments should provide. They have also the right to alter or add to the items in the 1st part of the schedule. When all this is done the figures about the altered revenue and the aggregate expenditure, as fixed by the Government of India, are communicated to the Local Government, and the first stage of a provincial Budget comes to an end.

With the second stage the rôle of the provincial Council begins. The draft financial statement when returned by the Government of India is submitted by the local Government to a committee of their council. This committee consists of officials and non-officials in equal number, the former nominated by the Government, the latter elected by their fellows. The Committee is presided over by the member of council in charge of the finance department, or, in provinces where there are no councils, by the financial secretary to the Government. The number of the Committee varies from 12 to 6. It busies itself with the 2nd part of the schedule already referred to: and provided it keeps within the aggregate expenditure fixed by the Government of India, it is free to make variations and even to insert new items occasionally. Though the discussion in the committee is free, and by the vote of the majority, the proceedings are private and informal. On the conclusion of its labours the Committee reports such changes as have been made to the local Government. The latter, after considering the report, revise their expenditure estimate, also their revenue totals if any changes are obvious, and report the figures under both these heads to the Government of India to be incorporated in the Imperial Budget. This ends the second stage.

The third stage begins with the presentation of the estimates as a whole to the provincial council. The figures of expenditure reported to the Government of India in the second stage would not, as a rule, have been altered by the latter, unless they were obliged to order a general reduction of taxation. The revenue figure would be brought upto date, and alterations in taxation, if required and practicable, are given effect to. These finally revised figures are incorporated in the Imperial Budget and communicated to the local Government. The latter then have their Budget printed, convene their council, and formally introduce the Budget in the whole council with a speech from the member in charge of finance. The Council considers the Budget in a committee of the whole council. They take the figures in groups as in the Imperial Council, and resolutions may then be moved on each group discussed. When all resolutions have been debated and voted upon, the result is reported to the local Government, who are, however, not bound to accept the recommendations. Here ends the third stage.

The fourth stage commences, when the local Government, after introducing such changes as have been found practicable within the limits of their powers, and after telegraphing the alterations to the Government of India, the final edition of the Budget is presented to the council. A debate follows, but no resolutions are in order, and the Budget being adopted the matter comes to an end.

XI. Summary of the Rules of Procedure in the Imperial Legislative Council.

The council meets ordinarily at about 11 a. m., and sits upto 4 p. m., unless the President should otherwise direct. The minimum number required is seven including the President, who is also given powers to adjourn, without discussion or votes, a meeting or business whether there is a quorum present or not. On all points of order a decision of the President is final. Members wishing to make observations on any subject must address the Chair. A curious provision of these rules is that members who are not able to speak in English may request any other member to speak on their behalf. On every motion before the council question is put by the President and decided by a majority of votes, and after the question is so put no further discussion upon the point is allowed. Members are entitled to call for any papers or returns connected with any Bills before the council; but the President has the power to determine whether such papers or returns can be given. It would seem also that the public have a right to petition the Governor-General in Council upon matters connected with any bill before the Council, in the form of a petition or by a letter to the Secretary. Such petitions or letters are required to be circulated among the members to help them in forming a judgment. Communications of this nature coming from Courts, except the High Court at Calcutta, officials, or public bodies must be sent through the Local Governments.

Questions.

Questions are allowed to be put generally to officers of the Government. They may be allowed also to the other members of the council. No question however is permitted on any matters touching the relations of the Home Government or of the Government of India with a Foreign State or with a Native State in India, or touching matters pending for decision before a Court of Law. As regards the form of questions, they must be so framed as to be merely a request for information, of moderate length, and free from arguments, inferences, or defamatory statements. Questions must neither be ironical, nor should they refer to the conduct or character of persons except in their official or public capacity. They, however, should not be made a handle for eliciting an expression of opinion, or a solution of a hypothetical proposition. As regards matters which are subjects of controversy between the Government of India and the Secretary of State or a Provincial Government, questions are not to be asked except as to matters of fact, and answers to such questions are confined to a statement of facts. Members desiring to ask questions must give notice in writing, at least 10 days before the meeting of the council at which he intends to put the questions, furnishing at the same time to the Secretary a copy of the questions. This rule about notice may be dispensed with by the President. The President is entitled to disallow any questions, without giving any reason, except that in his opinion it cannot be answered consistently with the public interest, or that it would be better put in the legislative council of a local Government. Questions cannot be followed by discussions in the council, but the member who has asked a question, may ask a supplementary question, if he finds the answer to the main question not sufficiently clear, in order to elucidate the subject. The supplementary questions need not be answered by the member in charge, since they are questions without notice, unless the member concerned waives his privilege.

Resolution.

For the discussion of matters of general public interest provision has been made by these rules. Matters of general public interest may include all subjects of administrative importance, with the exception of subjects removed from the cognizance of the Legislative Council, and also all matters affecting the relations of the English or the Indian Government with a Foreign State or a Native State in India, and in a matter which is pending for decision before a court of law. Subject to these restrictions, members are entitled to move resolutions relating to any matter of general public importance, provided that the resolutions are in the form of a specific recommendation addressed to the Governor-General in Council, worded in clear and precise language, raising a definite issue, and containing no arguments, inferences, ironical expressions, or defamatory statements. Notice of 15 clear days should be given by the member intending to move a resolution before the meeting of the council at which the same is desired to be moved, and a copy of the Resolution should be furnished therewith. As in the case of questions, the President may dispense with this rule about the notice, as he may also disallow any resolution, without giving any reasons, except that in his opinion it cannot be moved consistently with public interest, or that it should be moved in the legislative council of a local Government. The discussion on resolutions comes at the end of the business of the day, just as questions precede the business of the day. On every resolution the mover has the right to speak first, every other member in such order as the President directs, and at the end the mover has the right to reply. A time limit of 15 minutes is introduced; and members are not allowed to speak more than once on the same resolution, unless the President permits them to do so in order to make an explanation.

Amendments can be moved upon such resolutions, provided no amendment would be allowed which has merely the effect of a negative vote. After the resolutions have been sufficiently discussed in the opinion of the President, he may close the discussion by calling upon the mover to reply, and the member in charge to submit any final observations which he may wish to make. Resolutions, if carried, have the effect merely of recommendations to the Governor-General in Council, which are, however, not binding on the Governor-General in Council.

Bills.

Legislative business takes the shape of bills which must pass the council in various stages. Bills cannot be introduced in council without the permission of the council to that effect. A member desiring to introduce a bill must move the council for permission, and for such motion at least three clear days' notice must be given. When the permission is given, the bill is drafted, together with a full statement of objects and reasons, whether by the member independently, or by him in consultation with the Secretary. When the text of the bill together with its objects and reasons is ready, the Secretary has the bill printed, sending a copy to each member. The bill may be printed together with the statement of objects and reasons in Hindustani for the convenience of members unacquainted with English. The bill is then properly introduced in the council; and, unless the ordinary rules are suspended, if it happens to be a contentious measure it must pass through the following stages before it becomes law.

(1) A motion may be made to refer the bill to a select committee, of which the Law member is always a member, and of which other members are named by the council itself when the bill is referred to it, or at a subsequent meeting. On this motion the general principle of the bill is discussed. The Committee is generally presided over by the Law member and in his absence by the member in charge of the bill. When the members of the committee are equally divided the Chairman has a casting vote. After the bill is published in the Gazette of India, the committee considers the bill and makes its report thereupon, but not before at least three months have elapsed from the first publication in the Gazette of India unless otherwise ordered. If the bill is altered substantially the Committee may recommend republication as modified, and the republished bill must be sent to the department to which it refers. The report of the committee should be printed and a copy of such report should be sent to each member, and may also be printed in the Gazette of India with the amended bill if the committee or the President so directs. The bill is then taken into consideration either as a whole or section by section. At this stage the structure of the bill, as settled by the committee, is discussed by the council as a whole. Amendments may be moved at this stage upon any part of the bill provided sufficient notice—three clear days'—has been given for each amendment. After the amendments have been discussed and incorporated or rejected, the bill may be passed by the council. A copy of the bill so passed is signed by the President, who, as Governor-General, also signifies his assent to the bill by signing this copy. After this the bill is published in the official gazettes as an Act of the Governor-General-in-Council.

(2) Bills which are of the highest urgency may be passed through all the stages in the council at one and same sitting,

provided the rules of procedure have been suspended by the President.

(3) Bills involving large issues of policy are circulated among local Governments and other bodies for the purpose of eliciting public opinion on the principle and the provisions of these bills. After the opinions have been received the bill may again be referred to a select committee, and then goes through the same stages as any ordinary bill. Or it may be taken into consideration by the council at once, though this course would be rare and unprofitable.

In the case of provincial councils substantially the same procedure is followed, except that every proposed bill should be first submitted to the Government of India and the Secretary of State. For their own legislative proposals, the Government of India must also obtain a previous approval of the Secretary of State.

XII. The Summary of Changes.

To sum up the alterations effected by the act of 1909 it would be useful to have a view of the legislative council existing before that date and as it was extended in 1892. The legislative councils were created for India, Madras and Bombay in 1861, for Bengal in 1862, for the United Provinces in 1866, for the Punjab and Burma in 1898, for Bihar and Orissa in 1912 as also for Assam, and for the Central Provinces in 1913.

Under the Act of 1892 the Legislative Council of the Governor-General consisted of the ordinary members, and the additional members, not less than 10 and not more than 16, nominated by the Governor-General. The members were nominated for two years at a time. Not more than 8 of the members could be officials. The nomination of 5 members was to be made on recommendation of the Calcutta Chamber of Commerce, and the non-official members of the local legislative councils of

Madras, Bombay, Calcutta and Allahabad. The remaining seats, the Governor-General could fill in such manner as it appeared to him most suitable. In this respect the Act of 1909 introduced considerable changes. In the first place the additional members for legislation, instead of all being nominated, were to include persons so nominated, as well as members elected in accordance with the regulations made under this Act. Secondly the maximum number of members in the various councils was raised, in some cases doubled, and in some cases more than doubled. The resolution of the Government of India dated 15th November 1909, sums up thus the total effect of the changes in the constitution and functions of the legislative council.

"The Councils have been greatly enlarged. Their maximum strength was one hundred and twenty six. It is now 370. All classes and interests of major importance will in future have their own representatives. In the place of 39 elected members there will now be 135; and while the electorates of the old council had only the right to recommend the candidate of their choice for appointment by the head of the Government, an elected member of the new councils will sit as of right, and will need no official confirmation. Under the Regulations of 1892 the officials were everywhere in a majority; the Regulations just issued establish a non-official majority in every provincial council. Nor has reform been confined to the constitution of the councils; their functions also have been greatly enlarged. A member can now demand that the formal answer to a question shall be supplemented by further information. Discussion will no longer be confined to the legislative business and discursive and ineffectual debate on the Budget, but will be allowed in respect of all matters of general public interest. Members will in future take a real and active part in shaping the financial proposals for the year: and as regards not only financial matters but all questions of administration, they will have liberal opportunities of criticism and discussion and of initiating advice and suggestion in the form of definite resolutions."

XIII. Some Suggested Reforms.

A memorial signed by some 19 members of the Supreme Legislative Council, and presented to the Viceroy, has summed up the directions in which the Non-official public in India desires reform in the structure of the Government to proceed. They are as follows:—

In the words of the Memorial:

(1) "Under the first head we would take the liberty to suggest the following measures for consideration and adoption:- In all the executive councils, Provincial and Imperial, half the number should be Indians. The European element in the Executive council should, as far as possible, be nominated from the ranks of men, trained and educated in the public life of England, so that India may have the benefit of a wider outlook and larger experience of the outside world. It is not absolutely essential that the members of the Executive Councils, Indians or Europeans, should have experience of actual administration, for as in the case of the ministers in England, the assistance of the permanent officials of the department is always available to them. As regards Indians we venture to say that a sufficient number of qualified Indians, who can worthily fill the office of members of the Executive Councils, and hold port folios, is always available. Our short experience in this direction has shown how Indians like Sir S. P. Sinha, Sir Syad Ali Imam, the late Mr. Krishna Swami Iyer, Sir Shamsul Huda, and Sir Shankar Nair have maintained a high level in the discharge of their duties. Moreover, it is wellknown that the Native States, where Indians have opportunities, have produced renowned administrators like Sir Salar Jang, Sir T. Madhav Rao, Sir Sheshadri Iyer, Diwan Bahadur Raghunath Rao, not to mention the present administrators in the various states of India. The statutory obligation now existing that three of the members of the Supreme Executive Council shall be selected from the public services in India, and similar provisions with regard to the provincial councils should be removed. The elected representatives of the people should have voice in the selection of the Indian members of the Executive Councils, and for that purpose a principle of election should be adopted.

(2) All the Legislative Councils in India should have a substantial majority of elected representatives. These representatives, we feel sure, will watch and safeguard the interest of the masses and the agricultural population, with whom they are in closer touch than any European officer, however sympathetic, can possibly be. The proceedings of the various legislative councils, and the Indian National Congress and the Moslem League, bear ample evidence to the solicitude of the educated Indians for the welfare of the masses, and their acquaintance with their wants and wishes. The franchise should be broadened and extended directly to the people, Mahomedans or Hindus, wherever they are in a minority, being given proper and adequate representation, having regard to their numerical strength.

(3) The total number of the members of the Supreme council should be not less than 150, and of provincial councils not less than 100 for major provinces, and 60 to 75 for minor provinces.

(4) The Budget should be passed in the shape of money bills, fiscal autonomy being conceded to India.

(5) The Imperial Legislative Council should have power to legislate on all matters and to discuss and to pass resolutions relating to all matters of Indian administration, and the provincial councils should have similar power with regard to provincial administration save and except the direction of military affairs, of foreign relations, declarations of war, making of peace and entering into treaties other than commercial which should be vested in the Government of India. As a safe guard the Governor-General in Council, or the Governor-in-Council as the case may be, should have the right of veto, but subject to certain conditions and limitations.

(6) The council of the Secretary of State should be abolished. The Secretary of State should, as far as possible, hold in relation to the Government of India a position similar to that which the Secretary of State for the Colonies holds, in relation to the colonies. the Secretary of State should be assisted by two permanent under secretaries one of whom should be ar

Indian. The salaries of the Secretary and under secretaries should be placed on British estimates.

(7) In any scheme of Imperial Federation India should be given, through her chosen representatives, a place similar to the self-governing colonies.

(8) Provincial Government should be made autonomous as stated in the Government of India's despatch dated August 25th, 1911.

(9) The United Provinces as well as other provinces should have a Governor, brought from the United Kingdom, with an Executive Council.

(10) A full measure of local Self-Government should be immediately granted.

(11) The right to carry arms should be granted to the Indians on the same conditions as to the Europeans.

(12) Indians should be allowed to enlist as volunteers and units of a territorial army to be established in India.

(13) Commissions in the army should be given to the Indian youths under the conditions similar to those applicable to Europeans."

These 13 measures of reform are set out at length because they have been deemed important by the chosen representatives of the people. Of these the first 6 are by far the most important, the first dealing with the Executive Councils in India, the next four with the composition, functions and powers of the Legislative Councils, and the sixth with the India Council. Of the remaining 7, the 1st touches a problem of imperial politics, the next two matters of administrative detail, the 10th the question of local self-government, and the last three the right of Indians to carry arms, to be soldiers and officers in the Indian army.

To take the reforms in the order in which this work is planned, the abolition of the India Council is apparently a revolutionary proposal. In the existing state of things, it is quite true that the India Council has very little active power to promote or to prevent the better Government of India. And it must also be admitted, that, if we are right in understanding the nature of this council, it will always be unresponsive to the advanced tendencies in India. The more democratic the Government of India becomes, the less will be the chance of the council in London being sympathetic to the wishes of India. This presupposes that the constitution of the council remains unchanged. If, instead of being appointed, the members of India Council were elected by the people of India—directly or indirectly—this danger would almost be absent. But in case the members of the India Council are elected Indians, the question will become all the more acute. For that Council was originally established by Parliament, first to give expert advice to the Secretary of State, and secondly to watch, on behalf of the British Parliament, the interests of the people of India. This latter purpose is not so clearly realised as it ought to be. In the days after the Mutiny, when there was no idea, even among the most advanced radical, of Indians being associated with—let alone dominating—the Government of their own country, this council was admirably suited to be a check upon the autocratic Government of India. At the same time it was to be dominated by a personage who was the representative of Parliament, and therefore, one might say that the India Council, or rather the Secretary of State in Council, was the agent of the British Parliament to watch over the interests of the Indian people. But to-day the situation has changed. Indians are beginning to be associated in the government of their country. This memorial breathes the atmosphere of the day when they would be dominating their government. In that case the India Council would be quite superfluous, for its *raison d'etre* would have been over. The Secretary of State would have no need to check the views of the Government of India, since, presumably, they would be the views considered by the accredited leaders of the people to be the best in their interest; and so he would have no occasion to seek independent expert advice. Secondly, there would also be no need to act as the agent of British Parliament, because the Government of India would have ceased to be autocratic,

The question, however, would still remain as to what should be the relations of the Imperial Parliament with the Government of India. According to the tenor of this memorial there would seem to be no need for the exercise of that constant vigilance, which the English parliament deemed necessary in the past. Indeed, if the ideal of colonial self-government is realised in India–if India is ruled by the brains of her own sons as a member of the British Empire–Parliament may well delegate–if not abdicate altogether–its present position with reference to India. The English Parliament is admittedly unable, perhaps incompetenant–to govern the Empire of India as it governs the realm of Great Britain. Why should it not then relieve itself of a burden which: unable to carry itself, it may well entrust it to others, who would be grateful for the privilege ? But to do so the English people must be convinced that those aspiring to bear the burden are able to do so at least as well as they have done themselves. Suggestions, therefore, about the abolition of the Secretary of State's Council are of no avail if made to the Government of India. It is the English people who must be convinced of the necessity of resigning a trust which they have so well carried in the past.

Taking now the executive councils the proposal of the memorialists is open to criticism. If India's goal is self-government on colonial lines, she would want an Executive, whether elected or appointed, whether European or Indian or mixed, to conform to the wishes of the legislature. If it be secured that the wishes of the legislature shall prevail in every instance, it would be immaterial whether the Executive is Indian or European. To secure the supremacy of the legislative the principle of election in the executive may be all very well; but it would be opposed to every tradition of constitutionalism wherever British institutions have been copied. The right of the Crown to choose its own executive, provided that executive can command the support of a majority in the legislature, is unquestioned. That right is something more than a mere meaningless convention. It is very doubtful if that prerogative would be surrendered by the Crown in India, whether under a direct election of a certain portion of the executive, or by any system of panel. Besides, the suggestion misreads constitutional practice altogether. If a certain portion of the executive is elected and the rest nominated, there would be every chance of the elected members coming into conflict with the nominated members; and, as the authority of each section-each member-would presumably be equal, there would be no means possible to avoid a deadlock. The worst of all political deadlocks-it need hardly be mentioned-is the executive deadlock of this description. Again, if the right of the Crown to choose its own executive is not surrendered, the only other way to secure the supremacy of the Legislative is to copy that convention of the British Constitution, whereby the Crown selects its own ministers from among men who can command the support of a majority in the Legislature. To do so we need parties, which, for good or for evil, are almost unknown in India so far. There is, of course, no reason to imagine that self-government being once a reality in this country, parties will never emerge in India; but for the moment their absence makes it difficult, if not impossible, to copy faithfully the principles of the English or the colonial constitutions in India. It should be added, moreover, that if the convention of the English constitution, above referred to, is successfully copied in India, the suggestion that half of the Indian cabinets should consist of Indians, and half of Europeans would be superfluous and impracticable.

As regards the composition, functions and the powers of the Indian Legislatures, the memorial gives indications of the same hesitating tone. It is not merely enough that all legislatures in India should have "A substantial majority of elected representatives." They must be *exclusively elected* if the ideal of self-government is to be realised. The principle of representation according to races or interests should be abandoned; and means should be devised to secure adequate representation to important minorities. Increase in the numbers of members is inevitable as also the complete internal autonomy. There is nothing unreasonable in suggesting that the unity and integrity of the British Empire will in no wise be violated if the British Imperial Cabinet is confined to purely Imperial concerns, leaving the Local Governments in every part of the Empire a free hand in all their purely local concerns.

On the last seven points there can be hardly any criticism or disagreement, as they are all statements of general principles which no one denies altogether.

The reforms, then, which are both necessary and practicable, may be thus summed up:—

(a) The spheres of the activity of the British Imperial Cabinet and the Government of India should be accurately defined on the lines developed by the self-governing colonies. A clear definition of their respective spheres of activity would minimise misunderstanding, if not altogether eliminate every occasion for friction. At the same time it would render unnecessary the India Council. Each would, under such a definition, be supreme in its sphere; and so the Secretary of State would only be a common mouth-piece. In any scheme of Imperial co-operation such an official would be indispensable; and even in the absence of any Imperial federation, the necessity to England as well as to India of a Secretary of State is beyond question. But the powers and position of that official would be revolutionised. He would no longer be the dictator of the Government of India that he now is. He would scarcely be better than the chief Secretary to the Lord Lieutenant of Ireland.

(b) The Executive in India—if complete autonomy for internal purposes is geven—should be a completely parliamentary executive. One of the obstacles in the way of a fully parliamentary executive in India is the dependance of the Government of India on Home authorities. There is no hope of a Parliamentary executive in India so long as the Government of India are merely the agents of the Home Government. For so long as the Government of India are not sure of their policy prevailing in the end, a Parliamentary executive in India would serve only to embarrass and embitter the two governing authorities. Unless, therefore, the 1st condition of a clear definition of the respective spheres of authority of the Government of India and of the Home authorities is granted, there can be no chance of realising any ideals of self-government in India.

Assuming for the moment that a scheme of self-government is accepted, and the Government of India is given a tolerably free hand in the internal politics of India, there is no reason to doubt the possibility or the success of a Parliamentary executive. One condition for a successful working of the English Cabinet system is the existence of the parties. For every government in existence there is always possible a government in the alternative. In India so far we have had no parties. And, therefore, it might seem doubtful at first blush how we are going to realise a Parliamentary executive. It is, however, not too much to assert that the absence of the political parties in India to-day does not prove the impossibility of such parties ever appearing. To-day one single issue dominates and overshadows all others. If there be any parties in India at all to-day they are: the actual rulers and their popular critics. The latter are to-day almost unanimous on the great question of self-government in India. But once that self-government is granted there is every possibilty of active party spirit manifesting itself in India. Our problems of administration, whether of police reform or of Railway reform, whichattract the attention to-day are not, in themselves, great enough to create party divisions. But when those problems of social reform are taken in hand, as they must be one day taken in hand; when our rulers, instead of remaining deliberately neutral, actively busy themselves with such matters as the depressed classes and marriage laws, caste system and financial re-arrangement, India would not be able, however much she might desire, to avoid parties. And when parties arise successful working of a Parliament executive would be hardly difficult. The question may well be asked as to which should precede and which should follow. And though it is difficult to give an off-hand answer, it may yet be said that the grant of a scheme of self-government, even if it comes before the rise of parties, would not be impossible. It will, by habituating the people to self-rule, stimulate political thought and thereby bring about political parties.

At this stage the question of the Provincial Government may be introduced. It has already been treated of in these pages in some of its aspects. Here it may be added that the ideal of provincial autonomy does not by any means claim the unmixed support of every thinking man. The one strong argument in favour of raising our existing provinces to the dignity of semi-independent states is, that only by that means the governing machinery in India can be more popularised, and that each part of the country, being free, will be able to work out its own destiny. The argument is quite sound if it be remembered, that the autonomy of the provinces should not be purchased at the cost of weakening the central Government; nor should the development of any one province be allowed to be pushed on in such a way as to retard the country as a whole, whether by fostering provincial jealousy or by any other untoward, unexpected consequence. Besides, the experience of nearly every country in the last century betrays the necessity for every growing contry to have a strong central Government. Even in federations like the United States or Germany, Canada or Australia, the state sentiment is fading into back ground as against the Imperial or federal sentiment. A self-governing India would need a strong central Government more than ever the bureaucratic India needed it. If she is to be respected in the gathering of the Empire in proportiou to her size and population; if she is to make a stand against China and Japan, against Persia and Turkey in the industrial rivalry that is bound to dominate the current century; if she is to solve her own immence internal problems of social reform–some of which are not even perceived as yet–she must have a strong central government. And the ideal of provincial autonomy loses all its charm, when we have a fully popular government at the top, and completely self-governing institutions at the bottom. When for all local concerns there is the free popular assembly of the village or the district, and for all national concerns the Imperial Council—also a free and popular body—it is extremely doubtful if we would need provin cial autonomy on a scale which would make the provinces equal and independent states. That ideal was quite reasonable under bureaucratic government when there was an unmistakeable tendency of strong secretariats at the central head quarters to absorb all administrative work to interfere, to regulate, to dictate in all purely local affairs; and when there were reasonable apprehensions of the interests of individual provinces being not attended to. But if there is any prospect of a free popular Government being realised, much further decentralisation would be positively injurious. A complete provincial autonomy would prevent India from realising the consciousness of a single nationality; for to her already numerous principles of division—racial, religious and others, it would add one more—that of economic rivalry—among the various provinces,

(*c*) As regards the legislatures, the most urgent reform is that the councils should—one and all—be wholly elected. If some persons are excellent officers who fail to be elected, and who yet are too valuable to be dismissed, they may be allowed to attend in the councils, and speak. But they should have no right to vote. The elections should proceed on a popular franchise—of education, wealth or status. The membership in the councils should be increased—one member being elected by each district in the case of the Imperial council, and by a taluka or any other similar sub-division in the case of provincial councils. Officials, qua-officials, should not be allowed to have a seat, though in a few specified cases they may be eligible to the councils even after accepting those offices. The functions of the councils would necessarily increase, if the two previous conditions are realised, their sittings would be longer, their proceedings more varied. In the composition of the councils one very great reform would be to exclude the head of the executive Government from the deliberations of the Legislature. Almost in every democratic country—and particularly in the English speaking countries—the convention has been firmly established that the nominal head of the Executive Government should avoid any meddling with Legislative affairs. In India the presence of the Viceroy and the Governors as presidents of their respective councils was perhaps necessary in the beginning to secure decorum, to make the varied elements of the council harmonise. But with the increase in the freedom and the powers of the councils their presence would be undesirable. They might conceivably be reproached with partisan tendencies; they might–all unconsciously–become a restraint upon free and full discussion. Another reform of the like nature is the removal from the Regulations of certain arbitrary disqualifications for candidature to the Legislative Councils.

All these reforms are so connected one with another that there is no good in any one being effected while others are postponed. If they are to be introduced they had better be introduced all at the same time or be rejected altogether.

APPENDIX

TO

CHAPTERS II, III, IV & V.

INDIAN FINANCE.

Two important departments of State–Finance and Army–which in every other constitution receive the closest attention of the authors of the constitution, have not been specifically dealt with by this Act. Provisions of a financial character have no doubt been inserted in the chapters dealing with the Secretary of State and the Council of India; and reference to the Ligislative procedure has been made in the provisions relating to the Indian Legislatures. It is necessary, however, for a proper study of the system of Indian Government, to have a more connected account of the theory and practice of Indian finance, and some slight acquaintance with the important heads of revenue and expenditure; and this is, possibly, the most fitting place for inserting this account.

I. Financial Administration in India.

The general administration of finance in India, including the imposition of taxes, collection of revenue, and sanctioning of expenditure, is, (under the control of the Secretary of State in Council,) in the hands of the Government of India. The Executive Council of the Government of India has a member whose special duty it is to consider every question before the Government of India which has a financial aspect. Under him is the Accounts department, in the immediate charge of the Comptroller and Auditor-General, managing the civil accounts of the Supreme and the Provincial Governments. In this office all the accounts of the country are brought together and compiled. Subordinate to the Comptroller and Auditor-General are the Provincial Accountants-General, entrusted with the task of keeping the accounts of Imperial receipts and expenditure within their province, as well as the accounts of the local Governments. The accounts officers must see that no payment is made except upon proper authority, while another independent check is exercised by the Comptroller and Auditor-General through his own staff by means of test audits.

New Expenditure may be authorised and made by the governing authorities in India within the limits laid down in the case both of the Imperial Government and of the Provincial Governments by standing rules approved by the Secretary of State in Council. Any expenditure, outside these rules, requires the specific sanction of the higher authority. Under the existing rules the sanction of the Secretary of State in Council is required for creating any new permanent appointment, which would ordinarily be held by a gazetted civil officer recruited in England, and for raising the pay of such an appointment; for creating any other new appointment with a salary of over Rs. 800 a month; for revising a permanent establishment involving an additional expenditure of over Rs. 50,000 a year. The limits of the Provincial Governments are still narrower.

II. The Budget System.

Indian finance has been regulated by the Budget system since 1860. This system consists in preparing estimates for the revenue and expenditure one year in advance, and suggesting means for meeting the discrepancy, if any, between the revenues and expenditure of the country. In India the financial year ends on the 31st March. Under the new rules a financial statement is laid before the Imperial Legislative Council sometime before March to be discussed by that Council. The Budget proper, consisting of the estimates in their final form, as revised in the light of the latest information, and of the discussions on the preliminary estimates, must be presented to the Council by the Finance Member on or before the 24th March; while the Financial statement and Budget, with a report of the discussions in the Council, are laid before Parliament shortly afterwards.

The Indian financial statement and Budget include, besides the estimates for the coming year, the revised estimates of the year about to close, and the "actuals" or closed accounts of the previous year. There is almost always a considerable difference in the total estimates, as well as in the estimates for specific heads in the Budget, in the revised estimates, and in the actuals. This is due to the fact that the principal heads of revenue in India, depending as they do upon weather conditions, are proverbially uncertain; and the spending departments, too, are seldom able to keep rigidly to the exact limit set to their operations by the Finance department. The ideal of a Financial Minister is to try and make his budget estimates correspond as nearly as possible to the actual accounts; but for the reason given above this ideal is difficult to realise in India. Hence we have the constant phenomena of wide differences between the estimates and actuals, unexpected and heavy surpluses and deficits, and the consequent desire of the Finance Minister to make very cautious estimates, and to try and budget deliberately for a surplus. This is, of course, at variance with the sound maxim that no more revenue should be raised than is exactly necessary for expenditure; but it cannot be avoided by the Government of India, who have a fairly heavy debt in proportion to their revenues, who must therefore maintain their credit, if necessary, by budgeting deliberately for a surplus.

Another explanation of this phenomenon,(or, perhaps, we may regard it as another peculiarity of Indian Finance) is that the bulk of the Indian revenues are derived from non-tax sources. The table below would show that nearly one-half the revenue, if we regard the land revenue as not a tax, is derived from non-tax sources; the purely tax revenue being limited to about a fourth,

III. Revenue Table.

Revenue.	Accounts 1914–15	Revised Estimates 1915–16	Budget Estimates 1916–17.
Land Revenue	£ 21,221,539	£ 21,734,900	£ 21,932,100
Opium	1,572,218	1,881,200	2,286,900
Salt	3,910,790	3,490,500	3,987,600
Stamps	5,082,043	5,387,800	5,457,200
Excise	8,856,881	8,532,900	8,538,000
Customs	6,347,201	5,747,900	7,698,000
Other heads	5,151,321	5,178,300	6,107,400
Interest	1,023,307	1,076,000	1,155,300
Posts & Telegraphs ...	3,596,973	3,764,800	3,876,900
Mint...	69,498	74,000	72,900
Receipts by Civ. Dept. ...	1,505,120	1,546,300	1,549,900
Miscellaneous	677,750	645,100	565,100
Railways: Net	15,799,149	17,339,300	16,721,700
Irrigation	4,680,969	4,759,800	4,815,000
Other Public Works ...	288,219	288,500	269,700
Military Receipts	1,374,688	1,173,100	1,165,900
Total Revenue	81,157,666	82,620,400	86,199,600
Surplus + or deficit—	—1,785,270	—1,986,100	+1,052,400

Of these the Land Revenue, accounting for nearly ¼ of the total revenue, and being the largest single item, is fixed by settlements, which are, generally speaking, fixed permanently or subject to periodical revisions. The receipts under this head ought not, therefore, to fluctuate very much from year to year; but the uncertainty of yield, which depends very much on the character of the weather, and the consequent desire of the Government not to be very rigid in collecting this reveune, account for all variations. In a year of drought Government might have remitted, partially or totally, their revenue demand from the afflicted district, in which case the figures for that year would show a considerable decline. Or they might have only postponed their demand, in which case the figures for the following year would show a great improvement owing to the payment of arrears. On the whole the receipts under this head show a steady upward tendency owing to the value of the "assets" having increased with the extension in cultivation, growth in population, rise in prices and development in trade.

The receipts shown under the head of Opium are those arising from the sale of opium for export; the revenue derived from opium cousumed in India being credited under excise. Opium revenue is derived from a government monopoly. In normal times, before 1908, the revenue was subject to great fluctuations owing to variations in prices and changes in weather. Since 1908, following the Anglo-Chinese treaty in this respect, the Government of India have undertaken to reduce their exports progressively to China, and this revenue therefore is expected to fall very low in the near future.

The Salt revenue was, it is said, inherited by the British Government from native rule along with other transit dues. These transit dues were abolished, but the salt duty was consolidated and raised. Broadly speaking, one-half of the salt produced in India is manufactured by Government agency, while the rest is prepared under Government license. The North India Salt Department, a branch of the Finance department, controls the public manufactories in the Panjab and Rajputana, while in Madras and Bombay they are under the supervision of the local Governments. For the salt raised in native states there are special treaties, permitting, for a commuted payment to the states concerned, free movement of salt. The duty on indigenous salt was Rs. 2-8 between 1888-1903 per maund. It was reduced to Rs 2 in 1903, to 1-8 in 1905, and to Re. 1 in 1907. Owing to the exigencies of the present war the duty was raised to Rs 1-4 in 1916. The receipts under this head include the revenue derived from imported salt.

The Excise revenue in British India is derived from the manufacture and sale of intoxicating liquors, hemp, drugs, toddy and opium and cotton duties. The revenue is collected under provincial laws which have accepted the general principle of disposing of the right to maunfacture spirit for supplying a district by tender. The rate of still-head duty and the supply price to be charged are fixed in the contract, while the right to sell is separately disposed of. Foreign liquor is subject to an import duty at the tariff rates, and the revenue therefrom is included under the customs revenue.

The Stamp revenue is derived from two kinds of stamps: judicial or court fee stamps, and non-judicial or revenue stamps. The judicial stamp revenue constitutes more than $\frac{2}{3}$ of the total revenue; it is considered a kind of *quid pro quo*, rather than a tax properly so called. The revenue stamps are chiefly those charged on commercial documents.

The revenue under Customs is derived from duties charged on imported articles. Owing to financial stringency the customs schedule was completely recast in 1916-17. The general import tariff was raised from 5 p. c. to $7\frac{1}{2}$ p. c. *ad valorem*, except in the case of sugar which was taxed at 10 p. c. The old free list—containing articles not liable to any import duty—was materially curtailed. The customs revenue was further increased in this year by an export duty on tea and jute. The customs department is administered by an Imperial Customs service, responsible to the Imperial Government through the department of Commerce and Industry, but acting through the local governments.

Among the "other heads" of taxes may be mentioned the Income Tax which is the chief of the assessed taxes. Like the customs, this head also was considerably altered in 1916. The present Income Tax is levied on non-agricultural incomes of over Rs. 1,000 a year. Every such income of over Rs. 1,000 a year and under Rs. 2,000 a year must pay an income tax of 4 pies in the rupee, or roughly 2 p. c.; incomes between 2,000 and 5,000 must pay 5 pies in the rupee or $2\frac{1}{2}$ p. c.; incomes between Rs. 5,000 and Rs. 10,000 must pay 6 pies in the rupee or 3 p. c.; incomes between 10,000 and 25,000 must pay 9 pies in the rupee or $4\frac{1}{2}$ p. c. and incomes over Rs. 25,000 a year must pay 12 pies in the rupee or $6\frac{1}{4}$ p c. The total yield from this tax is estimated in 1916-17 at £ 2,912,800.

Among the remaining heads of revenue, receipts under Interest are derived from loans made to local Governments or native states or to local Boards and municipalities. The Posts and Telegraphs are another instance of a public monopoly in India, which is charging for its services the lowest possible rate, lower than any corresponding rate in the rest of the world, and which is worked mainly in the public interest.

The revenue derived from Public Works is given in the table under three heads: Railways, Irrigation and other public works. The Public Works Department originated from the military necessities of the Company's Government. Its activities have increased enormously since its institution in 1854; and at the present time, apart from the military branch, which, since 1899, has been finally separated from the civil branch and is now a part of the general military organization, it consists of three main branches: the Railways, the Irrigation works, and the Roads and Buildings branch. Of these the Railways form an Imperial department under a Railway Board represented in the Imperial Council by the member in charge of Commerce and Industry. The Board consists of a chairman and two members. The chairman has the status of a Secretary to the Government of India, with the right of independent access to the Viceroy. It is the duty of the Board to prepare the Railway programme for expenditure, and to consider all important questions of railway policy. The remaining two branches of the Public Works department are entrusted to the Provincial Governments, subject to the control of the Imperial Government. This control is exercised on the principle that all essential matters should be determined by the Imperial Government, while the local Governments should be left a free hand in all questions of detail. The selection and execution of individual works, for instance, are regarded as matters of detail, while the distribution of the available grants, the power to sanction projects costing over 10 lacs, the control and pay of the more important posts are regarded as essential matters and thus left to the Imperial Government.

The revenue from Railways is derived from: (*a*) the share of surplus profits falling to the State under the agreements with the railway companies, and (*b*) the direct profits of the State from lines owned or acquired and conducted by the State. The State in India is financially interested in almost every railway line in the country, in British India or Native States; and its credit has been staked to a very large extent in support of the railway enterprise. In the past it has suffered heavily through the railways, which were pushed on not always in strict confromity with the economic requirements of the country; since the beginning of the present century, however, the railways have turned the corner and are yielding an increasing—though varying surplus every year. It is calculated that by the middle of this century the Government of India would be owning a fine network of railways, each paying its own way and yet bringing a considerable profit to the State. The question whether, as the contract with each company falls through, the State should acquire the line and work it through a public department, or whether it should once again lease the line for working to a company securing more favourable terms for the State, is at present engaging the attention of the Government of India.

The revenue derived from Irrigation works is collected, generally speaking, along with the land revenue, and in the shape of an enhanced land revenue demand. It is also collected in some parts in the shape of specific rates levied on the owners or occupiers of the land benefiting by irrigation works. Unlike the railways, the major productive irrigaton works have all been constructed and worked directly by the State, and they have invariably proved profitable. A few irrigation works, however, have been constructed with a view to protection rather than to profit. But on the whole the public irrigation works have never caused a loss to the State.

In all these heads of revenue changes can be made by the Indian Legislature, though the Government are not bound to submit their proposals for financial changes to the Legislative Council and abide by the vote of the Council thereon. In practice, however, even before the changes of 1909, the Government carried out each proposed change by means of a special legislative enactment.

As regards expenditure, the following table gives

IV. The principal heads of expenditure:—

Heads of expenditure.	Accounts 1914-15.	Revised estimates 1915-16.	Budget estimates 1916-17.
Direct demands on revenue	8,939,330	9,383,100	9,450,600
Interest	1,191,257	1,135,400	989,700
Post and Telegraphs	3,257,263	3,221,000	3,503,500
Mint	141,682	86,000	90,300
Salaries and expenses civil depts.	18,909,977	19,067,000	19,323,300
Miscellaneous civ. charges.	5,311,384	5,131,200	3,283,300
Famine Relief	1,000,000	1,000,000	1,000,000
Railways: Interest etc.	13,641,115	13,990,800	14,217,100
Irrigation	3,754,268	3,769,300	3,770,900
Other Public Works	7,177,209	5,464,200	4,717,500
Military Services	21,809,603	23,015,800	23,165,900
Total Expenditure ...	85,133,038	85,263,800	85,512,100

Among these various heads of expenditure the most noticeable is the head of Interest on Debt, which amounted to £ 9,957,000 in 1916-17. The debt of India has arisen from two causes. (*a*) There was a huge legacy of debt left to the Crown by the East India Company in 1858, to which was added the value of the India stock in that year; so that the total debt amounted to Rs. 63·555 crores in 1859-60. This was almost wholly non-productive debt. In the years that followed, the rupee debt was gradually increased owing to wars, such as the 2nd Afghan war or the 3d Burmese war or the present European war, and to famines, such as those of 1878-79 and 1899-1900. (*b*) There was the need for fresh borrowing every year for the construction of productive public works. Under this head there is hardly any limit to the public borrowing in India, except the one set by the available supply of capital in the London and the Indian money-markets. Out of the total interest charge of £ 9,957,000 in 1916-17, Railways alone absorbed £. 8,147,000, while Irrigation accounted for £ 1,509,400, the interest on ordinary, unproductive debt amounting to only £ 298,200.

According as the loan is raised in India or in England, the public debt of this country is divided into Rupee debt and the Sterling debt. This distinction is not now of very great importance, since, for all practical purposes the rupee is a fixed fraction of the £ sterling; but before the value of the rupee was fixed, the distinction was full of a living importance, as the interest on sterling debt being payable in sterling, the amount in rupees payable for interest went on increasing as the exchange dropped. The rate of interest has also been gradually reduced. In 1822 the whole of the rupee debt carried interest at 6 p. c. and this debt was not finally paid off till 1860. Between 1823 and 1853 the Government borrowed in India at 5 p. c. The greater portion of this 5 p. c. debt was converted in 1856 to 4 p. c.; but the shock to the credit of the State owing to the Mutiny compelled the government to borrow at the higher rate of 5 p. c.; this debt was finally extinguished in 1871. In 1858-59, gevernment had to borrow even at 5½p.c.and this loan was paid off by 1878-9. The 4½ p. c. debt, first raised in 1856-7, was increased in 1871 owing to the conversion of 4½ p. c. loan;

and by 1878-79 nearly the whole rupee debt bore interest at 4½ or 4 p. c. *i. e.* Rs. 15.148 crores at 4½ p.c. and 61·388 at 4 p. c. The 4½ p. c. debt was converted to 4 p. c. by 1893 with the exception of Rs. 1 crore, which was borrowed from the Holkar, for the construction of the Indore State Railway, which cannot be converted till 1970. The 3½ p. c. debt dates from 1893 when a small loan of Rs. 3·55 crores was raised at that rate; and its success encouraged the Government for a further reduction of the rate of interest to 3½ p. c. on the 4 p. c. debt in the following year. In 1896-7 a loan of Rs. 4 crores was raised at 3 p. c. but the bulk of the debt in the following years, until the outbreak of the European war, was incurred at 3½ p. c. In 1915 Rs. 4½ crores were raised at 4 p. c. and in the following year Rs. 6·75 crores were added at the same rate. In the Budget of 1916-17 the total debt provided for was as follows:—

Sterling debt	...£ .180,282,858
Rupee „ —	
4 p. c.	Rs. 14,68,90,000
3½. p. c.	„ 138,53,25,400
3 p. c.	„ 7,72,75,500
Other debt	„ 1,00,14,300
Temporary Loans	„ 6,50,00,000
Savings Banks Balances...	„ 23,35,20,176

Against this the total interest payable was Rs. 5,80,25,000 in India and £. 6,088,700, in England.

The expenditure on the Army is greater than in the past owing to the European war. The organisation of the Army etc. are dealt with in another chapter.

The direct demands on Revenue include all costs of collection and production. This item has been steadily on the increase. The cost of collection of the land revenue constitutes over 60 p. c. of the total; the charges under that head include the cost of district administration of the departments of land records, and of survey and settlement operations,

The expenses of the civil departments have been continuously growing. They include charges for general administration, courts of law, Jails, Police, Ports and pilotage, Education, Ecclesiastical, Medical, Political, Scientific and other departments. The increase is most conspicuous under Education, Police, Medical and Scientific departments. The charges for general administration represent the cost of the whole civil administration down to the grade of commissioners of divisions. They include also the charges on account of the India Office, the Viceroy, the Governors, Lieutenant Governors and Councils in India. Such charges as those for the Coronation Durbar also come under this head. The Scientific and minor departments include the Survey of India, the Botanical and Geological Surveys, the Agriculture and Veterinary departments, Observatories, Inspectors of Mines and Factories and miscellaneous departments.

The Miscellaneous Civil charges include territorial and political pensions, civil furlough and absentee allowances, superannuation allowances and pensions, stationery and printing, and miscellaneous. Of these the first head is on the decline and the superannuation allowances are on the increase.

The charges for Posts and Telegraphs, Railways and Irrigation, Roads and Buildings, Mint &c. are incurred in connection with the working of these great commercial undertakings.

The Famine Relief and Insurance item dates from 1878. Prior to that date each famine was met as it occurred, and beyond that no regular machinery was provided. The experience of 1878 convinced the Government that the cost of famine relief should be treated as an ordinary charge on the revenue; and for that purpose a sum of 1½ crores of Rupees was to be set aside every year. This sum is applied first to the direct relief of famine; secondly to the construction and maintenance of "protective" railways and irrigation works; thirdly to the construction of "productive" public works which would otherwise necessitate additional borrowing. The amount used under the last-mentioned purpose is shown under the head of

Reduction or Avoidance of debt. Combating famine is primarily within the sphere of local Governments; but since 1907 the fixed assignments to Bombay, the Central Provinces, United Provinces, Bengal and Madras were increased by £ 250,000. This total is debited to the provincial revenues each year under the head of Reduction or Avoidance of debt, and the share of each province is entered to its credit with the Imperial Government. The provinces thus accumulate a reserve of credit which may be drawn upon in the event of famine. The charges then incurred are entered as Imperial expenditure.

V. Home Charges.

Another peculiarity of Indian Finance is that not the whole of the expenditure is incurred in India. A considerable portion, amounting to nearly £. 18 million, is spent in England, and is collectively described as the Home Charges. They include:–interest and management of the ordinary debt, interest and annuities on irrigation and railways account, payments in connection with civil departments in India, India Office charges, Army and Marine charges, stores, furlough allowances, and pensions and gratuities. Of these, interest accounts for nearly £ 7 million; India Office and Civil department charges for £ 500,000; Army and Marine charges over £ 1 million, stores a varying item, furlough allowances over a million and pensions and gratuities for nearly £ 5 millions. Indian public opinion regards this as a drain from India for the benefit of England. The defenders of the Government of India point out that (*a*) a good proportion of the Home Charges is used for paying the interest on debt, the greater portion of the money borrowed being used for productive purposes. Moreover the terms and conditions obtained by the Government of India in the London market are much easier than would be possible if India were an independent state. And such borrowing would be indispensable if India is to have all those means of modern material development, which many other countries, like Japan or the United States, have to bring about by borrowed money. To all these arguments Indian publicists retort that not the whole of the Indian public debt has been incurred for productive purposes, nor were the objects, assumed to be productive, equally or immediately productive. Besides, even if India had to borrow for all these material improvements, there is no ground for assuming that she borrows under better conditions under British dominion than she would otherwise, as the much more unsettled state of South American republics does not preclude them from borrowing in the same London market at pretty nearly the same terms as India. (*b*) It is further argued by those who see no drain in the Home Charges that the item of stores should not be included, since in this instance there is a tangible return in goods for India's money. Again (*c*) the item of pensions, gratuities and other charges of the kind is incurred for services rendered in the past, or being rendered now to the Indian peoples by the recipients of these allowances, and so here also it is unfair to describe the charge as a drain. To this the Indian publicists reply that the services of public servants are remunerated in India, admittedly the poorest country in the world, at a much higher rate than in any other country; that in those services the sons of India obtain a very slender proportion; and that the whole amount saved by English officials in India is taken away from India on their retirement, and may, therefore, quite reasonably be regarded as a drain. This subject, however, is too complicated, and involves too many considerations to allow us to do anything more than to summarise the arguments on either side in this work.

VI. The Decentralisation of Finance.

The third peculiarity of Indian finance is the division of financial authority between the Imperial and the Provincial Governments.

Originally under the Charter Act of 1833 a system of Financial administration was established, by which the revenues of the whole of India, although received in the treasuries and sub-treasuries of the various provinces, were all credited to the single account of the Government of India which distributed all the funds needed for the public services throughout India. "The Supreme Government" it has been said "controlled the smallest details of every branch of the expenditure: its authority was required for the employment of every person who was paid with public money, however small his salary, and its sanction was necessary for the grant of funds even for purely local works of improvement, for every local road, for every building however insignificant." The provincial Governments had no liberty and no incentive to economy. The distribution of the public income degenerated into a scramble in which the most violent—not the most reasonable—had the advantage.

This system was modified by Lord Mayo. The main principle introduced by that Viceroy was to make over to the provincial Governments a certain income by which they must regulate their expenditure, and to leave to them, under certain general conditions, the responsibility of managing their own local affairs. According to this principle the following heads of revenue and expenditure were made over to the local Governments: Jails, Registration, Police, Education, Medical services, Printing, Roads, Civil Buildings, and Miscellaneous public improvements. These were to be supplemented by a fixed annual Imperial grant varying according to the needs of each province. In case of a deficit the local Governments were to reduce their expenses or meet it by imposing taxation.

The system thus modified was improved under Lord Lytton, slightly altered under Lord Ripon, revised under Lord Lansdowne and made semi-permanent under Lord Curzon. The main principles of this scheme of gradual decentralisation of finance had been confirmed in the course of a generation and were summarised as follows by the Financial Secretary to the Government of India for the Royal Commission on Decentralisation:—

(*a*) The Imperial Government retained certain administrative services which were thought inexpedient to be handed over to the provincial Governments. They also reserved the revenues from such services, together with such a share of the other public revenues, as would meet the expenditure falling on them.

(*b*) The remaining administrative services were made over to the provincial Governments, each local Government was assured an income making it independent of the needs of the Government of India, and at the same time able to meet its normal needs.

(*c*) This income was given in the shape of a defined share of the revenues collected by the Local Government in order to allow the resources of the local governments to expand with their needs.

The Royal Commission on Decentralisation summarised the existing system in 1909 as follows:—

(1) The settlements had been declared to be quasi-permanent. The Government of India reserve the right of revision; but they had promised to exercise that power only when the variations from the initial relative standards of revenue and expenditure were, over a substantial term of years, so great, as to result in unfairness either to province itself or to the Government of India; or in the event of the Government of India being confronted with the alternatives of either imposing general taxation or seeking assistance from the provinces.

(2) The distribution of revenue between the provincial and central governments was made, except on occasions of grave emergency, with direct reference not to the needs of the central government, but to the outlay which each province might reasonably claim to incur upon services which it administered.

(3) The third feature of the system was the method by which the revenue accruing from the various sources was

distributed. The residue which was available for Imperial purposes was taken in the shape of a fixed fractional share in a few of the main heads of revenue which were known as the "divided heads". As, however, the distribution of these heads could never be so adjusted as to yield to a province, when added to the revenue from the purely provincial heads, the exact sum necessary to meet provincial charges, equilibrium was effected by means of fixed cash assignments--a deficiency being remedied by an assignment to provincial revenues from the Imperial share of the land revenue, and an excess by the reverse process.

In 1912 the settlements were made permanent, and provincial Finance in India is now governed by rules framed in that year. The settlements with all the provinces were revised, and, subject to the contingency of providing against famine, local Governments were informed that certain growing heads of revenue were placed once for all at their disposal from which to meet the future needs of their province. The following rules now govern the Provincial settlements.

(1) The settlements being permanent are not subject to revision. In the case of a serious famine the Government of India might render special assistance to the afflicted province. On the other hand provinces might be called upon to aid the Government of India in the case of a serious embarrassment.

(2) Whenever the fixed assignment to a province becomes unduly high it will, as a rule, be converted wholly or partially into a share of growing revenue.

(3) Whenever the Government of India have a surplus which is not required for remission of taxation or reduction of debt, they may make special allotments to the provinces and declare the purpose for which such special grant is to be used. But such grants are not to be made the occasion of a greater interference by the Supreme Government in the local concerns than before, nor should the grants be made without any regard to the wishes of the local Government, or should be made applicable in all the provinces to the same purpose.

(4) The local Governments are not allowed to budget for deficits, unless the excess expenditure is due to exceptional and non-recurring causes. And if the deficit results in the reduction of Provincial balances below the prescribed minimum, arrangements should be forthwith made to replenish the deficit. If a local Government exhausts its own balance, and is permitted to overdraw upon the general balance, the overdraft is regarded as a short loan, bearing interest and repayable in such modes as the central Government might direct.

(5) The corrections by the Government of India in future will be limited to the proposed totals of revenue and expenditure, and divided heads of revenue.

The same resolution which laid down these rules also considered the two further questions of the advisability of the provincial Governments imposing and altering taxes, 'and that of borrowing on their own credit. As regards the first the local Governments argued that the conditions of economic development in all provinces are not identical; and therefore, the uniform taxation levied by the central Government results in unfairness. The Imperial Government admitted that, in a vast country of varying conditions, imperial taxation must of necessity be limited in its range, since very few taxes are suitable for the whole Empire; that the incidence of an imperial impost might vary from province to province; that the right given to the provinces to tax their own citizens might balance such inequalities, and allow of tax experiments on a small scale which would be impolitic on a large scale. But all these were theoretical considerations only. In the absence of any practical scheme, the Government of India did not see fit to concede the right beyond admitting that the financial autonomy of provincial Governments must carry with it—whenever it came—the right to impose taxation. As regards the raising of loans by Local Governments, they are not permitted to raise them in open market, for they would compete with the Imperial loans. Besides it is considered undesirable to increase the unproductive debt of India. They may, however, have short term loans from Imperial revenues to meet the cost of non-productive works of obvious utility which they cannot finance from their own revenues.

Having already considered the question of the provincial autonomy, it is unnecessary to discuss in detail the financial policy of the Government of India in relation to the provinces. Suffice it to say that under the present circumstances it would be undesirable to make the provinces financially independent of the Government of India. That Government cannot concede the right of taxation or of borrowing without impairing its own supremacy, and no financial independence for thc provinces be complete without the right to tax and to borrow.

VII. Present Arrangement.

Revenue:—The Government of India take the whole of the revenue from opium, salt, customs, mint, railways, posts and telegraphs, military receipts, and tributes from native states.

The provincial governments take the whole of the revenues from forests, registration fees and the income from such spending departments as ordinary public works, police, education, medical, courts and jails.

The receipts from Land-revenue, Excise, Stamps, Income Tax, and Irrigation dues are divided equally between the Imperial and the Provincial Governments.

Expenditure:—The Government of India are exclusively responsible for Defence, Railways, Posts and Telegraphs, Interest on debt and Home Charges.

The Provincial Governments are similarly responsible for Land-Revenue and general administration, Forests, Police, Courts, Jails, Education and Medical.

Charges for Irrigation and other ordinary Public Works are common to the Imperial and Provincial Governments.

The arrangement varies from province to province but the general features are the same. It must be added that the principle of permanent provincial settlements applies only to the major provinces. British Baluchistan, and the North West Frontier Province have yet only a quasi-permanent settlement.

CHAPTER VI.

Public Services in India.

PART VII.

Salaries, Leave of Absence, Vacation of Office, Appointments &c.

85. (1) There shall be paid to the Governor-General of India and to the other persons mentioned in the Second Schedule to this Act, out of the revenues of India, such salaries, not exceeding in any case the maximum specified in that behalf in that Schedule, and such allowances (if any) for equipment and voyage, as the Secretary of State in Council may by order fix in that behalf, and, subject to or in default of any such order, as are payable at the commencement of this Act;

(2) Provided as follows:—

(*a*) an order affecting salaries of members of the Governor-General's executive council may not be made without the concurrence of a majority of votes at a meeting of the council of India;

(*b*) if any person to whom this section applies holds or enjoys any pension or salary, or any office of profit under the Crown or under any public office, his salary under this section shall be reduced by the amount of the pension, salary or profits of office so held or enjoyed by him;

(*c*) nothing in the provisions of this section with respect to allowances shall authorise the imposition of any additional charge on the revenues of India.

(3) The remuneration payable to a person under this section shall commence on his taking upon himself the execution of his office, and shall be the whole profit or advantage which he shall enjoy from his office during his continuance therein.

86. (1) The Governor-General-in-Council may grant to any of the ordinary members of his executive council, and a Governor-in-Council may grant to any member of his executive council, leave of absence under medical certificate for a period of not exceeding six months.

(2) Where a member of council obtains leave of absence in pursuance of this section, he shall retain his office during his absence, and shall, on his return and resumption of his duties, be entitled to receive half his salary for the period of his absence; but if his absence exceeds six months his office shall become vacant.

87. (1) If the Governor-General, or a Governor, or the Commander-in-Chief of His Majesty's forces in India, and, subject to the foregoing provisions of this Act as to leave of absence, if any ordinary member of the executive council of the Governor-General, or any member of the executive council of a governor, departs from India, intending to return to Europe, his office shall thereupon become vacant.

(2) No act or declaration of the Governor-General or a Governor or a member of an executive council, other than as aforesaid, except a declaration in writing under hand and seal, delivered to a Secretary to the Government of India or to the chief secretary of the presidency wherein he is, in order to its being recorded, shall be deemed or held as a resignation or surrender of his office.

(3) If the Governor-General, or any ordinary member of the Governor-General's executive council, leaves India otherwise than in the known actual service of the Crown, and if any Governor, Lieutenant-Governor or member of a Governor's Executive Council leaves the province to which he belongs, otherwise than as aforesaid, his salary and allowances shall not be payable during his absence to any person for his use.

(4) If any such officer, not having proceeded or intended to proceed to Europe, dies during his absence, and whilst intending to

return to India or to his province, his salary and allowance shall, subject to any rules in that behalf made by the Secretary of State in Council, be paid to his personal representatives.

(5) If any such officer does not return to India or his province, or returns to Europe, his salary and allowances shall be deemed to have ceased on the day of his leaving India or his province.

88. (1) His Majesty may, by warrant under his Royal Sign Manual, appoint any person conditionally to succeed to any of the offices of Governor-General, Governor, ordinary member of the executive council of the Governor-General, or member of the executive council of a Governor, in the event of the office becoming vacant, or in any other event or contingency expressed in the appointment, and revoke any such conditional appointment.

(2) A person so conditionally appointed shall not be entitled to any authority, salary or emolument appertaining to the office to which he is appointed, until he is in the actual possession of the office.

89. (1) If any person entitled under a conditional appoinment to succeed to the office of Governor-General, or appointed absolutely to that office, is in India on or after the event on which he is to succeed, and thinks it necessary to exercise the powers of Governor-General before he takes his seat in Council, he may make known by notification his appointment and his intention to assume the office of Governor-General.

(2) After the notification, and thenceforth until he repairs to the place where the council may assemble, he may exercise alone all or any of the powers which might be exercised by the Governor-General-in-Council.

(3) All acts done in the Council after the date of the notification, but before the communication thereof to the council, shall be valid, subject nevertheless, to revocation or alteration by the person who has so assumed the office of Governor-General.

(4) When the office of Governor-General is assumed under the foregoing provision, the vice-president, or, if he is absent, the senior ordinary member of the council then present, shall preside therein with the same powers as the Governor-General would have had if present.

90. (1) If a vacancy occurs in the office of Governor-General when there is no conditional or other successor in India to supply the vacancy, the Governor who was first appointed to the office of Governor by His Majesty shall hold and execute the office of Governor-General until a successor arrives, or until some person in India is duly appointed thereto.

(2) Every such acting Governor-General, while acting as such, shall have and may exercise all the rights and powers of the office of Governor-General, and shall be entitled to receive the emoluments and advantages appertaining to the office, foregoing the the salary and allowances appertaining to his office of Governor; and his office of Gevernor shall be supplied, for the time during which he acts as Governor-general in the manner directed by this Act with respect to vacancies in the office of Governor.

(3) If, on the vacancy occurring, it appears to the Governor, who by virtue of this section holds and executes the office of governor-general, necessary to exercise the powers thereof before he takes his seat in council, he may make known by notification his appointment, and his intention to assume the office of Governor-General, and thereupon the provisions of this Act respecting the assumption of the office by a person conditionally appointed to succeed thereto shall apply.

(4) Until such a Governor has assumed the office of Governor-General, if no conditional or other successor is on the spot to supply such vacancy, the vice-president, or, if he is absent, the senior ordinary member of the executive council, shall hold and execute the office of the Governor-General until the vacancy is filled in accordance with the provisions of this Act.

91. (1) If a vacancy occurs in the office of Governor when no conditional or other successor is on the spot to supply the vacancy, the vice-president, or, if he is absent, the senior member of the Governor's executive council, or, of where there is no council, the Chief Secretary to the local Government, shall hold and execute the office of Governor until a successor arrives, or until some other person on the spot is duly appointed thereto.

(2) Every such acting Governor shall, while acting as such, be entitled to receive the emoluments and advantages appertaining to

the office of Governor, foregoing the salary and allowances appertaining to his office of member of council or Secretary.

92. (1) If a vacancy occurs in the office of an ordinary member of the executive council of the Governor-General or a member of the executive council of Governor, and there is no conditional or other successor present on the spot, the Governor-General-in-Council or Governor-in-Council, as the case may be, supply the vacancy by appointing a temporary member of council.

(2) Until a successor arrives the person so appointed shall hold and execute the office to which he has been appointed, and shall have and may exercise all the rights and powers thereof, and shall be entitled to receive the emoluments and advantages appertaining to the office, foregoing all emoluments and advantages to which he was entitled at the time of his being appointed to that office.

(3) If any ordinary member of the executive council of the Governor-General, or any member of the executive council of a Governor, is, by infirmity or otherwise, rendered incapable of acting or of attending to act as such, or is absent on leave, then, if any person has been conditionally appointed to succeed to his office and is on the spot, the place of that member shall be supplied by that person; and, if no person conditionally appointed to succeed to the office is on the spot, the Governor-General in Council, or Governor-in Council as the case may be, shall appoint some person to be a temporary member of Council.

(4) Until the return to duty of the member so incapable or absent, the person conditionally or temporarily appointed shall hold and execute the office to which he has been appointed, and shall have and may exercise all the rights and powers thereof, and shall be entitled to receive half the salary of the member of council whose place he fills, and also half the salary of any other office which he may hold, if he hold any such office, the remaining half of such last named salary being at the disposal of the Governor-General in council or Governor-in-Council, as the case may be.

(5) Provided as follows:—

(*a*) No person may be appointed a temporay member of council who might not have been appointed under this Act to fill the vacancy supplied by the temporary appointment; and

(*b*) if the Secretary of State informs the Governor-General that it is not the intention of His Majesty to fill a vacancy in the Governor-General's executive council, no temporary appointment may be made under this section to fill the vacancya, nd if any such temporary appointment has been made before the date of the receipt of the information by the Governor-General, the tenure of the person temporarily appointed shall cease from that date.

93. (1) A nominated or elected member of the Indian Legislative council or of a local Legislative Council may resign his office to the Governor-General or to the Governor, Lieutenant-Governor, or Chief Commissioner, as the case may be, and on the acceptance of the resignation the office shall become vacant.

(2) If for a period of two consecutive months any such member is absent from India or unable to attend to the duties of his office, the Governor-General, Governor, Lieutenant-Governor or Chief Commissioner, as the case may be, may, by notification published in the Government Gazette, declare that the seat in council of that member has become vacant..

94. Subject to the provisions of this Act, the Secretary of State in Council may, with the concurrence of a majority of votes at a meeting of the Council of India, make rules as to the absence on leave of persons in the service of the Crown in India, and the terms as to continuance, variation or cessation of pay, salary and allowances on which any such leave may be granted.

95. (1) The Secretary of State in Council, with the concurrence of a majority of votes at a meeting of the Council of India, may make rules for distributing between the several authorities in India the power of making appointments to and promotions in offices under the Crown in India, and may reinstate officers and servants suspended or removed by any of those authorities.

(2) Subject to such rules, all appointments to offices and commands in India, and all promotions, which, by law, or under any regulations, usage or custom, are, at the commencement of this Act, made by any authority in India, shall, subject to the qualifications, conditions, and restrictions, then affecting such appointments and promotions, respectively, continue to be made in India by the like authority.

96. No native of British India, nor any subject of His Majesty resident therein, shall, by reason only of his religion, place of birth, descent, colour, or any of them, be disabled from holding any office under the Crown in India.

COMMENTS.

Ss. 85–96 (both inclusive).

The salaries of the Viceroys, Governors, and Members of Councils are fixed at the maximum in the first schedule of this Act. Originally they were so fixed by 3 & 4 Wm. IV, c. 85, s. 76; but the same Act declared that these salaries were subject to such reductions as the Court of Directors, with the sanction of the Board of Control, might at any time think fit. The salaries of the Commander-in-Chief and of the Lieutenant-Governors were fixed at 1,00,000 Company's rupees by 16 and 17 Vict. c. 95, s. 35, and they were made liable to the same provisions and regulations as the salaries fixed by the Act of 1833. At the present time it would seem that the salaries may be fixed at any amount not exceeding the amounts fixed by the Acts of 1833, and 1853. "The power to reduce", says Ilbert, "has been exercised more than once, but it is open to argument whether the power to reduce involves a power to raise subsequently." Besides the salaries thus fixed by law, a certain number of specified officers are entitled to an allowance for equipment and voyage to India, such as the Viceroy, the Governors of Presidencies, Commanders-in-Chief, Members of the Viceregal Council, Judges of High Courts, and Bishops of Calcutta, Madras and Bombay. These allowances are fixed by the Indian Salaries and Allowances Act of 1880, but they may be altered or abolished by the Secretary of State in Council. Under that Act the following allowances are paid to-day:—

Viceroy	£. 5,000
Governors of Presidencies...	„ 1,000
Commander-in-Chief	„ 500
Member of Council	„ 300
High Court Judges	„ 300
Bishops	„ 300

These allowances are paid, it should be further noted, only when the officer in question is resident in Europe at the time of his appointment. If he resides anywhere else a smaller allowance will be paid. No additional charge can be levied on the revenues of India under the Act of 1880, or for the purpose of these allowances.

PART VIII.

The Indian Civil Service.

97. (1) The Secretary of State in Council may, with the advice and assistance of the Civil Service Commissioners, make rules for the examination, under the superintendence of those Commissioners, of British subjects desirous of becoming candidates for appointment to the Indian Civil Service.

(2) The rules shall prescribe the age and qualifications of the candidates, and the subjects of examination.

(3) All rules made in pursuance of this section shall be laid before Parliament within fourteen days after the making thereof, or if Parliament is not then sitting, then within fourteen days after the next meeting of Parliament.

(4) The candidates certified to be entitled under the rules shall be recommended for appointment according to the order of their proficiency as shown by their examination.

(5) Such persons only as are so certified may be appointed or admitted to the Indian Civil Service by the Secretary of State in Council.

98. Subject to the provisions of this Act, all vacancies happening in any of the offices specified or referred to in the Third Schedule to this Act, and all such offices which may be created hereafter, shall be filled from amongst the members of the Indian Civil Service.

99. (1) The authorities in India, by whom appointments are made to offices in the Indian Civil Service, may appoint to any such office any person of proved merit and ability domiciled in British India, and born in British India of parents habitually resident in India and not established there for temporary purposes only, although the person so appointed has not been admitted to that service in accordance with the foregoing provisions of this Act.

(2) Every such appointment shall be made subject to such rules as may be prescribed by the Governor-General in Council and sanctioned by the Secretary of State in Council with the concurrence of a majority of votes at a meeting of the Council of India.

(3) The Governor-General in Council may, by resolution, define and limit the qualifications of persons who may be appointed under this section, but every resolution made for that purpose shall be subject to the sanction of the Secretary of State in Council, and shall not have force until it has been laid for thirty days before both Houses of Parliament.

100. (1) Where it appears to the authority in India, by whom an appointment is to be made to any office reserved to members of the Indian Civil Service, that a person not being a member of that service ought, under the special circumstances of the case, to be appointed thereto, the authority may appoint thereto any person who has resided for at least seven years in India, and who has, before his appointment, fulfilled all the tests (if any) which would be imposed in the like case on a member of that service.

(2) Every such appointment shall be provisional only, and shall forthwith be reported to the Secretary of State, with the special reasons for making it; and, unless the Secretary of State in Council approves the appointment, with the concurrence of a majority of

votes at a meeting of the Council of India, and within twelve months from the date of the appointment intimates such approval to the authority by whom the appointment was made, the appointment shall be cancelled.

I. The History of Public Service in India.

The service of the East India Company in India was composed of three grades:—Writers, Factors and Merchants. The pay and conditions of service, during the period that the Company was merely a body of merchants, may perhaps have been adequate; but as the Company began to be transformed into a ruling sovereign body, the emoluments of its servants became wretchedly insufficient, and the temptation to provide against a rainy day by illicit means became irresistible. The abuses thus creeping into the service had attracted the attention of authorities both at home and in India; and attempts were made by men like Clive and Hastings to check the rapacity of the Company's servants by removing the possibility of temptation from their way. Besides, the training of the Company's servants was utterly inadequate to help them in the discharge of their duties as administrators. It was not, however, till the days of Lord Cornwallis that the Public Service of the country was organised on a more satisfactory basis. Three main principles governed the new institution, to which the name of the Covenanted Service of the East India Company was given. These were: (1) that every civil servant should enter into a covenant not to engage into trade, nor to receive presents from the natives, and to subscribe for the pension fund. In return the Company bound themselves to provide a handsome scale of pay and regular promotion, as also a certain pension for every servant retiring after a certain number of years of service. The Company also undertook to set apart a certain number of the more important posts in its service in India for men so drafted. This principle is maintained almost intact even to-day. The civil servant of to-day has not only to enter into a covenant as before; he must also observe the Government Servants' Conduct Rules, which are applicable to every public servant in India, however chosen The scale of pay, allowances and pension remains almost unchanged. Every retiring Civil Servant–whether before his retirement he was a Lieutenant Governor, a High Court Judge or merely a District Officer–gets the same pension of £ 1000 a year; while the widows and orphans of the deceased members of the service are provided for by an annuity fund to which every civilian, married or single, must subscribe. As regards the number of posts reserved for the members of the covenanted service, the Act of 1793, modified by the Indian Civil Service Act of 1861, offered them the posts of Secretaries and Under-Secretaries to Government, Commissioners of Revenue, Civil and Session Judges, Magistrates and Collectors of Districts etc. The present Act reserves for them the offices of:—

1. Secretaries, Joint-Secretaries, Deputy Secretaries and Under Secretaries to the several governments in India, except the Secretaries, Joint Secretaries Deputy Secretaries and Under Secretaries in the Army, Marine and Public Works Department.
2. Accountants-General.
3. Members of the Board of Revenue in the Presidency of Bengal and Madras, the United Provinces, Bihar and Orissa.
4. Secretaries to those Boards of Revenue.
5. Commissioners of Customs, Salt, Excise and Opium.
6. Opium Agent.

Besides these in the Regulation Provinces the offices of:—

1. District and Sessions Judges.
2. Additional District or Session Judges and Assistant Session Judges.
3. District Magistrates.
4. Joint Magistrates.

5. Assistant Magistrates.

6. Commissioners of Revenue.

7. Collectors of Revenue or Chief Revenue Officers of Districts.

8. Assistant Collectors.

Though so many offices are reserved for the members of the Indian Civil Service—as the covenanted service is now called–they by no means exhaust the list. It has been said that nearly one fo-urth of the members of the service-now aggregating over 1300 men—are employed in posts not exclusively reserved for them. They serve in Native States, in the Post Office, in the Police department, in important Municipalities, and great Public Trusts like the Port Trust or the City Improvement Trust in Bombay. On the other hand it must be added that recent statutes, beginning from 1870, have enabled the authorities in India to appoint to posts reserved for the members of the Civil Service, men who have not passed the test of that service. Such appointments are made from amongst men of proved merit and ability in accordance with rules made by the Governor-General in Council, and sanctioned by the Secretary of State in Council with a majority of votes at a meeting of the India Council.

The second principle accepted in 1793 was that the first appointments to the service should be made by the Directors of the Company in England–without any interference by the authorities in India, while the subsequent promotion of men once appointed should depend entirely upon the authorities in India without any interference from home. This principle has been modified to some extent in the course of time. The right of nomination of the Directors was taken away in 1853 when the service was thrown open to competition among the natural born subjects of Her Majesty, and that system was maintained by the Act of 1858, and is accepted by the present Act. Still the principle remained that the first appointments should be made in England by the Secretary of State upon the recommendation of the Civil Service Commissioners. Even this was modified in 1870. The Charter Act of 1833 and the Queen's Proclamation of 1858 had distinctly promised that the public service will not be closed to the natives of the Country by reason merely of their caste, colour or creed, and that the only requirement for recruiting would be merit and efficiency. But the fact that the first appointments were to be made in England operated by itself as a bar to the admission of Indians in the service of their country. Men who were able to pass any, the stringest, test were, however, precluded from serving their country honourably and profitably because they were unable to bear the expense of a protracted residence in England and unwilling to run the social risks of a voyage to Europe. This was impressed upon the authorities at home, and the Act of 1870 was passed, which, after reciting that "It is expedient that additional facilities should be given for the employment of Natives of India, of proved merit and ability, in the Civil Service of, Her Majesty in India, " authorised the appointment of Natives of India to posts in the civil service irrespective of the statutory restriction, and subject only to rules made by the Governor-General in Council and sanctioned by the Secretary of State and a majority of his council. This Act, however, could not be carried into effect at once. It was not till 1879 that rules were framed by the Governor-General in Council which threw open to the natives of India of "proved ability and merit" one-sixth of the posts usually held by members of the Indian Civil Service. Thus in Bombay 2 posts of Collectors, 1 of Talukdari Settlement Office on th Revenue side, 2 posts of District and Sessions Judges, 3 posts of Assistant Judges, 1 post of the Registrar of the High Court once held by the members of the Indian Civil Service, are now open to natives of India, not belonging to the Civil Service proper. But the rules did not work satisfactorily in practice. Though the intention of the Government of India was sought to be given effect to by reducing to five-sixths the appointments made in England, between 1879 and 1889 only about 60 Indians could be appointed to this "Statutory Civil Service" as it was called. Already in 1886 a commission was appointed by the Government of India under the presidency of Sir C. Aitchison—" to devise a scheme which might reasonably be hoped to possess the necessary elements of finality, and to do full justice to the claims of natives of India to higher employment in the public service." The Commission was a representative body, and made recommendations under which the following scheme was framed.

"The Civil Service for the management of the higher branches of the executive and judicial administration is divided into 3 sections: first is the Imperial Civil Service, recruited in England by competitive examination and open to all subjects of the King-Emperor. It has its own conditions and standards, and a few natives have been able to pass its tests and obtain employment within its ranks. It fills the majority of the highest civil offices together with such a number of less important offices as would provide a course of training for the younger members of the service. The second is called the Provincial service, recruited in each province chiefly from among educated natives by nomination and sometimes by examination and promotion from the subordinate service. Admission to this branch of the service is regulated by rules framed by the Local Government and approved by the Government of India. The members of the provincial service are eligible for some of the offices reserved for the I. C. S., and lists of such posts open to them have been published. The third is the subordinate service which is recruited almost exclusively from the natives of the country and is entrusted with minor posts." (Strachey).

This arrangement, though satisfactory at the time, has not proved so definite and final as its authors intended it to be. There is a growing demand among the educated natives of India for a larger share in the actual administration of their country. Natural in itself, this desire has been encouraged and intensified by recent events. Lord Morley's tenure of the India office was memorable for the appointment of two Indians to the India Council, and one in the several executive Councils in India. If Indians could be appointed, with profit both to themselves and to the Government, to the highest and the most exalted posts, their practical exclusion from the general body of the superior service seemed quite unreasonable. Moreover half a century of experience both in British India and in the Native States had proved beyond the possibility of a doubt the fitness and aptitude of educated Indians for the administrative and judicial work of the highest order. The days were also gone when the natives of the country could be suspected of a want of integrity. Education and example had increased and confirmed their probity. And yet, as the following table shows, the position of the natives of India in the superior service of the country is far from enviable.

Appointments on less than Rs. 1000 a month.

Year.	Europeans.	Eurasians.	Hindoos.	Mahomedans.
1867	4128	2629	5078	948
1877	4706	3443	7432	1175
1887	5147	4164	9733	1388
1897	5017	4965	12249	1832
1903	5205	5420	14131	2152
1910	No figures.	No figures.	No figures.	No figures.

Appointments on Rs. 1000 or more a month.

Year.	Europeans.	Eurasians.	Hindoos.	Mahomedans.
1867	632	4	12	0
1877	995	5	18	1
1887	1007	0	24	3
1897	1227	11	56	13
1903	1263	15	71	21
1910	1721		134	27

For the highest offices for every native of the country in the public service there are more than ten Europeans and Eurasians. On the 1st of April 1913 out of a total strength of 1319 there were only 46 Indians in the Indian Civil Service. Or to put it differently, in 1903 the Europeans held 6468 posts for which they got the aggregate salary of £ 35,09,000, while the Hindus, who held 14201 posts, got only £ 3,21,16,000, and the Mahomedans who held 2173 posts got only £ 3,41,000. In other words the Natives of India who filled the majority of places 16374 got only £ 24,55,000, while the Europeans got nearly half as much again £ 35,90,000, for slightly more than one third of the posts—6468.

It was perhaps to remedy such a state of things that another Public Service Commission was appointed in 1912, nearly 25 years after the Aitchison Commission had made its recommendations. The Islington Commission was to examine and report upon the following matters in connection with the Indian Civil Service, and other Civil Services, Imperial and Provincial:—

(*a*) The methods of recruitment and the system of training and probation.

(*b*) The conditions of service, salary, leave and pension.

(*c*) Such limitation as still exist in the employment of non-Europeans and the working of the existing system of division of services into Imperial and provincial. And generally to consider the requirements of the public service, and to recommend such changes as may seem expedient.

On this Commission there were three Indian Gentlemen. It enquired into the conditions etc. of the Public Services in India as well as in England for nearly two years, and submitted a report in 1914. Owing to the War the publication of the Report was delayed, but it was at length published in January 1917. As no action has so far been taken on the report, further comment would seem unnecessary, though the general tenour of the Report shows a most deplorably retrograde tendency. If Indians had expected any great concessions as the result of this Report, they cannot but be disappointed.

The third principle adopted in 1793 was that regulations should be framed for insuring proper training and qualifications in the aspirants for the Indian Civil Service. These regulations are made, under the present Act, by the Secretary of State for India in Council, with the advice and assistance of the Civil Service Commissioners. These regulations should be submitted to Parliament, 14 days after their framing. They prescribe the age limit of the candidates and their qualifications as also the subjects of examinations. These have varied from time to time. For instance the age limit before 1906 were 21 and 23, while since 1906 the rule has been that the candidates appearing for the Civil Service Examination in London must not be under 22 years of age in August of that year and must not be over 24 years of age. A candidate once plucked is allowed a second attempt, but no one is allowed more than two attempts in all. Originally the nominees of the Court of Directors were sent direct to join their appointments, but the want of adequate previous training made them inefficient. Lord Wellesley sought to remedy this defect by opening a College at Calcutta in 1800 to give the necessary preliminary training to newly arrived Civilians; but this attempt was foiled by the Directors who started in 1805 a College at Haileybury. Till the day–1858–when this College was closed, nominees to the Indian Civil Service underwent there a course of two years training before proceeding to take up their appointments in India. At the present time the practice is a little different. After a candidate has shown the required proficiency at the Civil Service Examination, and has been recommended for appointment by the Civil Service Commissioners, he is encouraged to pass one year at an English University, to pursue there a prescribed course of study, and is given an allowance of £ 150 during that probationery year. At the end of that year there is another examination, failure to pass which might mean final loss of the service, while seniority in the service is determined by combining the results of the open competition examination and this final compulsory examination.

The principles, therefore, adopted in 1793, have all been maintained upto the present, with such slight modifications as the progress of the country demanded. There is practically the same covenants—if anything more strict than before; there are nearly the same posts reserved for them, though the increasing activities of the State have been met by the comparatively wider employment of Indians; there is nearly the same scale of pay, allowance and pensions, as also the general conditions of service. The first appointments are even now made in England, though there has been, since 1870, some authority delegated to the Government of India to make appointments under certain limitations. The regulations regarding the courses of study, age and qualifications have varied from the day that Lord Macaulay drafted the first regulations; but the general principle that there should be a certain standard of efficiency for every candidate is maintained. In addition to the Imperial Civil Service there are now also the provincial and subordinate Civil

Services, staffed in the main by the Indians, and governed by rules framed on the model of the rules for the Indian Civil Service.

II. Recent Changes.

Owing to the war, and the special measures which England has been forced to adopt to fight this war, it was felt that the old regulations of the Indian Civil Service would operate unfairly. A number of young men, who, in the ordinary course of events, would have offered themselves for the examination, have been called to arms, and so prevented from competition. Besides, if the old rules were allowed to remain unaltered, and if all the posts were to be filled by men in order of their proficiency at the competitive examination, there would be the risk of deterioration in the standard. On the other hand, the war had opened opportunities to Indians which, perhaps, they would not have had otherwise. Bearing in mind all these considerations an emergency bill was introduced in Parliament in October 1915, suspending the system of open competition and replacing by a method of recruitment which would be just to Indians, as well as to those Englishmen who had sacrificed their careers by obeying the call of duty. The main provisions of this Act "to enable persons during the continuance of the war, and for a period of two years thereafter, to be appointed or admitted to the Indian Civil Service without examination" were:—(1). The Secretary of State in Council may, with advice and assistance of the Civil Service Commissioners, make rules providing for the admission and appointment to the Indian Civil Service by the Secretary of State in Council, during the continuance of the present war, and for a period not exceeding two years thereafter, of British subjects possessing such qualifications with respect to age and otherwise as may be prescribed by the rules, not withstanding that they have not been certified as being entitled for appointment as the result of examination in accordance with the regulations and rules made under S. 32 of the Government of India Act 1858, and S. 97 of the Government of India Act 1915.

Provided that (*a*) not less than one-fourth of the persons admitted to the Indian Civil Service during such period as aforesaid shall be as certified as aforesaid; and (*b*) a person shall not be appointed to the Indian Civil Service, under the rules made under this section, unless the Civil Service Commissioners certify that by such means as may be prescribed by the rules they have satisfied themselves that in their opinion he possesses the necessary educational qualifications.

The effect of this temporary act was (1) not to suspend or abolish altogether the Civil Service Examination. Only instead of the whole number of vacancies in the service being filled by the successful candidates in the examination during the period described, one-fourth—at least one-fourth—shall be so filled. (2) The remaining vacancies may be filled by men who need not have passed the examination, but who must possess such qualifications as the rules, framed by the Secretary of State in Council and accepted by Parliament, lay down. (3) Further, no man can be appointed without success at the examination, unless the Civil Service Commissioners are satisfied that he possesses the necessary educational qualifications. (4) As regards the Indians, if among the one-fourth, which is to be still recruited by examination, there is not the same proportion of Indians as was usual in the last few years, then the deficit would be made up by the appointment of unsuccessful Indians, provided they satisfy the Commissioners about their educational and other qualifications. This was construed by the Government as showing their anxiety to be just and fair to Indians. On the other hand the critics of the Government pointed out that the whole Act was unjust since it limited the one opportunity Indians had so far to obtain admission in the service of their country in larger numbers. It must be added that the latter construction is not entirely unreasonable. At the same time Government could not ignore altogether the claims of these who were fighting for their country, nor suffer the standard of efficiency to deteriorate. Under the circumstances the measure was inevitable; and If it should operate unjustly upon the Indians the consolation is that the Act is only a temporary measure, and that, whatever be the recommendations of the Public Service Commission, we are undoubtedly on the eve of great and radical changes in this matter.

III. The Career of a Civil Servant.

Every young civilian, on joining the service in India, is attached to a district as assistant to the Collector. He is given the powers of a Magistrate of the lowest class, and is required to pass an examination in a vernacular language, local laws, and Revenue Procedure. When he has passed that examination he attains the full magisterial powers and holds charge of a revenue sub-division. At this stage he has two alternatives—to go into the Judicial branch of the service or the Executive branch. In the former line in the regular course of promotion he becomes an Assistant Judge and a District and Sessions Judge; but the last office he does not attain to, unless he has served for ten years. As District Judge he is the principal civil tribunal of the district and has considerable appellate powers. As Sessions Judge he tries the more important criminal cases. If he is intelligent and assiduous he may hope to rise and be on the High Court Bench or a Judicial Commissioner. In this branch of the service the highest available post is that of a High Court Judge.

If our Civilian elects to go in the Executive line in the regular course of promotion he becomes a Collector-Magistrate. In this branch the highest posts available are those of members of the Viceroy's Executive Council or even of a Lieutenant Governor. Civilians are now debarred from becoming Governors-General or even Governors of the presidencies. In general, however by the time that the highest grades in the offices of Collector or Judge are reached, the Civilian has nearly completed his 25 years of service, which are necessary before he can retire on a pension. Should he, however, elect to remain in service there are still ten years more, and he can hope to rise to higher posts. Every one must retire on completing 35 years of service or 55 years of life, except the Judges of the High Court who are allowed to complete 12 years on the Bench.

VI. Other Public Services.

"Besides this general service," says Sir Ilbert Courtney "there are special services such as the Education department, the Public Works Department, the Forest Department, and the Police Department." To these we might add the Agricultural service, the Pilot service, the Medical service and the Ecclesiastical service. In all those services there are generally speaking three main branches, *viz*:—the Imperial branch, recruited chiefly in England from Englishmen, the provincial branch recruited in India from Indians, and the subordinate branch. To take a bird's-eye-view of the conditions and prospects of some of the most important of the services:—

I. The Indian Agricultural Service.

The chief appointments in this service are:-Deputy Director of Agriculture, Agricultural Chemist, Economic Botanist, Mycologist, Entomologist and Professors of Agriculture in Agricultural Colleges. A few of these posts are directly under the Government of India, but a large majority is under the Provincial Governments. Sometimes the candidates are appointed directly to their posts, but as a rule they are appointed on probation or as supernumeraries. As such they undergo a course of training in Indian Agriculture, and will be appointed to permanent posts as they become vacant and as the candidates are specially suited for the posts. The qualifications as to age are that the candidates should not be under 23 nor over 30 years of age. Their specia qualifications may be (*a*) either a degree in honours in science, or a diploma of a recognised school of Agriculture; (*b*) qualifications in the special science according to the nature of the post to be filled and (*c*) practical experience. The salaries attached to posts in this department are: Rs. 400/- per month in the first year, Rs. 430/-in the second, Rs. 460/- in the third, and Rs. 500/- rising by annual increments of Rs. 50/- per month to Rs. 1000/- in the fourth and subsequent years.

2. The Ecclesiastical Establishment (Anglican.)

The Secretary of State makes appointments of chaplains on probation from time to time as vacancies occur. Candidates must be priests, between the age of 27 and 34 and must have been in Holy Orders for 3 years altogether. A chaplain is on probation for three years. If confirmed at the end of the period he is appointed a junior chaplain. While on probation he gets Rs. 5760/- per year and when confirmed he gets Rs. 6360/- per annum for five years, and thereafter Rs. 8160/- until promoted to be Senior Chaplain. He cannot be a senior chaplain until after ten years of service, and then he gets Rs. 10,200/- for the first five years and Rs. 12,000/- per year thereafter.

3. The Educational Department.

This service, like the Civil Service, has two main branches. The Imperial Educational Service is recruited from Englishmen in England and by the Secretary of State. It consists of two branches (*a*) the teaching branch, including principals and professors of Colleges and Head Masters in certain High Schools and (*b*) the Inspectors of Schools. They are all appointed by the Secretary of State as vacancies occur. As a rule candidates must not be under 23 years of age nor over 30. They must have a University Degree in honours, some experience as teachers, and qualifications in special subjects according to the nature of the appointment. The salaries paid are : Rupees 500 a month rising by annual increments of Rs. 50/- monthly to Rs. 1,000/- a month. When this point has been reached the increase of his emoluments depends upon his promotion, and is generally in the form of allowances varying from Rs. 200 to Rs. 500 in addition to the salary of Rs. 1000 a month. Besides, to this branch of the service are open the posts of the Director of public Instruction in the various Provinces, receiving a salary varying from Rs. 1,250 to Rs. 2,500.

The Provincial branch is recruited chiefly from Indian Graduates in India. It includes some principals and professors of colleges, head masters of schools and translators to the Government. The minimum pay is Rs 200 and maximum Rs. 750 in this branch of the service. The subordinate Educational service includes a few head masters, assistant Deputy Inspectors, and all the assistant masters in the Government High Schools and Middle Schools. The minimum pay in this service is Rs 40 and the maximum somewhere near Rs 400.

4. The Indian Medical Service.

This service is under the Government of India and consists of some 768 medical men and recruited in England by competitive examination. Its chief duty is the care of the Native troops and of the British officers and their families. In the course of time these duties have been amplified so that to-day they include the provision of medical aid to civil servants and their families, the administration of the civil Hospitals in large towns, and the supervision of numerous small dispensaries pubilc as well as private, the sanitation of large areas, the protection of water supply, the prevention of epidemic disease. The jails in British India are also in their charge.

The service dates from the earliest days of the East India Company. In 1766 it was divided into two branches, Military and Civil, though in the latter case the medical men were considered primarily as army officers temporarily lent to the civil Government, and liable to be called to duty at any time. In 1898 the officers of the service were given military rank and since 1906,the names of the officers serving in the different provinces are all combined in one list. Since 1853 the service has been thrown open to the Indians, and up to 1910 nearly 90 men of purely Indian extraction had been able to find employment within its ranks. And while in the Civil Service hardly three per cent. of the whole body were Indians in 1913, in the Indian Medical service the proportion of Indians is over 5 per cent and is yearly increasing. The service is recruited by open competition under rules and regulations framed by the Secretary of State in Council. The rules operating at present may be summarised as follows:—

The candidates must be of British or East Indian descent and subjects of His Majesty. They must be of sound bodily health, married or unmarried. They must possess a medical qualification registrable in the United Kingdom. No candidate is allowed to compete more than three times, while candidates for the examination in each year must be between 21 and 23 years of age. These examinations are held twice a year—in January and in July—and consist of the following subjects:—medicine, surgery, applied anatomy and physiology, pathology, and bacteriology, midwifery and diseases of women and children. Successful candidates are appointed as Lieutenants on probation, and, after two short courses of study at the Royal Medical College, Aldershot, are drafted in the regular service. At the head of the service is the Director General-sometimes called Surgeon-General—who is an official of the Government of India. The pay varies from Rs. 420 to Rs. 3000 a month.

5. The Public Works Department.

In this department the permanent establishment is recruited from:—

(*a*) Officers of Royal Engineers.

(*b*) persons appointed to the Imperial Service by the Secretary of State by selection from the United Kingdom.

(*c*) persons educated at the Government Civil Engineering College in India, and appointed to the provincial service by the Government of India.

(*d*) occasional admission of other qualified persons.

The Secretary of State in council appoints Assistant Engineers to the Public Works Department of the Government of India on the following rules:—

(1) Candidate must not be under 21 years and over 24 years of age.

(2) They must produce evidence that they have obtained a University Degree, or passed the A. M. I. C. E. Examination; or obtained some other satisfactory diploma or distinction in Civil Engineering.

In this Department the newly arrived officer begins as an Assistant Engineer with a salary of Rs 4560 a year, and has a regular increment of nearly Rs.500 every year till he becomes an Executive Engineer, when he gets Rs 10,200 a year with a regular similar increment. Over the Executive Engineer are the Superintending Engineers of the First, Second and Third class; and over them all are the Chief Engineers of the First and Second Classes. The highest officer—the First Class Chief Engineer gets Rs. 33,000 per annum.

Like other departments this department has also its provincial and subordinate branch of the service.

6. The Military Department.

This department has its own service. All officers of this department are not, however, always on active military duty. In non-regulation provinces they are frequently placed in charge of civil posts. The diplomatic service of India is also staffed to a great extent by the army officers. No Indian, however, has so far been allowed to hold commissions in the Indian Army, and so this department is of relatively little interest to an Indian writer. It is expected that as the result of this war, and perhaps upon the recommendation of the Public Service Commission this restriction will soon be removed, just as the distinction of the Victoria Cross was thrown open to the Indian soldiers by the King Emperor from 1912.

A survey of the various public services in India brings out prominently the following general features:—

(1) In almost every department the service is divided into three branches, the Imperial, the Provincial and the Subordinate branches.

(2) In almost every case all the higher ranks in the service are filled by Europeans, though, except in the army, there is no statutory disability upon Indians in every case. The lower ranks are filled by Indians-mostly Hindus.

(3) The conditions of pay and pension etc., are quite handsome. Compared to other countries, compared even to England, the public servants in India are extremely well paid.

(4) Almost all branches of the service are filled by men who have given sufficient, though varying, proofs of ability. This is done either by means of an examination, or by departmental rules for testing the ability of the candidates.

In general, then, the reflection is irresistible that in securing men for the public service in India, so much attention is paid to efficiency that every other consideration of economy or even justice has been sacrificed to this one dominating consideration of efficiency. The standards for admission are fairly high; and the reputation of the service almost unique in the world. In the general emulation which must and does result the whole body of public servants vie with one another in giving proofs of sterling integrity and marvellous ability. If efficiency were the only condition of good Government, there would be no hesitation in asserting that India is at present about the best governed country in the world.

CHAPTER VII.

Judicial Administration.

PART IX.

THE INDIAN HIGH COURTS.

Constitution.

101. (1) The High Courts referred to in this act are the high courts of judicature for the time being established in British India by letters patent.

(2) Each high court shall consist of a chief justice and as many other judges as His Majesty may think fit to appoint provided as follows:—

(i) The Governor-General in Council may appoint persons to act as additional judges of any high court, for such period, not exceeding two years, as may be required; and the judges so appointed shall, whilst so acting, have all the powers of a judge of the high court appointed by His Majesty under this Act;

(ii) The maximum number of judges of a high court, including the chief justice and additional judges, shall be twenty.

(3) A judge of a high court must be:—

(*a*) A barrister of England or Ireland or a member of the Faculty of Advocates in Scotland, of not less than five years standing; or (*b*) A member of the Indian Civil Service of not less than ten years standing, and having for at least three years served as, or exercised the powers of, a district judge; or

(*c*) A person having held judicial office, not inferior to that of a subordinate judge or a judge of a small causes court, for a period of not less than five years: or

(*d*) A person having been a pleader of a high court for a period of not less than ten years.

(4) Provided that not less than one-third of the judges of a high court, including the chief justice but excluding additional judges, must be such barristers or advocates as aforesaid, and that not less than one-third must be members of the Indian Civil Service.

(5) The high court for the North-Western Provinces may be styled the high court of judicature at Allahabad, and the high court at Fort William in Bengal is in this Act referred to as the high court at Calcutta.

102. (1) Every judge of a high court shall hold his office during His Majesty's pleasure.

(2) Any such judge may resign his office, in the case of the high court at Calcutta, to the Governor-General in Council, and in other cases to the local Government.

103. (1) The chief justice of a high court shall have rank and precedence before the other judges of the same court.

(2) All the other judges of a high court shall have rank and precedence according to the seniority of their appointments, unless otherwise provided in their patents.

104. (1) The Secretary of State in Council may fix the salaries, allowances, furloughs, retiring pensions, and (where necessary) expenses for equipment and voyage, of the chief justices and other judges of the several high courts, and may alter them, but any such alteration shall not affect the salary of any judge appointed before the date thereof.

(2) The remuneration fixed for a judge under this section shall commence on his taking upon himself the execution of his office,

and shall be the whole profit or advantage which he shall enjoy from his office during his continuance therein.

(3) If a judge of a high court dies during his voyage to India, or within six months after his arrival there, for the purpose of taking upon himself the execution of his office, the Secretaey of State shall pay to his legal personal representatives, out of the revenues of India, over and above the sum due to him at the time of his death, a sum equal to six months' salary.

105. (1) On the occurrence of a vacancy in the office of chief justice of a high court, and during any absence of such a chief justice, the Governor-General in Council in the case of the High Court at Calcutta, and the local Government in other cases, shall appoint one of the other judges of the same high court to perform the duties of chief justice of the court, until some person has been appointed by His Majesty to the office of chief justice of the court, and has entered on the discharge of the duties of that office, or until the chief justice has returned from his absence, as the case requires.

(2) On the occurrence of a vacancy in the office of any other judge of a high court, and during any absence of any such judge, or on the appointment of any such judge to act as chief justice, the Governor-General in Council in the case of the high court at Calcutta, and the local Government in other cases, may appoint a person, with such qualifications as are required in persons to be appointed to the high court, to act as a judge of the court; and the person so appointed may sit and perform the duties of a judge of the court, until some person has been appointed by His Majesty to the office of judge of the court, and has entered on the discharge of the duties of the office, or until the absent judge has returned from his absence, or until the Governor-General in Council or the local Government, as the case may be, sees cause to cancel the appointment of the acting judge.

Jurisdiction.

106. (1) The several high courts are courts of record and have such jurisdiction, original and appellate, including admiralty jurisdic-

tion in respect of offences committed on the high seas, and all such powers and authority over or in relation to the administration of justice, including power to appoint clerks and other ministerial officers of the court, and power to make rules for regulating the practice of the court as are vested in them by letters patent, all such jurisdiction powers and authority as are vested in those courts respectively at the commencement of this Act.

(2) The high courts have not and may not exercise any original jurisdiction in any matter concerning the revenue, or concerning any act ordered or done in the collection thereof according to the usage and practice of the country or the law for the time being in force.

107. Each of the high courts has superintendence over all courts for the time being subject to its appellate jurisdiction, and may do any of the following things, that is to say,

(*a*) call for returns;

(*b*) direct the transfer of any suit or appeal from any such court to any other court of equal or superior jurisdiction;

(*c*) make and issue general rules and prescribe forms for regulating the practice and proceedings of such courts;

(*d*) prescribe forms in which books, entries and accounts shall be kept by the officers of any such courts; and

(*e*) settle tables of fees to be allowed to the sheriff, attorneys, and all clerks and officers of court:

provided that such rules, forms and tables shall not be inconsistent with the provisions of any Act for the time being in force, and shall require the previous approval, in the case of the high court at Calcutta, of the Governor-General in Council, and in other cases of the local Government.

108. (1) Each high court may by its own rules provide as it thinks fit for the exerise, by one or more judges, or by division courts constituted by two or more judges of the high court, of the orignal and appellate jurisdiction vested in the court.

(2) The chief justice of each high court shall determine what judge in each case is to sit alone, and what judges of the court, whether with or without the chief justice, are to constitute the several division courts.

109. (1) The Governor-General in Council may, by order, trans fer any territory or place from the jurisdiction of one to the jurisdiction of any other of the high courts, and authorise any high court, to exercise all or any portion of its jurisdiction in any part of British India not included within the limits for which the high court was established, and also to exercise any such jurisdiction in respect of Christian subjects of His Majesty resident in any part of India outside British India.

(2) The Governor-General in Council shall transmit to the Secretary of State an authentic copy of every order made under this section.

(3) His Majesty may signify, through the Secretary of State in Council, his disallowance of any such order, and such disallowance shall make void and null the order as from the day on which the Governor-General notifies that he has received intimation of the disallowance, but no act done by any high court before such notification shall be deemed invalid by reason only of such disallowance.

110. (1) The Governor-General, each Governor, and each of the members of their respective Executive Councils, shall not—

(*a*) be subject to the original jurisdiction of any high court by reason of anything counselled, ordered, or done by any of them in his public capacity only; nor

(*b*) be liable to be arrested or imprisoned in any suit or proceeding in any high court acting in the exercise of its original jurisdiction; nor

(*c*) be subject to the original criminal jurisdiction of any high court in respect of any offence not being treason or felony.

(2) The exemption under this section from liability to arrest and imprisonment shall extend also to the chief justices and other judges of the several high courts.

111. The order in writing of the Governor-General in Council for any act shall, in any proceeding, civil or criminal, any in high court acting in the exercise of its original jurisdiction, be a full justification of the act, except so far as the order extends to any European British subjects; but nothing in this section shall exempt the Governor-General, or any member of his executive council, or any person acting under their orders, from any proceedings in respect of any such act before any competent court in England.

Law to be Administered.

112. The high courts at Calcutta, Madras and Bombay, in the exercise of their original jurisdiction in suits against inhabitants of Calcutta, Madras or Bombay as the case may be, shall, in matters of inheritance and succession to lands, rents, and goods, and in matters of contract and dealing between party and party, when both parties are subject to the same personal law or custom having the force of law, decide according to that personal law or custom, and when the parties are subject to different personal laws or custom having the force of law decide according to the law or custom to which the defendant is subject.

Additional High Courts.

113. His Majesty, may if he sees fit, by letters patent, establish a high court of judicature in any territory in British India, whether or not included within the limits of the local jurisdiction of another high court, and confer on any high court so established any such jurisdiction, powers and authority as are vested in or may be conferred on any high court existing at the commencement of this Act; and where a high court is so established in any area included within the limits of the local jurisdiction of another high court, His Majesty may, by letters patent, alter those limits, and make such incidental, consequen-

tial and supplemental provisions as may appear to be necessary by reason of the alteration.

Advocate General.

114. (1) His Majesty may, by warrant under His Royal Sign Manual, appoint an advocate-general for each of the presidencies of Bengal, Madras and Bombay.

(2) The advocate-general for each of those presidencies may take on behalf of His Majesty such proceedings as may be taken by His Majesty's Attorney-General in England.

COMMENTS.

I. History of the Courts of Justice.

The early charters of the Company gave a general authority to establish Courts of law in their possessions in India. Thus the charter of 1683 directed that a Court of judicature, consisting of a lawyer and 2 merchants, should be appointed at such places as the Company might appoint; and this was repeated in 1686 and 1698. But the necessity for a more regularly constituted judicial authority was not felt till **1726**, when the Company petitioned the King to establish *Mayor's Courts*. As a result three courts were created, one each at Bombay, Madras and Calcutta, consisting of a Mayor and 9 oldermen for the trial of actions between Europeans within those towns and their dependent factories. At the same time a sort of an appellate tribunal was created in the shape of the President and Council, who heard appeals from the Mayor's Courts; while from the Presidency Government an appeal lay to the King in Council in cases involving sums exceeding Rs. 4000. These Courts were re-established in *1753* by revised Letters Patent, and in the same year were established *Courts of Requests* for trying cases of value not exceeding Rs. 20.

This was the organisation in the Presidency Towns. As regards the Mofussil, under the Moghul rule in Bengal, the administration of justice was in the hands of the Nawab Nazim, who tried all capital cases himself, while his deputy, the Naib Nawab, tried all the other major cases, the minor cases being tried by Foujdars &c.

The Reforms of Hastings.

The series of English victories which followed the Battle of Plassey, and ended in the transfer of the powers of Government to the Company, changed this organisation. Under the arrangements made in 1765, the administration of civil justice was taken over by the Company, while that of criminal justice still remained in the hands of the Nawab. This state of things gave rise to considerable inconvenience which Hastings tried to avert by placing the organisation of justice on a more regular basis. He created a civil court—Diwani Adalat—for each district, presided over by a European *Z*illa Judge and aided by Hindu and Mahomedan law officers. For minor cases he appointed Registrars and Native Commissioners called Sadar Amins and Munsifs. To supervise over these he established four Civil Courts of appeal in four important centres, and over these was the Sadar Diwani Adalat or the Highest Civil Court of appeal consisting of the Governor and his Councillors assisted by native officers. As regards criminal justice corresponding reforms were effected at the same time. Nizamat Adalats—or Provincial Courts of Criminal Justice were instituted in each province, and Courts of Circuit, under the presideney of the judges of the civil appellate courts, were constituted as courts of criminal appeal. Along side the Sadar Diwani Adalat, a Sadar Nizamat Adalat was established as the Highest Court of Criminal Appeal.

The Regulating Act.

Soon after these reforms, the judicial system in India was complicated by the institution of the Supreme Court by Parliament in 1773. The new Court was a creature of Parliament, independent of the Company, and consisted exclusively of professional lawyers. It superseded the Mayor's Court but not the Court of Requests—and was vested with the most extensive jurisdiction, subject to an appeal to the Privy Council in cases involving Rs. 4,000 or more. The relations between the new Court and the Company's Courts were not defined, as also the relations between it and the Executive. At the same time the Supreme Court adopted without modification, English law and procedure, which were entirely unsuitable to the Indian conditions of the day. Hastings tried to remedy the antagonism between his adalats and the Supreme Court by appointing his friend, Sir Elijah Impey, the chief justice of the latter, to the Sadar Diwani Adalat; but his attempt failed; and by the Declaratory Act of 1781 the Supreme Court was obliged to recognise the Company's Courts, was debarred from interfering in cases relating to the Revenue or the regulation of the Government, while by the same Act the Governor-General and his Councillors were exempted from the jurisdiction of the Supreme Court.

The sequence of events in Madras and Bombay was very nearly the same. The evolution of the judicial system was worked out on the same lines. And the System established about 1783 lasted right upto 1861.

II. The Present System.

The present system was inaugerated by the Indian High Courts Act of 1861. On the establishment of the High Courts the old Sadar and Supreme Courts were abolished, and the jurisdiction of both was conferred upon the High Courts,

These were established at first in Bombay, Madras and Bengal, and later on in Agra at Allahabad, while a High Court was established for the new Province of Bihar and Orissa at Patna in 1915. The Judges of the High Courts are appointed by the Crown and hold office during the pleasure of the Sovereign. In this respect the practice in India is different from that of England, where the Judges are appointed during good behaviour. The difference between these two kinds of tenures is that, while the officers appointed during the pleasure of the sovereign can be removed by the king at any time he likes without giving any reasons, the officers appointed during good behaviour cannot be removed except if they commit such offences as render them unfit for their post in the eyes of a competent tribunal. The necessity of the independence of the Judges-to secure an impartial administration of justice, requires, that the Judges in India, as in England, be appointed during good behaviour, and be not removable except on an address to that effect by the Houses of Parliament, or by the Legislative Councils in India. Perhaps we can trace this principle of judicial appointments during the pleasure of the Sovereign to the necessity, which once existed, of the impartial authority of the Crown being given a power of removal of the obnoxious servants of the Company. That reason, of course, would not justify the present maintenance of this obsolete principle; but the composition of the Judicial bench makes it advisable that the principle be maintained even now. For at least one-third of the Judges of the High Court are members of the Civil Service; at least another third should be barristers or members of the Faculty of Advocates of Scotland, the remaining places being filled by members of the local bar. It is provided that the Chief Justice of a High Court shall always be a barrister, but that relates to the permanent occupant of the post, temporary or acting Chief Justices being indifferently drawn from the Civil Service or from the profession.

The Chief Courts and Judicial Commissioners.

The High Court is charged with the superintendance of all subordinate Courts within the Province. Corresponding to the High Courts of Bengal, Madras, Bombay, Allahabad and Patna, there are Chief Courts at Lahore for the Punjab, and at Rangoon for the province of Burma. Unlike the High Courts, the Chief Courts are established by the Governor-General-in-Council and derive their authority from him. The position and pay of the Judges of the Chief Courts are also inferior to those of the High Courts. In all other respects they are on the same level as the Chartered High Courts. In the remaining Provinces the highest judicial authority is vested in one or more Judicial Commissioners.

The Lower Civil Courts.

As regards the Subordinate Courts, the constitution and jurisdiction of the inferior Civil Courts varies from province to province. Broadly speaking, for each administrative district one Disitrict Judge is appointed to preside in the principal Civil Court of his district with original jurisdiction. Under the District Judge are the Subordinate Judges and Munsifs, the extent of whose original jurisdiction is not the same in the different parts of India. Generally speaking the Subordinate Judges are graded in three classses, with definite limitations on the powers and jurisdiction of a judge of each class.

Besides these inferior Civil Courts in the mofussil there are the Courts of Small Causes which are very important in the Presidency Towns of Madras, Bombay and Calcutta. They have powers to try money suits of Rs. 1,000, or, with the consent of the parties, suits upto Rs. 2,000 in value. The increasing pressure of original work upon the High Courts in the Presidency Towns has led to the suggestion that the jurisdiction of the Small Causes Courts be raised to money suits of Rs. 5,000 or less, and the suggestion is at present under consideration by the Government.

Generally speaking the District Judges are drawn from the Civil Service, while the Subordinate Judges and Munsifs are drawn from the Native Bar. The high character and remarkable attainments of the native members of the judicial service in India have deservedly procured them the warmest encomiums from all contemporary observers.

The Lower Criminal Courts.

As regards the Subordinate Criminal Courts, they are divided into Courts of Session and Courts of Magistrates. By the Criminal Procedure Code, every province, outside the presidency towns, is divided into sessions divisions. A sessions division does not always correspond to an administrative district. Frequently a sessions division includes more than one district. Each sessions division has a Court of Session, presided over by a Sessions Judge, with such assistance as the size of the division and the volume of the work may require. A Sessions Judge is usually also a District Judge at the same time. The Sessions Courts are competent to try all accused persons—committed to session by the Magistrates' Courts–and to inflict any sentence authorised by law; with this modification, however, that a sentence of death by a Sessions Court is subject to confirmation by the highest court of criminal appeal within the province. Trials before the Courts of Session are by assessors or juries. The former assist the Judge in framing a judgment though their opinion is not binding upon him. In the latter the verdict given by a majority prevails, if accepted by the presiding Judge. Though the verdict of a jury is usually binding on the Judge, he has power to refer a case to the highest criminal tribunal in the province, if in his opinion, the verdict of the jury is manifestly in opposition to the facts or the weight of evidence. The prerogative of mercy is vested in the Governor-General in Council and the loca

Government without prejudice to the superior authority of the Crown in this respect.

The Courts of Magistrates like the Courts of the Subordinate Judges on the civil side, are graded into three classes, each class of Magistrate having well defined powers. The Magistrate of the first class, for instance, can inflict a sentence of two years' imprisonment, or a fine of Rs. 1,000. For offences requiring more serious punishment, the Magistrates can only hold a preliminary inquiry, and commit such cases for trial by the Court of Sessions.

In the Presidency Towns there are Presidency Magistrates, with the powers of First Class Magistrates, to try the less important offences, and to commit the more important ones to the Sessions. Each Presidency Town is a Sessions Division by itself, and the Sessions Court in a Presidency Town consists of a Judge of the High Court sitting on the original side with the Criminal Jurisdiction of the High Court. Such Sessions Courts are held three or four times a year.

Besides the Presidency Magistrates, there are Honorary Magistrates in the Presidency Towns, any two of whom can form a bench to dispose of petty cases. Such Honorary Magistrates are now created in every important town.

Besides these officers, Coroners are appointed in Calcutta, Bombay and Madras to inquire, with the aid of a Jury, in cases of sudden and suspicious deaths, and to commit suspected persons for trial before the Sessions Court. In the mofussil the work of the Coroner is done by the ordinary staff of Magistrates and Police officers unaided by Jurors.

III. The Jurisdiction of the High Courts.

The High Courts in India have full civil and criminal, original and appellate jurisdiction. Its ordinary, original, civil jurisdiction is exercised, for the Presidency towns, in respect of all suits, except the minor money suits assigned to the Small Causes Court within the Presidency Town, by a single judge. An appeal lies from the decision of a Judge on the original side to a bench on the appellate side. In the case of those towns which—like Allahabad or Lahore—have a High Court or a Chief Court, the court has no such jurisdiction, their only ordinary orginal jurisdiction being confined to criminal proceedings against a British European subject. From the jurisdiction of the Indian High Courts, the Governor-General and the members of his council, as well as the Governors of the three presidencies, together with their councillors, are exempt; they can also be not arrested in connection with any suit or proceeding before a High Court. This exemption of theirs has probably arisen from the quarrels of Warren Hastings with the Supreme Court, as in the famous Nundkumar affair; and more particularly in the Cossijurah case. On the other hand for certain specified offences *e. g.* (1) oppression of any of His Majesty's subjects, (2) wilful disobedience of the orders of the Secretary of State, (3) engaging in trade, or (4) receipt of any bribe by way of a gift, gratuity or reward are made punishable as misdemeanours by the King's Bench Division of the High Court in London.

The extraordinary original jurisdiction of the High Courts consists of (1) the right to call for returns from all Subordinate Courts, (2) and the right to remove any suit on the file of a Subordinate Court, and try the same itself, either with the consent of the parties, or merely to further the ends of justice. The High Court exercises a constant control and supervision over the working of all the Subordinate Courts within its jurisdiction by examining their periodical returns, by sending for particular proceedings, calling for explanatinos &c. All this is altogether apart from that other power of supervision, which it exercises through the cases that constantly come before it for appeal. It also issues general rules for regulating the practice and proceedings before such courts, as well as prescribes forms.

The High Courts are Insolvency Courts for the Presidency Towns, and they act as Courts of Matrimonial causes for such of His Majesty's subjects as have their own marriage laws permitting divorce by such a public tribunal.

The Ecclesiastical Jurisdiction of the Indian High Courts relates only to the Established Church of England; while their jurisdiction with regard to offences on sea, and in connection with Prize Courts, was conferred upon them by a number of statutes and charters. In this connection it may be mentioned that for every offence committed on land, both the procedure and the substantive law to be applied are those of British India; and the same is the case for offences committed whether on land or on sea by British Indian subjects of His Majesty. The case is slightly different with regard to offences committed at sea by persons other than the natives of India. The proceedings in such a case will be regulated by the Code of Criminal Procedure, but English law will have to be applied to determine the nature of the crime and the extent of the punishment.

Under the Indian Criminal Law Amendment Act, 1908(XIV), persons accused of any of the offences specified there—chiefly offences which may be described as the terrorist attempts to overthrow the Government—may be tried in a High Court by a special bench of 3 Judges. As a rule offences are tried in the High Courts by a Judge and Jury; but in this case no jury is allowed—as also in all civil cases.

IV. The Revenue Courts.

The High Courts have no power to exercise original jurisdiction in matters concerning the revenue, or acts done in collecting the same. These cases are tried by a special set of courts, called the Revenue Courts, presided over by the chief Revenue Officers, the Collectors. The relations of these courts with the other civil courts in the country have given rise to serious difficulties in the past; and the balance of official opinion has inclined now in favour of one and now in favour

31

of the other. The present situation may be described thus: The civil courts are excluded from all cases concerning the assessment and collection of land revenue—and from other purely fiscal cases. But all questions of title to land—though closely connected with questions of assessment—are triable by the civil courts. And even in cases of rent disputes, *i. e.* disputes relating to the fixing and payment of rents between land-lords and tenants—the ordinary civil courts are supreme, especially in Bengal; and in those provinces where the local tenancy laws still leave such cases to be dealt with by the Revenue Courts, the procedure of these Courts is assimilated to that of the civil courts. Appeal from the Revenue Courts may be made to the Board of Revenue wherever this institution exists, and in provinces where it does not, such appeals probably lie to the officer in charge of the Land Records and Revenue Settlement.

V. The Privy Council.

As with the whole of the Empire, the final Court of Appeal for Indian cases is the Judicial Committee of the Privy Council. The prerogative of the Sovereign to hear appeals from his subjects beyond the seas, though regulated and modified by Acts of Parliament, local rules, and orders in council, is still maintained. In 1833 was constituted a Committee of the Privy Council to hear such appeals from British subjects beyond the seas. This Committee, though for all practical purposes a final Court of Appeal, adopts in its judgments the form of advising the Sovereign, who, therefore, stands out as the final dispenser of all justice. He has the right to refer any matter for advice to this Committee; but, apart from this, the conditions of appeal from India are regulated by the Charters of the High Court, and by the provisions of the Code of Civil Procedure as regards civil cases. In civil matters an appeal lies to the Privy Council from a final decree passed on appeal by the High Court or any court of final appellate jurisdiction; from a final decree of the

High Court in the exercise of its original jurisdiction; and from any other decree if the case is certified by the High Court as fit for appeal. In the first two cases the value of the subject matter of the suit in the court of first instance must be at least Rs. 10,000; and when the decree appealed from affirms the decision of the court immediately below, the appeal must also involve some substantial question of law. In criminal cases a right of appeal is given, provided the High Court certifies that the case is fit for appeal, from any judgment, order or sentence of a High Court made in the exercise of original jurisdiction, or in any criminal case where a point of law has been reserved for the opinion of the High Court. The Sovereign also may grant special leave to appeal.

VI. The Position of the European British Subject.

Every subject of the Crown is equal as far as the substantive criminal law is concerned; but in procedure certain distinctions have been maintained–thanks to the peculiar position the Company's servants occupied in India–as regards charges against, European British subjects. Upto 1836 every case, whether civil or criminal, in which a European was concerned as a defendant, could be tried only in the Supreme Court at Calcutta. This naturally gave rise to a great deal of injustice, for a European defendant or offender could compel the aggrieved party in a mofussil centre to go all the way, with all his witnesses, to Calcutta with all the dangers, hardships, and expenses of such a journey in those days, and take his chance of the proverbial blindness of justice. Under the circumstances very few natives could be found spirited and rich enough to pursue European offenders to justice. This situation was partly remedied in 1836 when the District Courts were given power to try all civil suits in which a European was concerned as a defendant. The anomaly remained intact with regard to criminal cases. An effort was made in 1872 to remove it partially, when it was enacted that European British subjects should be liable to be tried for any offences by magistrates of the highest class—who were also Justices of the Peace—and by judges of the Sessions Court, provided that in each case the trying judge was himself a European British subject. This provision made the anomaly greater than before. For it was obvious to every one concerned with the Government of India, that natives of India, who had passed the competitive examination and entered the Civil Service, would, in the ordinary course of promotion, become magistrates of the highest class and Sessions Judges; and would yet be debarred from trying European offenders, simply because they were not born of European parents. There was of course no question of the legal acumen or judicial impartiality of such men; they had already given striking proofs of their great learning and uprightness. On the bench of each High Court were to be found native lawyers of deserved repute-who, according to the rules of seniority,-may even become acting chief justices of the highest courts of justice in the country. The anomaly was that the men who could rise to the highest post in the service were not, however, deemed competent to try a certain class of His Majesty's subjects, to whom the same laws applied as to any other class, but whose skin was of a different colour.

It was this monstrous absurdity which Lord Ripon felt most acutely, and which he tried to remove most completely. The Government of India announced in 1883 that they had decided "to settle the question of jurisdiction over European British subjects in such a way as to remove from the code at once and completely every judicial disqualification which is based merely on race distinction." No sooner was this decision announced than a storm of protest was raised by the Anglo-Indian community, the like of which has never been witnessed in India before or since. The selfish jealousy of this small but powerful community would not allow them to submit to this simple act of justice to their fellow-subjects. Their arguments for maintaining the *status quo* were the merest travesty of logic or good sense; for they assumed and maintained that Indians, with the most liberal training that India or England could offer, having passed the most stringent tests, after a residence in England amongst English people of three or four years, could yet not understand the English mentality—the mentality of English criminals in India, while Englishmen, fresh from Oxford and Cambridge, without any acquaintance with the language, or literature, or customs, and habits of the people, without any previous training among or experience of the people, were deemed quite fit to tackle all kinds of judicial questions concerning the natives. The history of India in the last century and a half abounds in such instances, wherein the governing authority have ventured to lay hand on the unmerited and invidious privileges of this small class, and where that class has set an example of loyalty, which Indians would do well not to copy. From the day that Lord Clive forbade the Double Butta of the English officers to the day that Lord Ripon endeavoured to abolish the anomaly of a colour disqualification, the Anglo-Indian community have shown themselves prepared to maintain their rights by every means-even rebellion if need be-however injurious and unjust those rights may be. Before a strong, determined ruler like Clive they have had to yield; before weaker men, like Sir George Barlow, they have had their way. In the case of the Ilbert Bill the Government of Lord Ripon, frightened by this protest, agreed to a compromise, which is thus summarised by Sir John Strachey:- "The controversy ended with the virtual, though not the avowed abandonment, of the measure proposed by the Government. Act III, of 1884, by which the law previously in force was amended, cannot be said to have diminished the privileges of European British subjects charged with offences, and it left their position as exceptional as before. The general disqualification of the native judges and magistrates remains; but if a native of India be appointed to the post of District Magistrate or Sessions Judge, his powers in regard to the jurisdiction over European British subjects are the same as those of an Englishman holding the same office. This provision, however, is subject to the condition that every European British subject, brought for trial before the District Magistrate or the Sessions Judge, has the right, however trivial be the offence, to claim to be tried by a jury, of which not less than half the members shall be Europeans or Americans .... Whilst this change was made in the powers of the District Magistrates the law in regard to other magistrates remained unaltered." The disqualification of native Magistrates to try European offenders remains in practice, for in up country centres it is difficult, if not impossible, to empanel a jury of which half at least are Englishmen or Americans. The best thing that an Indian District Magistrate could do in such a case would be to depute one of his European subordinates to try the case.

At the present moment, therefore, the European British subject enjoys a privileged position in the following respects.

(1) He can only be tried, except for contempt in open court, before a judge or magistrate who is also a Justice of the Peace. Outside the presidency towns, only European British subjects can be appointed Justices of the Peace; but District Magistrates, Sessions Judges, High Court Judges and Presidency Magistrates are *ex officio* Justices of the Peace.

(2) When tried before a District Magistrate, a Sessions Judge, or a High Court, he can claim a jury of which not less than one half must be Europeans or Americans.

(3) If tried under the European Vagrancy Act he cannot be required to give any security for good behaviour under the ordinary law; but if declared a vagrant, or found guilty of certain offences, he comes under the provisions of the Act relating to Europeans who are not British subjects.

(4) He has the right to demand something like a writ of Habeas Corpus in any part of India, while the native Indian can get that protection only within the presidency towns.

(5) An order in writing of the Governor-General in council is no justification for any act complained against by an European, while such an order would be a complete justification against any Indian in any court of law,

N. B.—Europeans, whether they are British subjects or not, cannot be tried by the Courts in the Native States.

VII. The Combination of Executive and Judicial Functions.

Another question of constitutional importance connected with the administration of justice is the concentration of all the authority of Government in the hands of the same officer. The basic principle of Indian administration is the concentration of all authority with a view to promote efficiency. Thus the chief officer in an administrative unit is the head of the revenue department, directs the police, controls the Local Boards and Municipalities, and administers justice himself, or superintends his subordinates in the administration of justice.

This concentration of authority is open to attack from several points of view. Taking first the model of the British constitution, the practice in India seems to be at variance with the fundamental principles of the British constitution. Ever since King James I was foiled by Lord Coke in His Majesty's own court, the independence of the Judges was established; and the Revolution of 1688 secured it by law. The judges in England are, of course, subordinate to the sovereign authority of Parliament; but, they have nothing to do with the Executive. Between the Executive and the Judiciary in England there is no link at present, with the single exception of the Lord Chancellor, who is both a cabinet minister and a high judicial officer. But the Lord Chancellor never sits in any court of original jurisdiction; and he cannot, therefore, be placed in the awkward position of having advised certain proceedings in his capacity as executive minister, and being called upon to try the same case in his capacity as judicial officer. This is precisely what happens in India. The district officer is the head of the District Superintendent of Police, as far as the investigation of crime in a district is concerned. He is also the head of the Government pleader–the public prosecutor–of the District. The prejudices of the investigator of crime, and the preconceptions of the prosecutor are fatal to a judicial mind; and yet the District Officer–being the District Magistrate—may be called upon to judge important criminal cases in the district. It is not inconceivable that such judges may give sound justice; but it is also not inconceivable that the famous principle of English criminal law *viz.* "that it is better that ten guilty persons should escape punishment than that one innocent person should suffer," will not be maintained. It is alleged in answer to this criticism that in practice the District Officer does not try any important cases, because he has no time to do so. But, it may be urged, even if he himself does not try important cases, his subordinate magistrates have to try them: and there is no guarantee that the subordinates–whose promotion in the service depends upon the goodwill of their superior–will not try to please him, if he drops a hint about the guilt or innocence of men awaiting their trial. We cannot, of course, adduce any instances to support the view that District Officers do interfere with the judicial independence of their subordinates; for, by their very nature, such things take place behind the scenes. But there is nothing unreasonable or unnatural in assuming that the power of control,which the District Officers have by law over their subordinates, may be used to encourage the latter in proper subordination and a wholesome desire to please. It is also pointed out, by the advocates of the existing system, that the assumption is unwarranted that the District Officer allows his judgment to be coloured by the prejudices of the investigator and the preconceptions of the prosecutor of crime. It would, indeed, be a gross mistake if we assumed that the investigator, the prosecutor, and the judge are combined in the same officer. Still it is quite possible that the head of the administration is kept informed of all that takes place in the district; and that owing to this information he may, unknown even to himself, have formed opinions on a case, not strictly according to the merits of the case, but according to the bent of that information.

Another point of principle on which the present system is objectionable is that the Magistrates are primarily revenue officers and only incidentally judges. They are not trained lawyers, and cannot, therefore, be a match for all the subterfuges of legal practitioners. The criminal law of India, it is true, is contained in a simple code, which, after a few years' experience, any well educated man can administer. Still it is a serious handicap to a man who has never practised himself to administer even this simple code when confronted by acute practitioners. The plea that in the peculiar conditions of India a Magistrate with full local knowledge of the district would make a better judge than the lawyer pure and simple is equally inadmissible. For the bulk of the magistracy is recruited from men who know very little the language of their districts, and can therefore have but scanty knowledge of the customs and beliefs–of the psychology of the people. Moreover a professional lawyer, who is raised to the bench after years of practice, will not allow justice to suffer, either for want of common sense, or through an excessive regard for the letter of the law. For there is no profession in our modern society wherein, by constant contact with every shade of character, with every kind of villainy, weakness or virtue–men learn so well to appreciate their fellows at their proper value as in the profession of law. It is a profession which by destroying all ideals promotes one's common sense. And as regards excessive respect for the letter of the law, perhaps no one knows better than a lawyer when the letter of the law needs to be stretched, and how it should be stretched. Almost the whole of the English common law is a growth of such judicial interpretations and extension. Hence from the point of view of principle the present system is indefensible.

Even in practice there is nothing peculiar in the conditions of India to-day requiring a rigid observance of this antequated system. From the stand point of efficiency in administration the need for a separation seems all the greater. For it stands to reason that one and the same officer, encumbered with the duties of two distinct officers, will not do his work so well as two distinct officers. Both departments suffer, and a separation would make both departments benefit.

In 1899 ten leading Indian judicial officers presented a Memorial to the Secretary of State on this subject. The chief points of the Memorial were:—

(1) That the combination of judicial with executive duties in the same officer violates the first principles of equity.

(2) That while a judicial authority ought to be thoroughly impartial, and approach the consideration of any case without previous knowledge of the facts, an executive officer does not adequately discharge his duties, unless his ears are open to all reports and information which he can in any degree employ for the benefit of the district.

(3) That executive officers in India being responsible for a large amount of miscellaneous business, have not time satisfactorily to dispose of judicial work in addition.

(4) That being keenly interested in carrying out particular measures, they are apt to be brought more or less into conflict with individuals, and therefore that it is inexpedient that they should also be invested with judicial powers.

(5) That under the existing system, Collector-Magistrates do, in fact, neglect judicial for executive work.

(6) That appeals from revenue assessments are apt to be futile when they are heard by revenue officers.

(7) That great inconvenience, expense and suffering are imposed upon suitors required to follow the camp of a judicial officer, who, in the discharge of his executive duties, is making a tour of his district.

(8) That the existing system not only involves all whom it concerns in hardships and inconvenience, but also by associating the judicial tribunal with the work of the police and detectives, and by diminishing the safeguard afforded by the rules of evidence, produces actual miscarriage of justice, and creates, though justice be done, opportunities of suspicion, distrust and discontent which are greatly to be deplored.

The points, thus summed up by the memorial, make out a strong case for the separation of the executive from judicial functions. The last Decennial Report on the Moral and Material Progress of India says, "The question of carrying further the separation of executive and judicial functions has received much consideration in recent years. In Bengal some steps tending in this direction have been taken, in the course of the natural process of administrative development, by the appointment of additional district magistrates to relieve the pressure on the district officers, and by an increase in the number of outlying judicial centres in the mofussil. The very heavy expenditure that would be involved in the complete separation of the two classes of functions is necessarily an important factor in the case." To this it may be replied that the point at issue is not merely to relieve the pressure of work upon the District Officer; it is rather to bring about a complete divorce between executive and judicial functions. Magistrates should have only judicial work and nothing to do with any kind of executive duties. Merely appointing additional magistrates will not help the situation, unless the additional magistrates are debarred from taking part in any executive duties. And as regards the "very heavy expenditure," we may calculate that for the 250 districts which make up the whole of the British territories in India, an increase of Rs. 25000 a year—quite enough to bring about a complete separation in one district—would mean a total additional expenditure of Rs. 62·5 lacs. If the question at issue is one involving a great, fundamental principle, perhaps it would not be too great a sacrifice to incur this additional expenditure, and prevent those opportunities for "suspicion, distrust and discontent" which must necessarily arise under the present system, and which cannot but be deplored.

VIII. The Law Officers and the Organisation of the Bar.

The Government of India have their most important Law Officer in the Law Member of Council. Their Legislative Department has much in common with the office of the Parliamentary Counsel in England. All Government measures are drafted by that department; all bills before the Council, when referred to a Select Committee, are discussed by that Committee under the presidency of the Law Member. It publishes all the Acts of the Government, revises the Statute Book, drafts all statutory rules, and assists other departments with legal advice in certain specified questions of a non-litigious character. Legislation in the Provincial Councils is watched and guided by the same department. In spite of these duties, however, the Law Member of Council in India, does not correspond to the Attorney-General and Solicitor-General in England, the highest Law Officers of the British Crown. Their place is taken in India by the various Advocates-General, the most important of whom is the Advocate-General of Bengal. He advises the Government in legal matters, and conducts their litigation, and assists them in their legislative work. He is assisted by standing counsel and Government Solicitor. In Bombay and Madras there is also an Advocate-General for each province, who discharges the same functions in his province as the Advocate-General of Bengal. In Bombay he is assisted by a Government Solicitor, and to the Secretariat are attached a Legal Remembrancer (a Civil Servant) and a Deputy Legal Remembrancer (a practising Barrister).

IX. The Laws Administered in India.

The early English settlers in India established themselves in the country under license from native rulers. They ought, therefore, to have been subject to the native systems of law. But the two great indigenous systems of law are both systems of personal law, knowing no local limit, and binding upon individuals within their respective faiths, all the world over. There was, therefore, no *lex loci* to govern such aliens in race and religion which the English then were. Moreover, the system of Capitularies in force with Turkey, and recognised by the International Law of Europe in the XVII century, regarded European settlers in non-Christian countries as under the system of law in force in their own country. Hence the first Charters assumed that the English brought their own legal system in India, and the Charter of 1726 specifically introduced the Common Law and some of the older Acts of Parliament as applicable to Englishmen in India. As they grew to be a sovereign power the English inclined towards making their law the public and territorial law of India; and in 1773, with the establishment of the Supreme Court and the advent of English lawyers, they proceeded to apply the English law in its entirety to all the inhabitants within the Company's jurisdiction. The hardships which followed this indiscriminate application of English law are too well known, even to the ordinary student of Indian history, to need a detailed consideration here. In 1780 this was changed by a Declaratory Act, s. 17 of which required that Hindu Law and usage should be applied to Hindus, and Mahomedan law and usage to Mahomedans. This rule was in course of time extended to all the dominions of the Company.

The Government in India have thus accepted the indigenous systems of law, with such modifications as they thought India was fit to receive. The rigidity of the old systems has been considerably undermined by a variety of influences, the most important of which are the growth of education and enlightenment among the peoples themselves, the influence of Western ideas of Government, and of the case law emanating from courts established on English models. Acts of Parliament, and still more frequently, Acts of local legislatures, such as the Caste Disabilities Removal Act of 1850, or the Hindu Widows Remarriage Act of 1856, or the Age of Consent Act of 1893, have all tended in the same direction. Codes of

Procedure have been practically the creation of the present Government, as also the various laws relating to land-lords and tenants. At the present time, therefore, " Native law has been wholly superseded, as to criminal law and procedure and as to civil procedure, by the Indian Penal Code, the Indian Codes of Criminal and Civil Procedure, the Evidence Act and other enactments; and has been largely superseded as to other matters by Anglo-Indian legislation; but still regulates, as personal law, most matters relating to family law and to the law of succession and inheritance among the Hindus, Mahomedans, and other natives of the country". (Ilbert.)

The laws in British India may therefore, be either,

(*a*) English Common low, or (*b*) some old English statutes, or	In presideney towns applicable to Europeans.
(*c*) Hindu and Mahomedan law	Personal for Hindus and Mahomedans

or

(*d*) Acts of Parliament. (*e*) Acts of Indian Legislatures. (f) Statutory rules, orders and by-laws supplementing particular enactments.	Applicable to all persons in British India.

We may note in passing that a great portion of the statutory law of India is codified. The most important of these codes are the Indian Penal Code, passed in 1860, and in force to-day with very few modifications, the Codes of Procedure, and of Evidence, and the Law relating to Contract.

X. Comparison with the English System of Justice.

All our codes and our entire judicial system are said to be based on the English model. And yet a close study of the two systems of law and justice reveals many and fundamental differences. Most of these have already been described, and some of them critically examined. In this place we shall collect together all those features of the Indian judicial and legal system which, in a comparison with the English system, constitute the peculiarities of our system.

The one peculiarity of our system that has not yet been touched upon is contained in s. 113 of the present Act.

The order in writing of the Governor General in Council for any act shall, in any proceeding, civil or criminal in any High Court acting in the exercise of its original jurisdiction, be a full justification of the act, except so far as the order extends to any European British subject; but nothing in this section shall exempt the Governor-General or any member of his Executive Council or any person acting under their orders from any proceedings in respect of any such act before any competent Court in England.

Ever since the case of the Chancellor Lord Nottingham in the reign of Charles II, who pleaded an express order of the King for having affixed the great seal to an unlawful order, the principle has been well established in England that no order of the Crown shall grant an exemption to any minister or servant of the Crown for any wrongful act done in his private or official capacity. The above section goes entirely against the spirit of this principle, and is only defensible, if at all, on the ground that it was necessitated by the peculiar position of the Indian Government under the Company.

(2) The presence on the Judicial Bench of the highest tribunals in India of men who have never in their lives been practising lawyers constitutes another such peculiarity of the Indian system. The tenure, too, of judicial officers "during the pleasure of the Sovereign" is a marked departure from the recognised principles of the English constitution in this respect.

(3) The position of the "Jury", though an English institution, is too different from that of the same institution in Eng-

land to pass unnoticed. It is employed more sparingly, and is allowed less extensive powers than in England.

(4) The immunity of high officers of state from legal liability, the special privileges of whole classes of private individuals like the European British subjects, the existence of special tribunals exclusively empowered to try specified kinds of cases are all peculiarities of the Indian system of judicial administration unparalleled in England.

(5) To these may be added the combination in the hands of one and the same officer of executive and judicial functions.

There are other cases in which the Indian system differs from the English system; but, probably, the cases enumerated here are the only cases in which the difference is fundamental, while in other cases the difference is one of details.

XI. The Indian Police and Jails System.

For the effective administration of justice the existence of some form of police organisation is indispensable, both to carry out the punishment inflicted by courts of law, as well as to prevent the possibility of crime, and thus to minimise the occasions of the exercise of the punitive authority. After describing the judicial system of India we shall now proceed to give a brief sketch of the police organisation of India.

The police force in India may be divided into the regular police force and the Village police organisation. The regular police establishment is in most provinces a single force under the Local Government, and is formally enrolled. In Bombay each district has its own seperate police organisation. The force is in each province under the general control of an Inspector-General, who may be a police officer, or a member of the Indian Civil Service. Under him are the Deputy Inspectors-General of Police, holding charge of the portions of the province, each known as a Range. The most important unit of Police administration is the district, with a District Superintendent of Police, who is responsible for the discipline and the internal management of the force to his departmental superiors at the headquarters; while in all matters connected with the preservation of peace, and the detection and suppression of crime and its prevention he is the subordinate of the District Officer. He is assisted by one or more Assistant or Deputy Superintendents. The former are ordinarily recruited in England by competitive examination from among candidates who must be of European descent. In exceptional cases appointments may be made directly in India. The Deputy Superintendents constitute the Provincial branch of the Police service, and these officers are recruited in India partly by promotion from the rank of Inspectors, and partly by direct appointments of the natives of India who have the requisite educational qualifications. Their functions and departmental status is closely similar to those of the Assistant Superintendents. For Police purposes the district is divided into "circles" each in the charge of an Inspector; and the circle is again split up into areas in each of which there is a police station in charge of a Sub-Inspector of Police. The average area of a Police Station is nearly 200 sq. miles; and where the work of investigation is heavy additional Sub-Inspectors are appointed. In Bombay there are also subsidiary Police Stations, known as "outposts" in charge of head constables.

Besides the regular Police there is the old Indian village Police organisation, on whom the regular Police are dependent for information and assistance. Every Police Station comprises within its jurisdiction a number of villages, for each of which there is a Chokidar or watchman. This official, whether working under the orders of the village headman or directly under the regular Police officers, must report crime and aid the execution of justice. He is remunerated in different ways in different provinces, *e. g.* by fees, or by monthly payments, or by grants of free lands. Besides reporting crime, the Chokidar must keep a watch on suspicious characters, and give general aid and information to the Police.

In addition to the regular Police in the rural areas and the village organisation there are portions of the Police force in towns, organised more or less on the same lines. In the Presidency towns, however, and in Rangoon the Police are organised as a separate force, under a commissioner in each case, who is aided by a staff of European and Indian subordinate officers and constables. The Railway Police is another independent organisation, which, however, works in co-operation with the district Police. These last are, as a rule, concerned with the maintenance of watch and ward and order over railway property. The Railway Police charges are as far as possible, conterminous with the territorial jurisdiction of the local Governments, the force in each province being under a Deputy Inspector-General.

In addition to all these organisations there is the now famous Criminal Investigation Department, or the C. I. D. as it is more generally known. This department originated from the necessity to investigate those secret crimes associated with the Thugs in India. Upto 1904 there was a separate Thugee and Dacoitee Department; and, though the Thugs were wiped off the face of the earth long before that date, the duties of this department continued to be described by the title which suggested their principal original occupation before 1863. From 1863 to 1904 this department was concerned with the suppression of armed robbery in the dominions of the Nizam and of the Native States in Central India and Rajputana. In the latter year this department was abolished and replaced by a Central Criminal Intelligence Department under a Director. The duties of this department, with its provincial counterparts, is to collect and provide a systematic and full information as to important and organised crime, and to train up a small staff of detectives for investigation of crimes, the authors of which are not easily ascertainable by the ordinary Police. This department has of late earned an unpleasant notoriety by allowing its zeal to outrun its discretion in the task of securing the safety of the state and its important officers against the menace of the Anarchists, who carried on their activity in parts of India with the object of overturning the whole machine of the present Government by assassinating isolated officials. From being a protector of the state and its officers and a help to the citizens, this department has tended in every country, organised like India, to be a terror of the people, who will never aid men suspected not only of discovering criminals, but also of manufacturing crimes and creating criminals. The State may protect and maintain, but the people will distrust, an organisation, which, instituted to unearth unknown criminals, is often unable to fulfill that duty, but tries to shield its inability or incompetence by unnecessary and unfounded accusation to prove its vigilance and to earn its promotions, reckless of the mischief it causes between the rulers and the ruled. Those in power may be entirely innocent of any complicity with or encouragement of this side of the work of the C. I. D.; but, after the revelations of some of the anarchist trials in Bengal, it is hard to believe that the C. I. D. is an unmixed blessing to the people or to the State.

XII. Jails.

Jail administration in India is regulated by the Prisons Act of 1894, and by the rules issued under it by the Government of India and the local Governments. The Indian jails must provide accommodation for prisoners sentenced to penal servitude, rigorous imprisonment or simple imprisonment as well as for persons awaiting trial, and for civil prisoners. The Indian jails are accordingly divided into three classes, *viz*, the large central jails for convicts sentenced to more than one year's imprisonment; the district jails at the headquarters of each district; and subsidiary jails and lock-ups for prisoners awaiting trial and for short term imprisonment. The jail department in each province is under the control of an Inspector-General, who is an officer of the Indian Medical Service, and the superintendents of certain jails are usually recruited from that service. The district jail is in charge of the civil surgeon, and is frequently inspected by the district officer. In large central jails there are, under the superintendents, deputy superintendents to supervise the jail manufactures; and in all central and district jails there are one or more subordinate medical officers. The executive staff consists of jailors, warders, and convict petty officers.

As regards youthful offenders, *i. e.*, those under 15 years of age, the law provides alternatives to imprisonment, which consist in detention in a Reformatory School for a period of three to seven years, but not beyond the age of 18; whipping by way of discipline; discharge after admonition; and delivery to parent or guardian on the latter executing a bond for the good behaviour of the child. The Reformatory Schools are administered since 1899 by the Education department, and the authorities are directed to improve the industrial education of the inmates, to help the boys to obtain employment after leaving school, and as far as possible to keep a watch on their career.

Besides imprisonment, Indian Criminal Law provides another punishment *viz.*, transportation. At the present time the only penal settlement is Port Blair in the Andaman Islands.

CHAPTER VIII.

The Church in India.

PART X.

Ecclesiastical Establishment.

115. (1) The Bishops of Calcutta, Madras and Bombay have and may exercise, within their respective dioceses such episcopal functions, and such ecclesiastical jurisdiction for the superintendence and good government of the ministers of the Church of England therein, as His Majesty may, by letters patent, direct.

(2) The Bishop of Calcutta is the Metropolitan Bishop in India, subject nevertheless to the general superintendence and revision of the Archbishop of Canterbury.

(3) Each of the Bishops of Madras and Bombay is subject to the Bishop of Calcutta as such Metropolitan, and must at the time of his appointment to his bishopric, or at the time of his consecration as Bishop, take an oath of obedience to the Bishop of Calcutta, in such manner as His Majesty, by letters patent, may be pleased to direct.

(4) His Majesty may, by letters patent, vary the limits of the dioceses of Calcutta, Madras and Bombay.

(5) Nothing in this Act or in any such letters patent as aforesaid shall prevent any person who is or has been Bishop of any dioceses in India from performing episcopal functions, not extending to the exercise of jurisdiction, in any diocese or reputed diocese at the request of the Bishop thereof.

116. (1) The Bishop of Calcutta may admit into the holy orders of deacon or prie st any person whom he, on examination, deems duly qualified specially for the purpose of taking on himself the

cure of souls, or officiating in any spiritual capacity, within the limits of the diocese of Calcutta, and residing therein.

(2) The deposit with the Bishop of a declaration of such a purpose, and a written engagement to perform the same, signed by the person seeking ordination, shall be a sufficient title with a view to his ordination.

(3) It must be distinctly stated in the letters of ordination of every person so admitted to holy orders that he has been ordained for the cure of souls within the limits of the diocese of Calcutta only.

(4) Unless a person so admitted is a British subject of or belonging to the United Kingdom, he shall not be required to take the oaths and make the subscriptions which persons ordained in England are required to take and make.

(5) Nothing in this section shall affect any letters patent issued by his Majesty.

117. If any person under the degree of Bishop is appointed to the bishopric of Calcutta, Madras or Bombay, being at the time of his appointment resident in India, the Archbishop of Canterbury, if so required to do by His Majesty by letters patent, may issue a commission under his hand and seal, directed to the two remaining Bishops, authorising and charging them to perform all requisite ceremonies for the consecration of the persons so to be appointed.

118. (1) The Bishops and Archdeacons of Calcutta, Madras and Bombay are appointed by His Majesty by letters patent, and there may be paid to them, or to any of them, out of the revenues of India, such salaries and allowances as may be fixed by the Secretary of State in Council; but any power of alteration under this enactment shall not be exercised so as to impose any additional charge on the revenues of India.

(2) The remuneration fixed for a Bishop or archdeacon under this section shall commence on his taking upon himself the execution of his office, and be the whole profit or advantage which he shall enjoy from his office during his continuance therein, and continue so long as he exercises the functions of his office.

(3) There shall be paid out of the revenues of India the expenses of visitations of the said Bishops, but no greater sum may be issued on account of those expenses than is allowed by the Secretary of State in Council.

119. (1) If the Bishop of Calcutta dies during his voyage to India for the purpose of taking upon himself the execution of his office, or if the Bishop of Calcutta, Madras or Bombay dies within six months after his arrival there for that purpose the Secretary of State shall pay to his legal personal representatives out of the revenues of India, such a sum of money as will, with the amount received by or due to him at the time of his death on account of salary, make up the amount of one year's salary.

(2) If the Bishop of Calcutta, Madras or Bombay dies while in possession of his office and after the expiration of six months from his arrival in India for the purpose of taking upon himself the execution of his office, the Secretary of State shall pay to his legal personal representatives, out of the revenues of India, over and above the sum due to him at the time of his death, a sum equal to six months salary.

120. His Majesty may, by warrant under the Royal Sign Manual countersigned by the Chancellor of the Exchequer, grant out of the revenues of India, to any Bishop of Calcutta a pension not exceeding fifteen hundred pounds per annum if he has resided in India as Bishop of Calcutta, Madras or Bombay or Archdeacon for ten years, or one thousand pounds per annum if he has resided in India as Bishop of Calcutta for seven years, or seven hundred and fifty pounds per annum if he has resided in India as Bishop of Calcutta for five years, or to any Bishop of Madras or Bombay a pension not exceeding eight hundred pounds per annum, to be paid quarterly, if he has resided in British India as such Bishop for fifteen years.

121. His Majesty may make such rules as to the leave of absence of the Bishops of Calcutta, Madras and Bombay on furlough or medical certificate as seem to His Majesty expedient.

122. (1) Two members of the establishment of chaplains maintained in each of the presidencies of Bengal, Madras and Bombay must always be ministers of the Church of Scotland, and shall be

entitled to have, out of the revenues of India, such salary, as is from time to time allotted to the military chaplains in the several presidencies.

(2) The ministers so appointed chaplains must be ordained and inducted by the presbytery of Edinburgh according to the forms and solemnities used in the Church of Scotland, and shall be subject to the spiritual and ecclesiastical jurisdiction in all things of the presbytery of Edinburgh, whose judgments shall be subject to dissent, protest and appeal to the provincial Synod of Lothian and Tweeddale and to the General Assembly of the Church of Scotland.

123. Nothing in this Act shall prevent the Governor-General in Council from granting, with the sanction of the Secretary of State in Council, to any sect, persuasion or community of Christians, not being of the Church of England or Church of Scotland, such sums of money as may be expedient for the purpose of instruction or for the maintenance of places af worship.

COMMENTS.

Ss. 115-123 (both inclusive)

The East India Company were originally opposed to any settlement of Missioaries in India, partly because they feared the action of the Missionaries would give offence to the native population, by their proseletising zeal, and partly because they regarded missionaries as the forerunners of all insubordination among their subjects. It was not till 1813 that permission was first given by the Charter Act of that year for missionaries to settle in India, and to carry on such educational and other activities as they chose. By the same Act three bishops were appointed for the cities of Calcutta, Madras and Bombay; and these provisions were confirmed by the Charter Act of 1833. The present Act retains those provisions. Hence the bishops only of the three Presidency Towns are appointed under an Act of Parliament, the remaining bishops for the Dioceses of Lahore or Nagpur for instances are appointed by letters patent.

"In the ordinary acceptance of the term, there is no established Church in India. An Ecclesiastical Establishment is maintained for providing religious ministrations, primarily, to British troops, secondarily to the European civil officials of Government and their families. Seven out of the eleven **Anglican Bishops** in India are officers of the Establishment, though their episcopal jurisdiction is much wider than the limits of the Ecclesiastical Establishment. The stipends of the three Presidency Bishops are paid entirely by Government, and they hold an official status which is clearly defined. The Bishops of Lahore, Lucknow, Nagpur and Rangoon draw from Government the stipends of Senior Chaplains only but their episcopal rank and territorial titles are officially recognised. The Bishops of Chota Nagpur, Tinnevelly, Madura, Travancore, Cochin, Dornakal and Assam are not on the Establishment. The new Bishopric of Assam was created in 1915. In its relations with Government it is subordinate to the see of Calcutta. But the maintenance of the Bishopric is met entirely from voluntary funds.

The **ecclesiastical establishment** includes four denominations—Anglican, Scottish, Roman and Wesleyan. Of these, the first two enjoy a distinctive position, in that the Chaplains of those denominations (and in the case of the first-named the Bishops) are individually appointed by the Secretary of State and rank as gazetted officers of Government. Throughout the Indian Empire there are 134 Anglican and 18 Church of Scotland chaplains whose appointments have been confirmed. The authorities in India of the Roman Catholic church receive block-grants from Government for the provision of clergy to minister to troops and others belonging to their respective denominations. The Wesleyan Methodist Church has a staff of military chaplains in India who receive a fixed salary from Government, and 25 chaplains working on a capitation basis of payment by Government. Churches of all four denominations may be built, furnished and repaired, wholly or partly at Government expense.

In the Anglican Communion a movement towards **Synodical Government** was making great progress, when, in the course of the year 1914, serious legal difficulties were encountered. The Bishops were advised that their relations with Canterbury and the Crown precluded the establishment of synods on the basis adopted by the Anglican Church in America, Japan, South Africa and other countries where it is not established by the State. It is stated that in course of time those relations may be modified so as to admit of the establishment of synodical government in India. Meanwhile Diocesan Councils are being adopted as a make-shift measure. These Councils possess synodical characteristics, but are devoid of any coercive power.

So far as the European and Anglo-Indian communities are concerned, the activities of the Church are not confined to public worship and pastoral functions. The **education** of the children of those communities is very largely in the hands of the Christian denominations. There are a few institutions such as the La Martiniere Schools, on a non-denominational basis; but they are exceptional. In all the large centres there exist schools of various grades as well as orphanages, for the education of Europeans and Anglo-Indians under the control of various Christian bodies. The Roman Catholic Church is honourably distinguished by much activity and financial generosity in this respect. Her schools are to be found throughout the length and breadth of the Indian Empire; and they maintain a high standard of efficiency. The Anglican Church comes next, and the American Methodists have established some excellent schools in the larger hill stations. The presbyterians are also well-represented in the field, particularly by the admirable institution for destitute children at Kalimpong, near Darjeeling. Schools of all denominations receive liberal grants in aid from Government, and are regularly inspected by the Education Departments of the various provinces. Thanks to the free operation of the denominational principle and its frank recognition by Government; there is no religious difficulty in the schools of the European and Anglo-Indian communities." (Indian year Book.)

CHAPTER IX.

Local Government in India.

The subject of local Government, though not introduced in the main Act, is yet too important to be left out in any work on Indian administration. The principle of local government is far too deeply established on the Indian mind to need any historical sketch. In common with the other offshoots of the Aryan race the Hindus had a form of free local self-government long before they had a centralised state. Every village in ancient India was an autonomous political unit. The officers of the central government, when it came into existence, were content to accept the village collectively as a unit for such of their administrative duties as had reference to the inhabitants of the locality. It was of such villages that Sir Henry Maine speaks in his village communities, which endured in spite of wars and changes of dynasties, in spite of every revolution in the principles of government.

But this old-time independence and autonomy is a thing of the past. The village tribunal of local elders no longer distributes justice, for are there not the King's Courts of Law ? The village chaukidar and his assistants are no longer the amateur detectives who traced criminals by their foot-prints–and professional watch keepers–who went on crying 'Khabardar' at every hour of the night, for has not the State established a new police organisation ? The village council no longer estimates and assigns the local burdens, for the settlement officer has learnt the value of individual assessment. The powers which made the village organisation effective and efficient have been destroyed by the roads and the railways which would tolerate no isolation, however inoffensive, which would respect no passivity however ancient

And yet the village remains—even to-day—the first unit of administration. True the principle village functionaries, the headman, the accountant, the watchman, have become in ever increasing numbers the subsidised officials of a central government. Their functions in the administration of the village have also been altered by law. Their natural, traditional, independence has been stultified by artificial organisations-such as the Union Punchayets of Madras—which are formed to discharge specific duties. Notwithstanding all this the village endures as a unit of administration. Even in the "severalty or Raiyatwari" village, where the revenue is collected from individual cultivators, and where there is no joint responsibility of the village as a whole, government is vested in the patel or Reddi, who is responsible for law and order, and who collects the government dues. He recalls, however faintly, the primitive headships of the town or the caste which founded the village. In the joint or landlord village the position is cleared. The demand of the state used to made upon the village as a whole, its incidence upon individual villagers being determined by the local council. A certain amount of collective responsibility still remains. The village site is owned by the proprietory body, where permission is necessary for the settlement in the village of artisans, traders or others. The waste land belongs to the village, and, when required for cultivation is partitioned among the share-holders. The government of such a village, used to be by a punchayet.

The Royal Commission on Decentralisation recommended "While, therefore, we desire the development of a punchayet system, and consider that the objections urged thereto are far from insurmountable, we recognise that such a system can only be gradually and tentatively applied, and that it is impossible to suggest any uniform and definite method of procedure. We think that a commencement should be made by giving certain imited powers to punchayets in those villages in which circumstances are most favourable by reason of homogeneous conditions natural intelligence and freedom from internal feuds. These powers might be increased gradually as results warrant, and with success here, it will become easier to apply the system in other villages. Such a policy which must be the work of many years will require great care and discretion, much patience and judicious discrimination between the circumstances of different villages; and there is a considerable consensus of opinion that this new departure should be made under the special guidance of sympathetic officers".

In accordance with this recommendation an Act was passed in 1912 to provide for the establishment of the punchayets in the Punjab. But in that province, the ancient home of the Indo-Aryans, the ideal of village self-government has never been abandoned. Custom has vested the village organisation there-even under the present regime of centralisation-with a degree of independence which is almost unknown in other provinces. It was futile to seek to strengthen this already all powerful tradition. Besides the sphere of the proposed punchayet would be larger than a village, and yet its functions would be limited to the disposal of civil suits of a petty character. The latest expression of policy on the subject is contained in the following passage of the Resolution of the Government of India of May 28, 1915. "Where any practicable scheme can be marked out in co-operation with the people concerned full experiment must be made on the lines approved by the local government or the administration concerned." In marked contrast with other parts of the same resolution-issued by the Government of Lord Hardinge-this breathes an air of pessimism which may fairly be taken to mean that the re-suscitation of the old Indian village autonomy is as impracticable as the revival of the Anglo-Saxon Shiremoot in the twentieth century in England.

I. The Municipalities.

As the villages in India have a long and sad story, so the towns—now called Municipalities—have a short but a fairly glad history. The Presidency towns of Bombay, Calcutta and Madras had received some form of local self-government as early as 1726. In the country at large, however, the Company's government attempted to introduce no new form of local Municipal institutions, nor tried to modify or develop the existing institutions before 1842. In that year Bengal got an act on the subject, but it was found to be useless—and was followed in 1850 by another act for the whole of British India. Under this Act a number of Municipalities was established, and commissioners were appointed to administer their affairs with power to levy some taxes. Since, however, the commissioners were all nominated, the act effected no great progress from the point of view of self-government. With the introduction of a scheme for the decentralisation of finances in 1870 the problemof extending self-governing institutions became more prominent, and between 1871 and 1874 new Municipal acts were passed extending the elective principle.

It was not, however, till the days of Lord Ripon that local government in India was constituted on a more scientific basis —whether in the town or in the country. "It is not primarily with a view to improvement in administration that this measure is put forward and supported. **It is chiefly desirable as an instrument of political and popular education.** His Excellency in council has himself no doubt that in course of time, as local knowledge and local interest are brought to bear more freely upon local administration, improved efficiency will in fact follow." In these famous and eloquent words was laid the foundation of the system of local government in India. Lord Ripon's Government were quite aware, to quote the same resolution,-that, "at starting there will be doubtless many failures, calculated to discourage exaggerated hopes, and even in some cases to cast apparent discredit, upon the practice of self-government itself. If, however, the officers of Government only set themselves, as the Governor-General-in-Council believes, they will, to foster sedulously the small beginnings of independent life; if they will accept loyally and as their own the policy of the Government, and if they come to realise that the system really opens to them a fairer field for the exercise of administrative tact and directive energy than the more autocratic system which it supersedes then it may be hoped that the period of failures will be short, and that real and substantial progress would very soon become manifest." In accordance with the policy thus laid down acts were passed by the various local governments, which defined and extended the powers and functions of local self-governing bodies.

Taking the Municipalities—the three Presidency Muncipalities of Calcutta, Madras and Bombay are the most important. Their constitution and functions vary considerably. Thus in Calcutta the Municipal administration is entrusted to the Corporation, consisting–under the Act of 1899–of a chairman nominated by the local government, and 50 Commissioners. Of these 25 are elected at triennial ward elections, while the remaining 25 are appointed as follows:—

The Bengal Chamber of Commerce	4
The Calcutta Trades Association	4
The Port Commissioners	2
The Government of Bengal...	15
	25

Besides the Corporation there is the General Committee, consisting of the Chairman and 12 Commissioners, 4 of whom are elected by the ward Commissioners, 4 by the other Commissioners, and 4 nominated by the local government. The entire executive power is vested in the Chairman subject to the approval or sanction of the Corporation or the General Commit tee. The Corporation fixes the rates of taxation and has other general functions of the kind. The General Committee is a sort-of a buffer between the Executive and the Legislative. It deals with those matters which the Corporation as a whole cannot. discuss and which are yet too important to be left to the Chairman alone. The Government of Bengal, also, has the power to command the Corporation to take action under certain circumstances, while its sanction is necessary for undertaking large projects.

In Bombay the Municipal Corporation dates from 1872, and its present form is regulated by the Act of 1888 as amended. It consists of 72 councillors, 36 of whom are elected by the wards and 16 by the Justices of the Peace. The Fellows of the Bombay University elect 2, and 2 more are elected by the Bombay Chamber of Commerce. The remaining 16 are nominated by the Government. Judging from this constitution the Corporation of Bombay is the most liberal and may well be envied by other towns. The general municipal government is vested in the Corporation, while the ordinary business is transacted by a Standing Committee of 12 Councillors, of whom 8 are appointed by the Corporation and 4 by the Government. The President of the Corporation is elected by that body, but is not, like the Chairman of the Calcutta Corporation, an Executive officer. The Chief Executive Authority is the Municipal Commissioner, who is appointed by the Government, usually an I. C. S.-but is removable by a vote of 45 Councillors.

In Madras the last Act regulating the Corporation was passed in 1904. Under this Act the number of Municipal Commissioners consists of 36 besides the President. Of these 20 may be elected at divisional election, 3 are nominated by the Madras Chamber of Commerce, and 3 by the Madras Trades Association. The remaining 10 are nominated—2 each by such associations, corporate bodies, or classes of persons as the local government might direct. The President is nominated by the Government, and is the sole executive authority but removable by a vote of 28 Commissioners. A Standing Committee of the President and 8 other Commissioners is mainly concerned with finance and building questions.

Of these constitutions that of Madras is by far the least liberal, while that of Bombay with an elective majority, and elective chairman, and only one nominated official executive officer, with large discretion in administration and large powers of taxation within the limit of the law—the most advanced. In their latest resolution on the subject the Government of India seem to recognise and recommend the Bombay constitution as a model for the Presidency Municpalities though they were not prepared to grant a similar constitution to Rangoon.

II. Mofussil Municipalities.

The total number of mofussil municipalities has altered very little in the last 15 years. New municipalities have been formed from time to time, but some also have been removed from the list. In fact between 1902–12 there was a marked decrease, the number in 1911–12 being actually less than 30 years before. This was due to reduction to "notified areas" of a large number of the smaller municipalities in the Punjab and the United Provinces. (The "notified areas" are small towns not fit for full municipal institutions, but to which parts of the Municipal Acts are applied, their affairs being administered by nominated Committees). Taking the municipalities as a whole the number of elected members in 1911–12 was rather more than half, while in 1901–2 it was slightly less than half. The proportion of non-officials and Indians, high in 1901. become higher still in 1902, Elected members are in a majority in the cities of Bombay, Madras and Rangoon and in the towns of Bengal, Bihar and Orissa, and the United and the Central Provinces. Taking the Municipalities individually some of the members are elected in most cases—election being by wards or classes of the community or both combined. Voters must be male residents of a certain age or more, possessing the requisite property of status qualification. It is interesting to note that in some municipal areas in Bombay women possessing the prescribed qualifications are entitled to vote, and in some other cases they are not expressly excluded though they seldom exercise the right. The Chairman of the Corporation is sometimes nominated and sometimes chosen by the Commissioners from among themselves. In the Central Provinces, Madras, Bengal, and Bombay there is a majority of non-official elected chairmen.

The control of the Government is exercised in a variety of ways. Thus (1) Municipalities cannot borrow without the sanction of the local Government and beyond certain limits. (2) Municipal budgets, and changes in Municipal taxation must also obtain the previous approval of the local Government or of a Divisional Commissioner. (3) Government may provide for the performance of any duty which the Commissioners neglect, and, (4) may suspend them in case of default, incompetence or abuse of power. (5) The sanction of the Government is required for the appointment of certain officers like the Health Officer or the Engineer.

The following is a table of Municipal statistics, showing the number of members-elected or not-officials or not and the incidence of taxation.

Province.	No. of Municipalities.	Members			Employment.		Total number.	Incidence of taxation.	
		Ex-officio.	Nominated.	Elected.	Official.	Nonofficial.			
District Municipalities								s.	d.
Bengal ...	111	108	531	887	190	1336	1526	2	5
Bihar and Orissa	55	78	225	469	100	672	772	1	4
Assam ...	18	37	98	62	50	147	197	2	4
Bombay ...	158	387	830	913	457	1673	2310	3	3
Madras ...	62	77	392	492	137	824	961	2	0
United Provinces ...	86	93	211	877	175	1006	1181	2	5
Punjab ...	104	217	419	543	237	942	1179	3	5
Central Provinces ...	56	9	270	483	161	597	762	2	11
Burma ...	44	181	282	97	198	362	560	3	2

III. Municipal Functions and Finance.

Municipal functions are classified under the heads of public safety, public health, public convenience and public instruction. Under these four heads the duties of the municipalities are many and varied. The chief of these are:-(*a*) the construction, maintenance, and lighting of streets and roads; (*b*) the provision and up-keep of public and municipal buildings; (*c*) preservation of public health by medical relief, vaccination, sanitation, drainage, water-supply and measures against epidemics; (*d*) public instruction chiefly of an elementary description.

Municipal revenues are derived from four main sources: taxation, municipal property, Government subventions and public borrowing. Of these the last is permitted under certain restrictions as to the previous sanction of the Government, specific security to the lender and the amount. Generally speaking, excluding the Presidency towns, municipalities borrow from the Government. Municipal loans, therefore, though not unknown in India, cannot be said to be of the same importance here as they are in some European countries. In those countries, the idea of Municipal trading has been carried so far that the municipalities supply not only light and water, but also bread and meat, wine and milk, amusement in the dancing house, the race-course, the lottery office and even the municipal restaurants. They build houses for their citizens on land owned by themselves, cultivate fields for procuring the raw material, work forests and mines for their profit, own baths and spas, hotels and boarding-houses, serve as tourist agencies, receive, and invest their money, act as educator, doctor and research student. In India on the other hand the utmost activity of the municipalities is confined to providing indifferently clean and irregularly copious water and some slight drainage works. While the western municipalities need large funds, which they procure without hesitation by borrowing, to carry on their vast and multifarious activities, Indian town governments whenever they desire to borrow a small loan are viewed with suspicion by the Government,

Being restricted in borrowing, they cannot have the same extent of municipal property which is so common in the west. Their utmost possessions are a market, a few school buildings, a slaughter-house, and in rare cases profitable water-works or a town-hall. Picture-galleries and museums, zoological gardens and libraries, tram-lines or lighting plant, theatres or cages are all conspicuous by their absence or rarity in India as municipal undertakings. Hence the item of their revenues from their own property is also very insignificant.

Of the two remaining items Government subventions are as degrading to the municipalities as they are unprofitable to the central government. And yet they are by no means an insignificant item. For the municipalities to be dependent on Government aid is to sacrifice an independence. For such aid will not of necessity be granted without humiliating conditions. Nor that is no room for the subvention from the central authority. Undertakings like the provision of secondary education–or even compulsory primary education which are of universal importance–may fitly be manintained at a high level by central assistance, as also the Police force. But in such cases the aid would be claimed and obtained under conditions prescribed once for all for every local body without discrimination. Such aid is both legitimate and necessary. But the aid which is given to each municipality on the merits of each case necessarily results in making it weaker and more dependent every day. The restriction in practice upon Indian municipalities as regards borrowing in the public market may have a political justification in the expediency of maintaining unimpaired the credit of the central Government. But it does result also in a complete and perpetual tutelage of the municipality—so hostile to the development of really beneficent civic spirit and civic pride.

As regards taxes, tolls and fees the most important are:—

(*a*) Taxes on arts, trades, callings, professions etc.

(*b*) Taxes on buildings, lands and holdings.

(*c*) Taxes on water, drainage, sewage, conservancy etc.

(*d*) Taxes on vehicles, boats, palanquins, animals etc.

(*e*) Taxes on property.

(*f*) Taxes on private menials and domestic servants.

(*g*) Taxes on private markets.

(*h*) Octroi on animals, or goods, or both within town limits.

(*i*) Tolls on vehicles and animals entering the town limits.

(*j*) Fees on registration of cattle sold within town limits.

The resolution of the Government of India, dated 28th April 1915, from which the above have been taken goes on to add, "The taxes provided for in the acts vary, however, in the different provinces, and not all these taxes are actually levied in any one province. Any tax, other than those specified in the acts, which is proposed to be levied, ordinarily requires, and should continue to require the sanction of the Governor-General in Council. The most important taxes now in force are octroi duties, levied principally in Bombay, the United Provinces, the Punjab, the Central Provinces, the North West Frontier Province, and the tax on houses and lands which holds the chief place in other provinces as well as in Bombay City." The right of taxation within municipal limits is granted subject to the approval and sanction of the Government of India in every case of a new tax. The following table shows the proportion of the various heads of municipal income in the different provinces in 1912-13:—

Province.	Percentage of toal income from rates and taxes, from:—								Perceentage of total income excluding loans and advances from.				
	Octroi.	Tax on houses.	Animals etc.	Trades etc.	Tolls.	Water rates.	Conservancy	Other taxes.	Taxation.	Under Special Acts.	Municipal property.	Grants from Government.	Miscellaneous.
Madras. ...	...	45.	10.2	8.6	19	16.8	...	0.4	44	0.3	15.1	36.4	4.2
Bombay.	46.9	16.3	3.2	0.3	4.5	16.9	8.	3·9	62.6	0.5	16.4	17.1	3.4
Bengal. ...	...	37.2	5.5	1.8	2.1	13.9	25.1	14.4	75.8	2.1	8.4	11.5	2.2
United provinces. ...	69.2	5.4	1.	3.8	2.8	6.6	1.1	10.1	62.8	1.6	19.7	13.6	2.3
Punjab. ...	89.7	6.8	0.8	...	...	1.3	1.2	0.2	63.1	0.8	19.3	13.7	3.1
Burma. ...	...	42.5	3.7	...	14.	9.2	20.6	10.	38.1	1.1	42.3	17.2	1.3
Behar and Orissa. ...	1.7	40.7	9.5	1.8	5.6	3.5	21.6	15.6	62.5	1.4	9.9	25.1	1.1
Central Provinces. ...	61.6	3.3	4.3	0.1	1.2	15.3	10.9	3.3	60.3	2.7	16.3	16.4	4.3
Assam. ...	...	40.5	7.6	...	9.9	11.6	22.1	8.3	36.8	4.	10.8	47.3	1.1
N.W.Frontier Provinces.	98.	0.6	0.1	...	...	1.2	0.1	...	42.1	0.2	15.9	41.1	0.7

The aggregate income of the 701 municipalities in 1912-13, not counting the Presidency Towns and Rangoon, was £ 3,282,845 apart from loans, sales of securities and other extraordinary receipts. Of this, considerably more than half in most provinces, and three-fourths in Bengal, was derived from taxation, one-sixth to one-fifth-in Burma, over two-fifths was derived from municipal property, and a varying proportion–from one-tenth in Bengal to nearly half in Assam–was derived from Government grant.

The following is a more detailed analysis of Municipal revenues in the Bombay Presidency.

1911-12 Revenue Table.

Revenues.	BOMBAY.	
	Presidency Town.	District Municipalities.
Octroi (net)	£ 115,792	£ 185,953
Tax on houses etc.	£ 331,755	£ 56,511
		£ 54,174
Water rate.	£ 138,408	£ 72,977
Other rates.	£ 124,485	
Special Acts.	£ 10,163	£ 3,064
Municipal property. ...	£ 64,407	£ 94,276
Government Grants...	...	£ 97,628
Miscellaneous. ...	£ 29,292	£ 12,531
Total	£ 814,301	£ 577,123

Of the taxes the octroi duties are most important wherever they obtain. They have their own merits and defects. They are familiar to the people, are likely to grow with the prosperity of the town, and, being collected in small amounts, are not felt as burdens. On the other hand they undoubtedly furnish occasion for fraud and oppression, are very expensive to collect, and, lastly, they are likely to degenerate into mere transit duties and so obstruct trade, inspite of the provisions for refunds. Attempts have been made to substitute these duties by some form of direct taxation or by a terminal tax in the United Provinces. The Government of India have approved these attempts on condition that the rate of such a terminal tax is lower, that there are conditions which make such a tax specially inevitable, and that it is meant to effect the transition from a system of indirect to that of direct taxation. Where the octroi tax prevails precautions are taken to confine the tax only to those articles actually consumed in the town. The articles so taxed are generally commodities of local consumption *e. g.* the articles of food. Taxes on land and houses, trades and profession, animals and vehicles, water dues and road tolls, lightening charges and conservancy rates are more by way of variety than as important sources of revenue.

The average incidence of municipal taxation per head of municipal population in British India 1911-12 was Rupees 2.95. If we leave out of account the Presidency Towns, where the incidence is higher, the average from province to province varies being Rs 3.08 in the North West Frontier Province, Rs. 2.38 in the Punjab, Rs. 1.35 in Madras and Rs. 1.02 in Coorg. In the Presidency towns the incidence is highest in Bombay being Rs. 11.67, and lowest in Madras being Rs. 4.44. Calcutta comes between with Rs. 9, if we do not include Rangoon as a Presidency town with its average incidence of Rs. 10.5.

As regards municipal expenditure it corresponds necessarily to municipal functions. The one item of expenditure which is connected with no single specific function is the item of general administration and collection. These amount to something less than 10 per cent. Municipalities have in every case been relieved of the Police charges, while in case of famine relief, or extraordinary epidemics, their responsibility is shared also by the State. The construction of light railways-whether a privilege or a burden, will be noted later on. The total municipal expenditure in British India in 1911-12 was £ 4,844,734 distributed as follows:—

1. General administration and collection charges. £ 416,210.
2. Public safety (lighting, fire etc....) ... £ 294,565.
3 Public health and convenience:—
    (*a*) Water supply. ... ... £ 576,889

(*b*) Drainage ... ... £ :385,092

(*c*) Conservancy ... ... £ 843,261

(*d*) Other heads *e. g.* roads and hospitals £ 1,250,591

4. Public Instruction ... ... £ 304,747

5. Contributions etc., including interest on loans ... ... £ 8773,37

The total debts of the municipalities amounted to £. 9,597,826.

IV. Municipal Policy.

The whole subject of the Urban Local Government in India was thoroughly examined by the Royal Commission on Decentralisation (1909), and various recommendations were made. They may be summarised as follows:—

(*a*) Municipal boards should be constituted on the basis of a substantial elective majority, nominated members being limited to a number sufficient to provide the due representation of minorities, and official experience. On this point the Government of India—six years after the Commission had reported—accepted the principle. The change, however, they thought, could not be introduced all at once; and in the absence of suitable candidates perhaps the change might not be introduced at all where suitable candidates cannot be had. In this respect it must be remarked that real progress of municipal government is impossible without full play being given to the elective principle.

(*b*) Municipal chairmen should be elected non-officials, Government officers should not be allowed to stand for election, and only where any other chairman but a nominated chairman would be impossible should they be allowed a chance. This principle also is accepted by the Government of India, though they would like to leave to the local Governments the discretion to nominate non-official chairmen.

(*c*) The Bombay system of an elected chairman, acting as the official mouthpiece of the corporation, with a full time nominated official entrusted with the executive, subject to the control of the Corporation and its Standing Committee should be adopted every where in the presidency municipalities. One wonders why the Government of India, if they really desired to liberalise municipal government, should have demurred to this suggestion.

(*d*) The functions of municipalities need an all round extension, and, consequently, also their finances. We find indications and proofs that municipal trading on a large scale is not only profitable to the municipality itself, but beneficial to the citizens individually, both in the cheapness of the service rendered as well as in the wholesomeness of the article supplied, wherever that system is adopted. But the commission above referred to did not find it within the scope of their reference to make a specific recommendation on the subject; and in the absence of such a recommendation the Government of India can hardly be blamed for not incorporating it in their famous resolution. Nevertheless, it must be added, that there is no stimulant to civic spirit and civic pride like the extension of municipal functions. It is true we are yet beginners in that field. But that proves only the necessity of supervision and suggestion from outside, not a limitation of functions altogether. As regards the Budget, the Government of India are willing to give a free hand to the municipalities provided a prescribed minimum balance is kept.

V. Rural Local Self-Government.

If the municipalities in India have a comparatively short history, the institutions of self-government in the rural parts of the country has a shorter history still. Before 1858 there were no such institutions, though there were some semi-voluntary funds in Madras and Bombay for local improvements, while in Bengal and the United Provinces there were consultative committees to assist the district officers in the use of funds for local schools, roads and dispensaries. In 1865 Madras led the way by a law to impose cesses on land for such purposes, and Bombay followed the lead in 1869. Two years later came the financial decentralisation scheme of Lord Mayo; and, in consequence, various acts were passed in the provinces for the levy of rates and the creation of local bodies—here and there with some tinge of the elective principle—to administer those funds. Under Lord Ripon the rural institutions flourished along with the municipal. Under the Resolution of 1882 the existing local committees were to be replaced by local boards extending all over the country. The principle observed in the creation of these boards was that the lowest administrative unit was to be small enough to secure local knowledge and interest on the part of each member of the board; the various minor boards of the district were to be under the control of a general District Board, and were to send delegates to a District Council for the discussion of measures common to all. The non-official element was to preponderate, and the elective principle was to be cautiously recognised. The resources as well as the responsibilities of the boards should be increased by transferring to them items of provincial revenue and expenditure.

VI. The Present System.

As the conditions in the different provinces varied immensely the Government of India could do no more than lay down the general principles—with a large measure of discretion to the Local Governments. Hence the systems introduced in the different provinces under the acts of 1882-4 varied considerably. The Madras organisation most nearly resembles the pattern set in the original orders. It provides for three grades of local boards;

(*a*) Important villages or groups of villages are organised as Unions, each controlled by a Panchayet. The duties of these bodies are chiefly in connection with sanitation, and they have powers to levy a light tax on houses. Next in order (*b*) come the Taluk boards–entrusted with the conduct of local works in the subdivisions of the district. Above them all (*c*) comes the District council with general control over the administration of the district. In Bombay there are only 2 classes of boards, the District and the Talukas. In Bengal, the Punjab and the N. W. Frontier Province the law requires the establishment of a District Board in each district, but leaves it to the Local Government to establish subordinate local boards. In the United Provinces the sub-district boards have been abolished since 1906, while in the Central Provinces the system resembles that prevailing in Madras.

The elective principle has been introduced in varying degrees everywhere, except in the North West Frontier Province where it has been abolished since 1903. On the whole, however, the principle of representation is much less developed in the rural than in the municipal area. In Madras the elective principle, previously confined to the District Boards, was extended to the Taluk Boards, while in the United Provinces and the Central Provinces there is a majority of elected members. The following table shows the general constitution of the boards in each province (1913–14).

Province.	District Boards.	Local Boards	Total Members.	By appointment.			By employment.	
				Ex-Officio.	Nominated.	Elected.	Officials.	Non-Officials.
Madras ...	25	96	2401	222	1161	1018	684	1707
Bombay ...	26	216	3690	651	1395	1644	725	2965
Assam ...	2	19	318	76	58	184	79	239
Bengal (1912-13)	25	72	1361	188	581	592	246	1115
Behar Orissa ...	18	41	883	174	460	249	205	678
United Provinces ...	48	...	897	3	270	624	250	647
Punjab ...	28	13	1406	270	559	579	284	1122
N. W. Frontier ...	5	...	219	51	163	...	51	108
Central Provinces ...	19	80	1858	27	503	1328	220	1627

VII. Local and District Boards Finance.

The income of the rural self-governing institutions is derived from sources much narrower and less elastic than those of the municipalities. The bulk of their income is derived from a cess on land over and above the land revenue and usually not exceeding one anna in the rupee on the annual rental or the Government assessment. This due is collected along with the land revenue by the Government agency. Since 1905 Government have granted a special contribution, amounting to one-fourth of the income from the land cess, chiefly for education and sanitation. In addition to these special contributions there are other grants made by the Provincial Governments to the District Boards for specific purposes. Besides these all the boards derive a small percentage of their income from their educational and medical establishments, pounds and ferries, and, in Madras, road tolls. Except in that province, the Sub-District Boards have generally no independent source of income, their only receipts being such sums as the District Boards might allot to them.

The total income of the District and Local Boards in 1911-12 amounted to £ 3.434.219, and was distributed as follows:—

1. Provincial rates.......£ 1,541,919 nearly 47 per cent.

2. Education fees and contributions..........£ 448,629 „ 12 per cent.

3. Medical fees and contributions...............£ 97,763 „ 3 per cent.

4. Railways, Irrigation— and Navigation. ....£ 44,948 „ 1.6 per cent.

5. Police (Pounds and Ferries)...................£ 128,648 „ 4 per cent.

6. Civil Works & Contributions...................£ 882,547 „ 25 per cent.

There are some miscellaneous sources of income as the receipts from land-revenue, interest, public gardens, exhibitions and fairs.

VIII. Functions.

The principal normal functions of these boards are the maintenance and improvement of roads and other communications, education–especially in its primary stages, upkeep of medical institutions, vaccination, sanitation, veterinary work, the charges of pounds and ferries. They may also be called upon to devote their funds to famine relief. The total expenditure of £ 3,303,670 in 1911-12 was distributed as follows:—

1. Education	£	777,106	nearly	24 per cent.
2. Medical	£	340,256	„	11 per cent.
3. Civil Works.	£	1,758,479	„	52 per cent.
Buildings.	£	213,225		
Communications. ...	£	1,112,066		
Water supply. ...	£	88,474		
Drainage.	£	6,438		
4. Miscellaneous.	£	427,829	„	12 per cent.

The miscellaneous groups included general administration, cattle pounds, Veterinary work, public gardens, fairs and exhibitions.

IX. Recommendations of the Decentralisation Commission.

On the subject of rural local government the following recommendations were made by the Decentralisation Commission. Under each recommendation the policy adopted by the Government of India in their resolution of April 28, 1915 is also noted.

(1) Sub-district Boards should be established every where, and should be made the agency of rural boards administration. For this purpose the boards should have adequate funds and a large measure of independence; and their jurisdiction should

be so limited as to ensure local knowledge and interest on the part of the members, and be at the same time a well-known unit to the people. These requirements were best met by a Tahsil or a Taluka. On this point the Government of India, finding a great divergence of opinion among the local Governments due to varying conditions of each provinces–have decided to leave the matter to them.

(2) The proposal that district and sub-district boards should contain a large preponderance of elected members—the nominated members being just enough to secure the due representation of minorities and official experience, was accepted by the Government of India.

(3) The chairman of these boards should be an official as at present–since, in the opinion of the commission, the dissociation of the District Officer from the general administration of the district including education, roads etc., which must inevitably follow the election or appointment of non-official chairmen, would be prejudicial to the interests of efficiency in administration. The Government of India accepted this view though they made no objection to non-official chairmen being retained where they already existed, or to the appointment of such where the Provincial Government desired to try the experiment.

(4) As regards the financial resources of these boards, the commission would not allow the land cess to be increased beyond one anna in the rupee; and the Government of India accepted that proposal. But they proposed that the District Boards should be allowed to levy a railway or tramway cess of 3 pies in the rupee of land rental or assessment, in order to help the Districts to build light railways and thus to improve communications. The Government of India accepted the principle and have authorised local governments to undertake the necessary legislation, though they believe that the actual imposition of the cess would not be necessary. The mere power to impose

would be a sufficient guarantee. The construction of light railways by District Boards in Bengal and especially in Madras has shown that the financial results of carefully selected schemes will in a few years materially strengthen the resources of the District Boards. Assam has already undertaken such legislation and the Punjab Government has similar legislation under consideration. Finally financial and other Budget restrictions, should the Government desire, be gradually released.

X. General Remarks.

At the very commencement of their resolution of May 28, 1915 the Government of India remark "The results have on the whole justified the policy out of which local self-government arose. The degree of success varies from province to province and from one part of a province to another, but there is definite and satisfactory evidence of the growth of a feeling of good citizenship, particularly in the towns. The spread of education is largely responsible for the quickening of a sense of responsibility and improvements in the machinery. In certain provinces beneficial results have followed the elaboration of a system of local audit. On all sides there are signs of vitality and growth." But the same resolution goes on to say "The obstacles in the way of realising completely the ideals which have prompted action in the past are still, however, by no means inconsiderable. The smallness and inelasticity of local revenues, the difficulty of devising further forms of taxation, the indifference still prevailing in many places towards all forms of public life, the continued unwillingness of many Indian gentlemen to submit to the troubles, expense and inconveniences of election, the unfitness of some of those whom these obstacles do not deter, the prevalence of sectarian animosities, the varying character of Municipal area–all these are causes which cannot but impede the free and full development of local self-government."

37

Even apart from these obstacles, however, the progress of self-government in India has been impeded for other reasons. (1) In the first place all these institutions are new in India, in spite of the fact that India was not unfamiliar with self-government in the past. They are really an attempt to familiarise this country with institutions which have had the most marked success in England. The old indigenous local institutions of India—like the famous, almost immortal village-community—have been abandoned and superseded if not altogether suppressed; and progress is sought to be achieved on unfamiliar lines. The new institutions were established suddenly and such success as they have achieved is due to the now rapidly growing consciousness of local interests among the people, and not to any intrinsic merits of the institutions themselves.

(2) The scope for self-government whether in the municipalities or in the rural areas is very limited, quite in conformity with the character of these institutions as experiments in self-government. The principle adopted in India is to leave to these institutions such functions as would ensure interest as well as knowledge on the part of the members. But the functions themselves, however important they may sound in the West, are either novel or limited and restricted so much as to preclude the possibility of genuine interest. The class of citizens who can and will participate in local affairs is not only limited; but among them the necessary knowledge and experience is wanting. If the functions were enlarged possibly they would attract a larger class with more knowledge and more brains. Perhaps it is the limited extent of self-government allowed, more than any other factor, which can explain the want of interest displayed by the municipal public of even such a large and wealthy city as Calcutta. Out of 25 seats filled by election in Calcutta, only 2 were contested in 1903, in 1906 and 8 in 1909. Seldom has the contest there been so keen as the elections for the London County Council or even that which Bombay witnessed during the famous caucus elections.

(3) The limited scope allowed to the principle of election may also explain in part the lack of adequate interest on the

part of the native public. In the old Indian institution there was literally self-government when all the villagers voted on the questions affecting all. In the new institutions there is not even a full representative government. The presence of a fairly large proportion of officials of these councils, the domination of the official presidents tend towards apathy among the able, want of independence among the incompetent, and the routine for the rest.

(4) The financial resources of these bodies are narrowly circumscribed. Besides they must all depend upon Government aid to eke out their expenses. Government contributions being naturally dependent on the action of the local bodies being approved of by the Provincial Government, they are inevitably under official leading strings. Government control, whether by way of Budget restrictions or approval for new undertakings or new officers, though slightly relaxed, is not yet so modified as to permit a free development.

CHAPTER X.

The Indian Army.

I. History of the Indian Army.

The great Indian army of to-day had the most modest beginning in the guards enrolled for the defence of the treasuries and factories of the East India Company at Surat, Masulipatan, Armagam, Madras, Hoogly &c. These corresponded more to the *Ramoshis* and *Bhaiyas*, which great personages in India maintain for purposes of show as well as safety even in our days, than to the Police sepoy of to-day, much less to the regular soldier, enrolled for fighting. The native army of India proper may be said to have begun in 1748, when Major Stringer Lawrence, the "Father of the Indian army", following the example set by the French, enrolled some sepoys for fighting the French and their native allies. The army thus begun fought many a pitched battle in the service of the "Company Bahadur", defeated one after another their own countrymen who had not the advantage of the officers and equipment that the Company's sepoy had, and carried the flag of the Company from the Hoogly to the Jumna, from the Jumna to the Setlej, from the Setlej to the Kabul, reversing the tide of invasions for centuries past, conquering the conquerors of India, asserting their prowess and the English dominion even on the banks of the Nile against the soldiers of Bonaparte. The fidelity of the native soldiers to the Company for more than a century was unbroken by any serious rebellion; and the fact is all the more remarkable when we remember that in the same period they had fought some of the hardest battles for the Company with always a very small proportion of the English soldiers to aid or to overawe them, when in the same period the English section of the army, both officers and men, had been guilty of more than one rebellion in more than one centre for quite selfish reasons, and when we remember that all through that period they were serving an impersonal master, different from them alike in race, religion, and language. And even in the great rising of 1857, the disaffected soldiers of the Company revolted not for any personal selfish reason, as their European comrades had done in the past, but for safeguarding their caste and their religion, which, they honestly, though erroneously, believed was in danger. Even in the Mutiny of 1857, not the whole army had rebelled; there were none braver in the attack on Delhi than the Sikhs from the Punjab, and the native cavalry under Sir Hugh Rose was second to none in putting down the mutineers in Central India.

Under the Company the armies of each Presidency were necessarily mutually independent and self-contained units. They consisted of native and European soldiers in unequal proportions, Indian soldiers forming chiefly the infantry. There were, besides the soldiers in the service of the Company, some officers and men in the service of the English Crown. The armies of the Company were organised on a definite principle for the first time in 1796. The European troops numbered 13000 and the native soldiers 54000. To describe this reorganisation fully would take us far into military details, not easily intelligible to a mere civilian; it would be enough, therefore, to give a sketch of the organisation as established in Bengal, the other provinces more or less copying that plan. The Bengal, army in 1796 had:—

European artillery, 3 battallions of 5 companies each;

" Infantry, 3 regiments of 10 companies each;

regular native cavalry, 4 regiments of 6 troops each;

" " infantry, 12 regiments of 2 battalions each;

Each cavalry regiment had a commanding field officer, 15 officers including the regimental staff, 4 European non-commissioned officers, and 39 Indian non-commissioned officers, 12 native officers and 426 troops. In each infantry regiment there was a colonel commandant, 2 lieut. colonels, 2 majors, 8 captains, 22 lieutenants, 10 ensigns, 2 European non-commissioned officers, 40 Indian officers and 200 non-commissioned Indian officers, and 1600 sepoys with 40 drummers and pipers.

The strength of the army as fixed in 1796 was continually increased all through the period ending in the Mutiny of 1857. On the eve of the Mutiny the army in India consisted of 39,500 British soldiers, including 2686 cavalry, 6769 artillery, and 30,045 infantry; and 311,038 sepoys, including 37,719 cavalry, 11,256 artillery, 3,404 sappers and miners, 211,926 infantry. Thus the native army was as 8: 1 of the European force. After the Mutiny 2 important questions had to be decided by the Government of India; first the form of the European army for service in India, and secondly reconstruction of the native army. As to the first there were two opinions; Lord Canning, the Viceroy, proposed a local European army, entirely at the disposal of the Government of India. He thought that plan would be not only more economical, but politically more advisable, as the officers and men would identify themselves more closely with the country and its inhabitants. On the other hand it was suggested that the British army should be a truly imperial army, whose interests should in no way be divided by their having to serve two masters, and whose traditions would be impaired if any section of it was to be permanently localised in India. Just at that time there occurred what was known as the "White Mutiny" on account of the European troops objecting to being transferred to the Crown without their wishes in that respect being first considered: and the advocates of a local army were once for all placed in a hopeless minority. It was accordingly decided that the European army of the Company should be transferred to the Crown, the infantry becoming regiments of the line, and the artillery being amalgamated with the Royal Artillery and Royal Engineers. It was further laid down that this British force should be maintained at a strength of 80,000, and that the native troops should not exceed it by more than two to one in Bengal and more than three to one in other provinces. The native regiments were to be recruited by a general mixture of all classes and all castes The proportion between the European and Indian soldiers as thus laid down was maintained pretty closely, but the general mixture system in recruitment was found impracticable, and so was eventually abandoned, though those who proposed it fancied it to be a source of great strength to the Government in as much as soliders so recruited could never all combine against the Government.

As regards the European section of the army in India, since the amalgamation, regiments and batteries have been sent to India for a definite period, to be relieved at the end of that period by other regiments and batteries, on the same system as for any other part of the Empire, In this way almost all regiments and batteries go round the Empire, the tour taking 9 years for cavalry, 16 for infantry, and from 11 to 15 for artillery. While in India, these troops are in many respects under Indian regulations as regards pay, equipment &c., and the Government of India pays for them at a capitation rate of £7 s.10. The period of service in India for such units averages 5 years and 4 months By 1863 the Indian Army was reorganised on a reduced footing, the reduction amounting to nearly 40 per cent as compared to the strength before the Mutiny. The question of officering this new army was solved by the institution of a Staff Corps while the total complement of officers for each regiment of cavalry and infantry was increased. In 1886 two important changes were made. The "linked battallion" system was introduced to guarantee a ready supply of trained units for regiments in the field, and an Indian army reserve was formed. The greatest of all changes came in 1893 when the separate organisation of each Presidency army, which was more than a century and a half old was abolished by an Act of Parliament.

II. Administration of the Army.

The supreme authority over the army in India is vested in the Governor-General in Conucil, subject to the control of the

Crown exercised through the Secretary of State. Until 1906 the Governor-General's Council had a military member, who was in direct charge of the administrative and financial business relating to the army. As a consequence there were frequent differences of opinion between the Commander-in-Chief, the official head of the army, and the military member of the Council. Lord Kitchener the Commander-in-Chief in India from 1902, opposed this arrangement, and proposed to place all matters relating to the army directly under the official head of the army. Lord Curzon, the then Viceroy, opposed this proposal on the ground that it tended to subvert the civil control over the army, which was such a distinctive feature of the British constitution. To some extent Lord Curzom was right, though Lord Kitchener pointed out that his position did not necessarily involve the ousting of the civil control over the army, as the commander-in-chief would himself in future be under the Governor-General in Council. He objected to the Military member of the Council, himself an army officer, and therefore a subordinate of the Commander-in-Chief, sitting in judgement on the military proposals submitted by the superior officer, under cover of advising the Governor-General in Council. Lord Curzon pleaded for the necessity of independent advice to the civilian chief of the Government; but he was at length overruled, and the Military Department was abolished. Its place was taken between 1906 and 1909 by the short-lived Military Supply Department which took over some portion of the work relating to the army. From 1909 every question relating to the army goes to the army department the head of which is the Commander-in-Chief, an extraordinary member of the Viceregal Council.

III. Strength of the Army.

On the 1st April 1914 the sanctioned and actual strength of the army in India were as follows:—

Troops under the orders of the Commander-in-Chief:—

	Sanctioned	Actual.
British officers	5,017	5,001
British warrant and non-commissioned officers and men	73,323	73,155
Indian officers, non-commissioned and men	160,313	150,574
Troops not under the orders of the Commander-in-Chief:—		
British officers....	9	9
Indian officers, non-commissioned and men	24,466	23,077
Total	263,128	251,761

The different portions of the army in India are governed by different laws. The British Forces in India are under the English Army Act, which is passed every year by the British Parliament. The Indian troops are governed by the acts of the local legislature, though their officers are governed by the Imperial Army Act.

IV. Reorganisation, Redistribution and Rearmament.

The name of the late Lord Kitchener will for ever be associated with the wholesale schemes of reoganisation and redistribution of the army in India, with which during his tenure of office as Commander-in-Chief he identified himself. After the abolition of the separate Presidency armies in 1895, the army of India was divided into 4 large commands corresponding to the provinces of the Punjab, Bengal, Madras and Bombay, to which, since 1903-4, was added the Burma command. These commands were subdivided into districts, but they were in no way capable of expansion; while their territorial organisation made it extremely difficult for them to take the field against an external foe. There were no organised army corps, nor brigades, the troops in case of war having to be drawn from all parts of the country, the various units being sorted out into brigades and divisions after they had reached the base of operations, and being provided with a scratch lot of officers just for that occasion. The whole force was in fact organised more for the purpose of internal defence than with any intention to its possible use against an invader. Lord Kitchener set to reorganise with a view to make the army of India equal to any demands that might in reason be made upon it. The units of the Indian army were renumbered, presidency and local distinctions were abolished, and a homogeneous army, free to serve in any part of India wase stablished. The entire army, was formed into 9 divisions, exclusive of the Burma divison, each with its proper complement of artillery, cavalry, and infantry, under its own general and staff complete. These were organised for war; each division could take the field by itself and yet enough troops would be left behind to guarantee the defence of the country. For the better training of candidates for staff appointments in India, a staff college was established, at Deolali first, and afterwards at Quetta. The strength of the army was also increased and the artillery section as well as the Flying corps were established. The Indian Army Reserve was substantially augmented, and 350 officers added to the army. The equipment of individual soldiers was altered to suit the altered conditions and the manufacturing establishments of the Ordnance branch were improved. The pay of all ranks was increased, and the general conditions of service were revised. At the Coronation Durbar in 1911 the coveted distinction of the victoria Cross was thrown open to the Indian soldiers.

V. Volunteers.

The right to volunteer for the defence of the country was, until quite recently, confined to the Europeans or Anglo-Indians in this country. They include foot and mounted regiments, light horse, garrison artillery, together with some companies of electrical engineers. Their role is to defend ports, railways, cantonments, and civil stations. On the outbreak of the War a general desire was manifested that a volunteer brigade should be raised for active service at the front. For the present, however, they were kept in India though many were sent to the front in the motor-cycle or machine gun detachments. The volunteer force has considerably increased in number and importance; and the latest legislation of the Government of India permits volunteering to the children of the soil. Though this measure is apparently only a war measure, and declared to last for the duration of the War and six months thereafter, it is to be hoped that the policy of distrust which has so long dominated the Government of India in this respect would once for all be consigned to oblivion. The services of the Indian soldiers at the various theatres of war, and the remarkable loyalty of all classes of Indians in this world War, may not unreasonably be taken to be sufficient proof that there is no room for a policy of distrust in new India. The other grievance of Indians in this department, *viz.*, that they are not allowed to become commissioned officers in the army of their country, will similarly, it is to be hoped, be remedied.

VI. Imperial Service Troops.

In 1887 the Nizam led the way by an offer to create and maintain at his own cost a body of troops for the defence of the Empire. His example has been warmly taken up by the other rulers of Indian Native States. The troops belong to the several states, and are recruited from their subjects. They are officered by native officers, under inspection by British officers, and available for Imperial Service when placed at the disposal of the Government of India by the rulers. The troops are armed and equiped in very nearly the same way as the Indian army, and in a number of campaigns they have shown a remarkable degree of military excellence. The total strength of these troops is approximately 22,271 contributed by 29 states. They include 10,000 infantry, 7,500 cavalry, with transport and camel corps. Almost all these troops were placed at the disposal of the Government of India on the outbreak of the War, and many of them were dispatched to one or the other theatre of war.

VII. The Imperial Cadet Corps.

This corps was formed in 1901 with the object of providing military training for the scions of ruling and noble families. It consists of about 20 young men of noble birth who have been educated at the Chiefs Colleges, and have received instruction in military exercise and military science.

VIII. The Officers of the Indian Army.

On the reorganisation of the Indian army in 1861, its British officers were organised into 3 "staff corps," one for each of the 3 Presidency armies of Bombay, Bengal, and Madras. At first these officers were only transferred from the Company's army; but later on they were drawn from British regiments. In 1891 the separate corps were combined into one, and were styled thenceforth "The Indian Staff Corps". Ten years later the term "staff corps" was dropped, and the officers came to be known as the officers of the Indian army. They number about 3500, and are drawn partly from the British regiments stationed in India, but chiefly from the candidates at the Royal Military College of Sandhurst. An officer in the army must pass an examination in the native languages and in military subjects before he is eligible for staff employment of company in any part of India. These officers of the Indian army are employed not only in their proper military posts, but are often given civil posts and they are sometimes lent to the Native States. They also hold a number of political posts chiefly under the Foreign Department, and make up the greater portion of the diplomatic service of India.

IX. Commissions in the Indian Army.

The question as to who is the proper authority to grant commissions in the Indian Army does not seem to be free from doubt. The King—Emperor, of course, is the final and undisputed source of all authority in the Army. But is the highest civil authority in India, the Governor—General, alone or in Council, competent to grant such commissions. Before 1858 the Company's Governor-General used to grant commissions to the officers of the East India Company, the power to do so being presumed to be derived from the Company's Charters and other Acts relating to the Company. On the abolition of the separate European army, Sir Charles Wood informed the Gevernor-General (1862) that local commissions should be granted, wherever practicable, by the Field-Marshall commanding-in-chief on the recommendation of the Government of India preferred through the Secretary of State. If in any case the Government of India thought it necessary to bestow commissions without any such previous reference, the commissions so granted should be made conditional on the approval of the Crown. Two years later, 1864 the same Secretary of State informed the Government of India that as royal commissions were granted to all officers of H. M.'s Indian forces and staff corps, local Governments in India, and the commander-in-chief in India need not issue any further commissions. The Indian Volunteers Act of 1869 introduced a modification. Though that Act itself is silent about the grant of commissions to volunteer officers, in practice these commissions were signed by the Governor-General alone, or in Council. As regards the regular army, the Crown is the supreme authority from whom alone military rank and powers of command can be obtained. As a rule the commander-in-chief in India is authorised by his commission to grant commissions, pending the intimation of the sovereign in that behalf; but such commissions are granted by a military, and not by a civil, authority; and they are granted under specific powers. The existing Army Act (44 & 5 vict, c. 58) gives no authority to the Governor-General to grant commissions.

X. The Royal Indian Marine.

The Government of India have no navy of their own, though they give a small subsidy to the Imperial British Navy of about £ 100,000 a year. India has, however, a substitute for a navy, the socalled the Royal Indian Marine, which dates from 1612, and which has rendered naval services in the past of the highest importance. The marine at present renders service as transport. It is in charge of a Director.

The questions of constitutional importance in connection with the military forces in India are twofold; *viz.*, those relating to the status of Indians in the military forces of their country, and those relating to the authority of the Government of India over these forces. As regards the first, though Indians as such were never debarred from entering the army as privates, they could not hope to rise to the ranks of commissioned officers in their native army. Until quite recently, therefore, the army was a closed profession to Indians born in India. The new defence force is based on a measure which is admittedly of such a temporary character that no assertions can be based on that. We may, however, regard it as an indication of the tendency of the times; and if we are right in that the hope may be expressed that even in the permanent, regular army the status of Indians will improve after this War.

In this connection we might also mention the Arms Act which disables native Indians from carrying arms ordinarily.

The injustice of this measure is far too universally admitted at this time to require any lengthy argument to establish it; and the hope may be expressed here that as a consequence of this War, as a lesson of this War, this permanent and undeserved disgrace on Indian name will be removed.

The other question about the control over the Indian army has not, so far, taken that actually painful aspect, which the similar question with regard to the navy had taken in Canada just before the outbreak of this War. Provisions of the present Act no doubt require that Indian troops shall not be used outside the frontiers of India without the consent of Parliament. But such provisions cannot solve the grave question as to what authority is ultimately supreme in connection with the local forces of defence of any one particular part of the Empire. The supremacy of the King is only theoretical; but it is just possible that the Government of England may, sheltering themselves behind the name of the King, endeavour to use the local forces of the different parts of the Empire for their own purposes. And if these purposes are not, or cannot be, approved of by the Government of that particular part, must they always yield to the English Government, and allow their forces to be used in English quarrels, merely because the English Government claim to speak in the name of the sovereign? This grave question did not arise in the present War because every part of the Empire has made England's quarrel its own. But there is no ground to assume that such an identity of interest and sentiment would occur in every future war. This question is necessarily very grave already for those parts of the Empire, whose Governments enjoy a substantial measure of local autonomy, and it is relatively unimportant for countries like ours whose Government have no real independence. It is nevertheless, even for Indians, a grave constitutional question of the first importance. Within the scope of this work, we can but indicate this question, for it trenches upon the much wider problem of the constitution of the entire British Empire, which we cannot discuss here.

CHAPTER XI.

The Native States of India.

A study of the Indian system of Government, however brief, would be incomplete without some account of the relations of the Government of India with the Native States. They form an integral part of India, and though at first sight they may seem to be excluded from the scheme of Government in British India, the interests of the Native States, of the princes as well as of their subjects, are so closely interwoven with the interests of the population of the rest of this mighty country, that we cannot brush aside, as a prominent leader of political thought in India is reported to have done, as of no consequence, the question of the Native States, their present position and their place in the India of a generation hence.

In studying this question the student is confronted at the very outset with a very serious difficulty. The relations of the Government of India with the native princes are to a large extent conducted without that publicity which characterises the proceedings of the Government in other departments. This is of course no peculiarity of the Indian Government: even in England the complaint is very frequenly made that the foreign policy of the country, on which depends so much the prosperity of a trading nation like Britain, is conducted without any reference to Parliament. To some extent this policy is not unreasonable, since, though the days of the bedchamber politics are over, the foreign relations of every country require such a delicate handling that the fierce light of popular criticism would throw the whole mechanism out of order. On the other hand it is justly contended that publicity would do away with many of those trivial but yet portentous misunderstandings which often result in the most disastrous wars. And it is all the more dangerous when what is claimed to be entirely confidential leaks out, and not always in its true form, thereby causing endless confusion, misunderstanding, distrust and hatred. If in Europe they cannot always guard such secrets of state policy against official indiscretion, or journalistic impudence, the Native States in India cannot be blamed very much, if in the laxer atmosphere that prevails there, state secrets including the relations with the suzerain, leak out, and are none the better for the slight editing that they receive in the process of transmission from mouth to mouth. While, therefore, we can say very little authoritatively, beyond what we can glean from the various treaties and sanads, about the way the relations between the princes and their suzerain are determined. We know or we fancy that we know a lot about what takes place behind the scenes, which, if published, would place an entirely different complexion upon certain matters from the version which the official gazettes deign to place before the public. This state of chronic and confirmed doubt and suspicion is naturally very dangerous to every one concerned, but in the existing state of things it seems to be inevitable. The student of this part of the governing machinery in India must beware against saying too little as well against saying too much; he must weigh every word, and consider every phrase in all its possible and even its impossible meanings; for the latter are even more to be dreaded than the former, as, exactly because an interpretation is impossible it would be deemed to be the most likely, and would therefore be adopted.

I. The Origin of the Native States.

Confining ourselves only to the British period, the native states, as we known them to-day, did not originate until the days of Lord Wellesly. The Company had no doubt entered into relations with the princes of India long before that date;

but their position at the native courts, in the days before Wellesly, was hardly superior to that of suppliants or military adventurers, little better than the French soldiers of fortune who continued to baffle the English long after the French were ousted from India as an organised power. Even where the relations were those of equals, as in the case of the Nawab of Carnatic or the Nizam, the position of the Company was far too uncertain, and their territorial possessions far too inadequate to their pretensions of a later day, to allow us to regard them as really the equals of their native allies. In a sense that idea of equality, which we now associate with the alliance of two modern sovereign powers like England and France, never appeared in India, at least as far as the East India Company were concerned. They passed too rapidly from the position of dependents to that of dictators for that idea to materialise. The Subsidiary Alliances of Wellesly laid the foundations of our modern protected states in India. By requiring them to maintain at their cost a considerable British army, ostensibly to aid them in their perennial dynastic quarrels, possibly to keep them in check against any design that they might be misled to entertain against the Company; by compelling them to surrender all control over their foreign relations; by stipulating that they should entertain no European in their service without the consent of the Company's government; by inducing them to agree to the arbitration of the Company in all their differences with the friends of the Company; Wellesly managed to render them entirely innocuous for future mischief. Naturally all the consequences of this grand policy were not clearly apprehended from the first even by the author himself. No wonder that those who followed him, or those who opposed him, could not see in this net-work of alliances anything but an irresistible force which would steadily impel the Company, in spite of themselves, from one frontier to another, till at last they would have to succumb under the very load of their greatness; and consequently tried to set aside this grand and silent scheme of conquering India without shedding a drop of unnecessary blood. It is difficult to say what Wellesly thought to be the probable results of such a policy in the end:

would he have regarded it only as a prelude to total annexation of the native territories, when the Company were strong enough to venture on annexation without unnecessarily exposing themselves? or did he consider his scheme as an ultimate and permanent solution of the political problems of India in his day? Certain it is that while his policy had inspired the weaker among the native princes with hopes of their own continuance in power, it provided no obvious solution to the riddle which faced his immediate successors as to what should be done in the event of internal anarchy, or external molestation of those who had not allied themselves with the Company yet; nor did they know what to do when a prince, secured in his own possessions by the aid of the Company, used his security to his own undoing by extravagant misrule in his own dominions.

Lord Hastings carried the policy of Wellesly a step further; and, while arranging treaties with the native princes for safeguarding and improving the position of the Company, he made it clear that the obligations of an alliance with the Company included a reasonable measure of decent Government within a prince's own dominion. The direct extension of British territory, which this Governor-General was instrumental in bringing about, was also due to the same general idea of securing a modicum of good Government to the peoples of India whether directly under British rule or not. In his time he had no distinct opportunity to make this principle clear, but under his much more pacific successor, Lord William Bentinck, the principle was carried out in the case of Coorg, which was annexed to the dominions of the Company, on the reigning prince showing himself utterly incompetent to improve his Government. In the Mysore case the same Governor-General adopted a slightly different principle; the Mysore territories were placed under the administration of the Company's officers, though the Government was conducted in the name of the prince himself. The prince was given a fixed income to support his position, and beyond that he had nothing to do in the affairs of his principality.

In the twenty years that followed the departure of Lord William Bentinck from India, the policy of the Company's government fluctuated in this respect. The important native states of the Punjab, of Nagpur, of Oudh and of Sind were all annexed for one reason or another; and for a while it seemed that the supreme power in India had made up its mind to abandon the role of King Log and commence the part of King Stork. The annexatinns of Sind and of the Punjab were dictated by reasons of imperial defence; they lay so temptingly in the way of India's centuries old channels of invasion, and of the Company's natural line of advance, that the authorities in India as in England decreed their annexation. In the case of the Punjab there were no doubt other considerations. Under the late ruler Punjab had been a strong and reliable barrier between the English possessions and the old invaders of India; his successors were too weak to preserve their own authority; and so to remove once and for all this danger of the pretorian bands of the Punjab Government, Dalhousie decided for annexation, only two years after Hardinge had, on a similar occasion, decided for maintaining the local prince in subordinate alliance with the Company. In the case of Sind there was not the ghost of a reasonable excuse; and it was much more of a "humane piece of rascality" than the facetious Sir Charles Napier was aware of. The fundamental reason was in both these cases imperial necessity; the others were only temporary pretexts, the hollowness of which was not disguised from the superior authorities at home. The same may be said for Nagpur. It lay so inconveniently between the different parts of the Company's dominions, and prevented so effectually the linking up of the various presidencies and provinces with one another, that the doctrine of lapse received all the sting and importance which the ingenuity of lawyer could devise and the necessities of the statesman could suggest. We cannot give the same explanation for the annexation of Oudh; there the reason given was the prevailing and apparently irremediable misrule of the native government. The principle was at that time deliberately asserted that by supporting a prince on his throne against all opposition, whether from his own subjects or from his external enemies, the Company's Government had made themselves responsible for the proper discharge of the duties of the sovereign towards his subjects; and that the sovereign who failed to improve his administration inspite of repeated warnings could not, in justice to his subjects, be maintained in power by the Company without their being held responsible for that misrule.

These annexations of Lord Dalhousie occasioned a natural and general alarm. The Mutiny which followed was regarded by many as the direct result of the many and injudicious annexations of the preceding Governor-General; though it is a fact of history that the rebel forces received no substantial aid from the native princes, that may have been due to the distrust of the rebel leaders and of their motives more than to any settled affection for the Company's suzerainty. The suspicions of the Company's intentions were much too generally entertained, and far too reasonably founded for the new Government of India under the Crown to ignore altogether the problem of the Native States. The Queen's proclamation allayed all doubts that might have been felt by the Native princes by specifically promising that the Native States would be maintained in their integrity, and that the honour of the native princes would be preserved by the English sovereign as the honour of the English Crown.

II. The Present Position.

Before trying to speculate on the actual position of the Native States in the Indian polity to-day, as well as their future, it would perhaps be better if we summarise the existing obligations of the Government of India towards the Native States and vice versa, as far as we can learn them from the published treaties and arrangements between the two. Among themselves the Native States show every variety of size and importance, and perhaps the summary given below may not apply in its entirety to every state irrespsctive of its size and its past record. Generally speaking, however, the mutual obligations sketched below hold true.

Every state in India is protected against aggression from without, while a solemn assurance is given that their protector, the paramount power, will respect their rights as rulers. Hence in all questions of foreign relations the paramount power acts for them. Within their own dominions, the inhabitants of those territories are regarded as the subjects of their rulers; with the exception of the personal jurisdiction over British subjects, and the "residuary jurisdiction" these rulers and their subjects are free from the control of the laws of British India. The police of British India, for instance, cannot arrest criminals escaping from British India to the adjoining Native States, but they must be arrested by the authorities of the native state and handed over to the British police, or the latter might be permitted to arrest itself. The native princes are secured not only against the menace of an aggressive neighbour; the paramount power will, it is well understood, intervene when the internal peace of their territories is seriously threatened. They also enjoy as a matter of course all the benefits which the paramount power secures by its diplomatic relations, as for instance in commerce, railways, ports and markets of British India. Though a customs line is not entirely abolished, it is none of the most stringent; while as regards the movements of the people of India from one part of the country to another no passport is required, and no barriers created. According to the strict letter of the law, until quite recently, the subjects of the Native States were foreigners in British India; but they were admitted practically to all the privileges of British Indian subjects, and since the last Act on the subject even this slight difference is done away with.

Against these rights the Native States have corresponding obligations. Thus as regards the Foreign relations, the Native States have practically no foreign relations except those with the Government of India. They have no international existence. Not only they cannot deal with any foreign prince or state by themselves, but they cannot treat one another among themselves without the intervention of the paramount authority. This exclusion from all international relations is carried so far that the Native States cannot employ any European or American without the previous permission of the British Government in India. They cannot receive any diplomatic agent from any foreign power, nor accept any title or mark of honour from such foreign powers except with the consent of the Imperial Government. The subjects of a Native State cannot obtain a passport from their own prince for purposes of foreign travel; and they are regarded for all practical purposes, when travelling in foreign parts as subjects of His Britannic Majesty. As for foreigners resident in a Native State, it is the British Government, and not the Government of the state, which has jurisdiction over such persons. If the supreme Government enters into any treaty with a foreign Government, which cannot be carried into effect without the participation of a Native State, that state shall do all in its power to give effect to that treaty. Amongst themselves all disputes must be referred to the arbitration of the paramount authority. In all such interstate questions, as boundary disputes, or the mutual extradition of criminals, or the completion of an interstate line of railway, the paramount power must arrange the matter, and its arrangement is binding upon the Native States.

As the princes have no foreign relations and no occasion to fall out with their neighbours, they need not keep up a large military force. The Instrument of Rendition of the Mysore State lays down that the military force maintained in Mysore "for the maintenance of internal order and the Maharaja's personal dignity, and for any other purpose approved by the Governor-General in Council, shall not exceed the strength which the Governor-General in Council may from time to time fix." Though this provision is not specifically incorporated in the treaties with other States it is well understood that the army maintained by the native princes shall ordinarily be confined to the police needs of the State and for the proper show of the ruler's dignity. The British Government in India maintains an army which is organised not only for the defence of British India, but also of the territories of the native princes. On the other hand it is expected of these states that they shall render a proper account of themselves in the event of the necessity of Imperial defence. They must co-operate actively in securing the efficiency of the Imperial army, and at the same time do their allotted share of the defence of the empire. Under these principles the Native States must not fortify or garrison their own strong places for that the Imperial Government may have cause for anxiety. They must allow the British forces in their dominions camping facilities, find them supplies, and arrest their deserters. They must submit to the Imperial control over the means of communications like the railways or the post and telegraph office within their territories. As regards their active help in time of war that depends on treaties partly, and partly upon good understanding and loyalty, to which is trusted the solution of all doubtful points when the occasion arises. In the present War for instance the Native States, one and all, have rendered the most magnificent service to the British Empire, in excess in many cases of their paper obligations. At the present time several states in Rajputana, Central India, and in the Punjab, as well as Cashmere, Hyderabad, and Mysore habitually maintain what are known as the Imperial Service Troops.

In all the matters relating to the obligations of the Native States in connection with foreign relations and the defence of the country, the position of every state is generally speaking the same. It is otherwise with the questions relating to the internal administration of the several states. Several old and unrepealed treaties require that the British Government shall have nothing to do with the Maharaja's dependents or servants "with respect to whom the Maharaja is absolute". The usage of more than half a century has confirmed the principle that the Government of India is not precluded "from stepping in to set right such serious abuses in a native government as may threaten any part of the country with anarchy or disturbance, nor from assuming temporary charge of a Native State when there shall be sufficient reason to do so". (Lord Canning's Minute of April 30, 1860). As to when that necessity may be said to have arisen is in the discretion of the Governor-General, subject to such control as may be provided by Parliament. It is well known now that the Government of India will intervene in all cases of grave internal misrule. They would also intervene, it is felt, to prevent the dismemberment of a state by divisions among the sons of a prince or by means of a legacy.

In the name of public order the paramount power would intervene to stop disputes about succession and to prevent rebellion. So also to put a stop to such inhuman practices as female infanticide, or sati, or slavery or barbarous punishments. On the other hand in such cases as the reforms in administration in prosecuting works of material development of the country, the co-operation of the Native State would be invaluable to the British Government, but in this respect the latter would ordinarily content themselves with advice, and wait for the willing co-operation of the local prince.

The dissimilarity in the relative position of the different princes is the greatest in matters of local jurisdiction. It is not difficult to understand that the paramount power should claim jurisdiction in connection with its own subjects resident in the Native States as also in connection with the foreign subjects resident in those territories. But in some states the jurisdiction exercised by the suzerain goes far beyond this, and extends sometimes to a population which neither consists of British officials nor of British subjects. This jurisdiction is sometimes conceded by treaty, but frequently it is the result of long usage and acquiescence.

III. The Future of the Native States.

The brief sketch of the present position of the Native States in the scheme of Indian polity is sufficiently intriguing not to raise the inquiry as to their future. The policy of their gradual absorption in the British territory, under pretexts which could always be discovered or created, has, however, too definitely been dropped by the suzerain to permit us in indulging in speculations as to the possible merits of a policy of gradual sequestration of even the remnants of sovereign authority that the Native States enjoy to-day. Had it been intended to bring the whole of India gradually under one undisputed authority, the occasions were not wanting in the case of some of the most improtant states in the last 60 years or so to carry that policy into execution. It may perhaps be said that the obligations with the Gaekwar family were far too deep and enduring to allow the suzerain the exercise of the last authority of paramount power on the mere pretext of a laxity in the personal conduct of a native ruler in the nineteenth century in India. The graver charge of the attempt to poison the representative of the British Majesty, not being proved to the satisfaction of the Indian commissioners in the commission of inquiry in that case, the Government of India decided in that case to dethrone the prince but to maintain his principality, utilising that occasion for a clear enunciation of the mutual rights and obligations. But the best proof of the intentions of the Government of India in favour of maintaining the native princes is, perhaps, afforded by the restoration of the State of Mysore to the Maharaja, who had been for more than 50 years deprived of his princely authority in the administration of his territories. The Rendition of that state, after fifty years of direct administration by British officers, to the native ruler may well be cited as an example, evidencing the trend of policy in favour of the maintenance of the native rule. There are many reasons why the Government of India may not merely tolerate but actively support the native rule in certain parts of India. Even apart from the treaty obligations, which cannot be treated by a modern civilised power as mere scraps of paper without endangering its own reputation in the family of nations, even though in the particular case at issue the power tempted to set at naught its treaties may have nothing to fear; the British Government has many distinct advantages in their preservation. The States bear an appreciable portion of the cost of the defence of the Indian Empire, and provide a sort of indefinite but yet a reliable reserve to be drawn upon in case of emergency. And people are not wanting who allege that there is a more deep-seated reason, a more subtle influence, requiring the British Government to tolerate and even to actively support the Native States: the Native States provide an admirable foil, by their relatively backward system of Government, to set of in all its advantage the British form of Government. Perhaps this does but scant justice to the motives of such distinguished statesmen like Lord Curzon, who endeavoured, even at the risk of being misrepresented, to infuse a new spirit of vitality in the administration of the Native States. Said he at the Rajkote Durbar in November 1900, "I am a firm believer in the policy which has guaranteed the integrity, has ensured the succession, and has built up the fortunes of the native states. I regard the advantages accruing from the secure existence of those states as mutual. In the case of the chiefs and the states it is obvious. ....But to us also the gain is indubitable, since the strain of Government is thereby lessened, full scope is provided for the exercise of energies that might otherwise be lost to the government, the perils of excessive uniformity and undue centralisation are avoided, and greater administrative flexibility ensured. So long as these views are held,–and I doubt if any of my successors will ever repudiate them,—the native states should find in the consciousness of their security a stimulus to energy and well doing......If the native states, however, are to accept this standard it is obvious that they must keep pace with the age. They cannot dwadle behind and act as a drag upon an inevitable progress. They are links in the chain of Imperial administration. It would never do for the British links to be strong and the native links to be weak and vice versa......... I therefore, think,......that a very clear and positive duty devolves upon them. It is not limited to the perpetuation of their dynasties or the maintenance of their Raj. They must not rest content with keeping things going in their time. Their duty is one, not of passive acceptance of an established place in the imperial system, but of active and vigorous co-operation in the discharge of its onerous responsibilities."

It would be manifestly unjust to such views to assume that the men at the head of affairs in India are interested in keeping the government of the states deliberately backward. On the other hand it cannot be denied that the Native States are by their very nature impervious to the modern western ideas of good government. Whatever be the intention of the Viceroys and Governors in India, they are but the birds of passage whose influence cannot endure beyond the period of their own sojourn in the country. Unless therefore it be made a maxim of public policy to try and make the Native States keep up the pace they would invariably lag behind. But such efforts at making them keep up their rate of progress are apt to lead into too detailed, and not always pleasant, interference into what may be regard-as the purely domestic concerns of a prince. And such interference had best be avoided-for obvious reasons. To the British official, who really desires the uplift of the land he serves, it may no doubt seem an onerous condition that the equal and simultaneous progress of all parts of India is rendered impossible for what he might well deem to be preventible causes. To the Indian nationalist also, the presence of the Native States as so many relics of a deplorable past is insupportable. Impotent to do any good, incapable of assimilating modern ideas of good Government, constitutionally averse to all ideas of progress, the Native States cannot but appear to the impatient nationalist as so many hindrances in the way of India's regeneration. He is but too apt to forget that the Native States offer, in the existing circumstances of this country, about the only chance for displaying administrative talents or genius to the inhabitants of India. He also forgets that the Native States are the only section of the Indian community, who can, if they would, promote materially the regeneration of India. He thinks but of the few but fascinating examples of royal license and recklessness; he remembers their misrule in the past and broods upon their apparent absolutism in the present, and hastens to dub them from such evidence as entirely unsympathetic with the hopes and aspirations of the rising generation of India. Curiously, therefore, if at this time there are any advocates of the mediatisation, or even total annexation of the Native States, they are to be found in the ranks of the young and ardent nationalists.

From the point of view of the princes themselves, also, it must be observed, the position of the rulers of the native states is not quite enviable. To the thinking portion of them it cannot but be evident that their powers are in most directions so narrowly circumscribed, by formal engagements, or by the silent force of usage and acquiescence, that they are unable to govern according to their inclination. They are not in reality the equal members of an imperial federation, in which the interest and authority of each partner are equal, though expressions are often given utterance to by responsible officials which might perpetuate that misunderstanding. Between them and the suzerain there is no independent tribunal to judge; and the decisions of one of the parties to a dispute, sitting as a judge in the dispute, cannot be expected to be always palatable to the other party. They are also not in the position of a powerful aristocracy, as is sometimes believed: for they have yet that much of the sovereign in them which, while rendering them entirely innocuous as sovereigns, yet prevents them effectually from assimilating the mentality of a class of citizens, however privileged that class may be. Probably no one would repudiate more emphatically than the princes themselves the idea of regarding them as merely the hereditory, titular, privileged subjects of the British Crown, entrusted with the task of administering their patrimony in trust for and on behalf of the British Crown. Those in the ranks of the Indian publicists, who hope for the salvation of India through the action of these our aristocracy, are destined to bitter disappointment if they go on cherishing their delusion.

These considerations make the task of forecasting the future of our Native States all the more difficult. They are not members of a federation; they are not the landed aristocracy of India corresponding to the barons of England and the Junkers of Prussia; they are unable to march ahead and yet they would not be suffered to lag behind. They are not respected as their natural leaders by the people, and yet not treated as their collaborators by the government; they are incapable of uniting among themselves, and yet powerless to resist by themselves a determined attack on their position. Under these cricumstances the student of our system of Government must tasign the task of offering a possible or even a plausible solution of this enigma, and leave it to be decided by the man of the moment.

CHPTERX XII.

Miscellaneous.

PART XI.

Offences, Procedure and Penalties.

124. If any person holding office under the Crown in India does any of the following things, that is to say,—

(1) If he oppresses any British subject within his jurisdiction or in the exercise of his authority; or

(2) if (except in case of necessity, the burden of proving which shall be on him) he wilfully disobeys, or wilfully omits, forbears or neglects to execute, any orders or instructions of the Secretary of State; or

(3) if he be guilty of any wilful breach of the trust and duty of his office; or

(4) if, being the Governor-General, or a Governor, Lieutenant-Governor or chief commissioner, or a member of the executive council of the Governor-General or of a Governor, or Lieutenant-Governor, or being a person employed or concerned in the collection of revenue or the administration of justice he is concerned in, or has any dealings or transactions by way of, trade or business in any part of India, for the benefit either of himself or of any other person, otherwise than as a share-holder in any jointstock company or trading corporation; or

(5) if he demands, accepts, or receives, by himself or another, in the discharge of his office, any gift, gratuity or reward, pecuniary or otherwise, or any promise of the same, except in accordance with such rules as may be made by the Secretary of State as to the

receipt of presents, and except in the case of fees paid or payable to barristers, physicians, surgeons and chaplains in the way of their respective professions,

he shall be guility of a misdemeanour; and if he is convicted of having demanded, accepted or received any such gift, gratuity or reward, the same, or the full value thereof, shall be forfeited to the Crown, and the court may order that the gift, gratuity or reward, or any part thereof, be restored to the person who gave it, or be given to the prosecutor or informer, and that the whole or any part of any fine imposed on the offender be paid or given to the prosecutor or informer, as the court may direct.

125. (1) If any European British subject, without the previous consent in writing of the Secretary of State in Council or of the Governor-General in Council or of a local Government, by himself or another,—

(*a*) lends any money or other valuable thing to any prince or chief in India; or

(*b*) is concerned in lending money to, or raising or procuring money for, any such prince or chief, or becomes security for the repayment of any such money; or

(*c*) lends any money or other valuable thing to any other person for the purpose of being lent to any such prince or chief; or

(*d*) takes, holds, or is concerned in any bond, note or other security granted by any such prince or chief for the repayment of any loan or money hereinbefore referred to,

he shall be guilty of a misdemeanour.

(2) Every bond, note, or security for money, of what kind or nature soever, taken, held or enjoyed, either directly or indirectly, for the use and benefit of any European British subject, contrary to the intent of this section, shall be void.

126. (1) If any person carries on, mediately or immediately, any illicit correspondence, dangerous to the peace or safety of any

part of British India, with any prince, chief, landholder or other person having authority in India, or with the Commander, Governor, or president of any foreign European settlement in India, or any correspondence, contrary to the rules and orders of the Secretary of State or of the Governor-General in Council or a Governor in Council, he shall be guilty of a misdemeanour; and the Governor-General or Governor may issue a warrant for securing and detaining in custody any person suspected of carrying on any such correspondence.

(2) If, on examination taken on oath in writing of any credible witness before the Governor-General in Council or the Governor in Council, there appear reasonable grounds for the charge, the Governor-General or Governor may commit the person suspected or accused to safe custody, and shall within a reasonable time, not exceeding five days, cause to be delivered to him a copy of the charge on which he is committed.

(3) The person charged may deliver his defence in writing with a list of such witnesses as he may desire to be examined in support thereof.

(4) The witnesses in support of the charge and of the defence shall be examined and cross-examined on oath in the presence of the person charged, and their depositions and examination shall be taken down in writing.

(5) If, notwithstanding the defence, there appear to the Governor-General in Council or Governor in Council reasonable grounds for the charge and for continuing the confinement, the person charged shall remain in custody until he is brought to trial in India or sent to England for trial.

(6) All such examinations and proceedings, or attested copies thereof under the seal of the High Court, shall be sent to the Secretary of State as soon as may be, in order to their being produced in evidence on the trial of the person charged in the event of his being sent for trial to England.

(7) If any such person is to be sent to England, the Governor-General or Governor, as the case may be, shall cause him to be so sent at the first convenient opportunity, unless he is disabled by illness from undertaking the voyage, in which case he shall be so sent as soon as his state of health will safely admit thereof.

(8) The examinations and proceedings transmitted in pursuance of this section shall be received as evidence in all courts of law, subject to any just exceptions as to the competency of the witnesses.

127. (1) If any person holding office under the Crown in India commits any offence under this Act, or any offence against any person within his jurisdiction or subject to his authority, the offence may without prejudice to any other jurisdiction, be inquired of, heard, tried and determined before His Majesty's High Court, and be dealt with as if committed in the county of Middlesex.

(2) Every British subject shall be amenable to all courts of justice in the United Kingdom, of competent jurisdiction to try offences committed in India, for any offence committed within India and outside British India, as if the offence had been committed within British India.

128. Every prosecution before a High Court in British India in respect of any offence referred to in the last foregoing section must be commenced within six years after the commission of the offence.

129. If any person commits any offence referred to in this Act he shall be liable to such fine or imprisonment or both as the court thinks fit, and shall be liable, at the discretion of the court, to be adjudged to be incapable of serving the Crown in India in any office, civil or military; and, if he is convicted in British India by a High Court, the court may order that he be sent to Great Britain.

COMMENTS.

The provisions of all these sections can be traced to the consciousness of the difficulty of governing India-as befits a great country–through the servants of a company of merchants. The trial of Hastings at the bar of the House of Lords revealed but too clearly the lengths to which the servants of the Company in India could go with impunity. The interest of the Company often served as a valid excuse for official iniquity; and British justice often proved powerless to reach such high-placed offenders as the Company's chief officers in India. The Government of India by the Crown direct had, for reasons of policy, to maintain the privileges of Indian officials as against the courts of justice in India; but these sections attempt to provide effectively agains the possible misuse of these official immunities. As no instancest have occurred to the knowledge of the public further comments are superfluous.

PART XII.

SUPPLEMENTAL.

Repeal of Acts.

130. The Acts specified in the Fourth Schedule to this Act are hereby repealed, to the extent mentioned in the third column of that Schedule;

provided that this repeal shall not affect:—

(*a*) the validity of any law, charter, letters patent, order in Council, warrant, proclamation, notification, rule resolution, order, regulation, direction or contract made, or form prescribed, or table settled, under any enactment hereby repealed and in force at the commencement of this Act, or

(*b*) the validity of any appointment, or any grant or appropriation of money or property, made under any enactment hereby repealed, or

(*c*) the tenure of office, conditions of service, terms of remuneration or right to pension of any officer appointed before the commencement of this Act.

Savings.

131 (1) Nothing in this Act shall derogate from any rights vested in His Majesty, or any powers of the Secretary of State in Council, in relation to the Government of India.

(2) Nothing in this Act shall affect the power of Parliament to control the proceedings of the Governor-General in Council or to repeal or alter any law made by any authority in British India, or to legislate for British India and the inhabitants thereof.

(3) Nothing in this Act shall affect the power of the Governor-General in Legislative Council to repeal or alter any of the provisions mentioned in the Fifth Schedule to this Act, or the validity of any previous exercise of this power.

132. All treaties made by the East India Company, so far as they are in force at the commencement of this Act, are binding on His Majesty, and all contracts made and liabilities incurred by the East India Company, may, so far as they are outstanding at the commencement of this Act, be enforced by and against the Secretary of State in Council.

133. All orders, regulations and directions lawfully made or given by the Court of Directors of the East India Company or by the Commissioners for the affairs of India, are, so far as they are in force at the commencement of this Act, deemed to be orders, rules and directions made or given by the Secretary of State under this Act.

Definitions, Short Title and Commencement.

134. In this Act, unless the context otherwise requires,—

(1) "Governor-General in Council" means the Governor-General in executive council;

(2) "Governor in Council" means a Governor in executive council;

(3) "Lieutenant-Governor in Council" means a Lieutenant-Governor in executive council;

(4) "Local Government" a Governor in Council, Lieutenant Governor in Council, Lieutenant-Governor or Chief-Commissioner;

(5) "Office" includes place and employment;

(6) "Province" includes a presidency; and

(7) references to rules made under this Act include rules or regulations made under any enactment hereby repealed, until they are altered under this Act.

135. This Act may be cited as the Government of India Act, 1915, and shall come into operation on the first day of January one thousand nine hundred and sixteen.

SCHEDULES.

Sections 63 (2), 74 (1), 76 (1).

FIRST SCHEDULE.

MAXIMUM NUMBER OF NOMINATED OR ELECTED MEMBERS OF LEGISLATIVE COUNICL.

Legislative Council.	Maximum number
Indian Legislative Council	Sixty.
Local Legislative Councils—	
Bengal Legislative Council	Fifty.
Madras Legislative Council	Fifty.
Bombay Legislative Council	Fifty.
Bihar and Orissa Legislative Council . . .	Fifty.
United Provinces Legislative Councils . . .	Fifty.
Punjab Legislative Council	Thirty.
Burma Legislative Council	Thirty.
Assam Legislative Council	Thirty.
Central Provinces Legislative Council . . .	Thirty.
Legislative Council of the Lieutenant-Governor of any province hereafter constituted . . .	Thirty.

SECOND SCHEDULE.

Section 85.

OFFICIAL SALARIES ETC.

Officer.	Maximum annual salary.
Governor-General of India . .	Two hundred and fifty-six thousand rupees.
Governor	One hundred and twenty-eight thousand rupees.
Commander-in-Chief of His Majesty's forces in India.	One hundred thousand rupees.
Lieutenant-Governor . . .	One hundred thousand rupees.
Ordinary member of the Governor-General's Executive Council.	No statutory maximun has been fixed.
Member of a Governor's Executive Council	Sixty-four thousand rupees.

THIRD SCHEDULE.

Section 98.

OFFICES RESERVED TO THE INDIA CIVIL SERVICE.

PART I—GENERAL.

1. Secretaries, joint secretaties, deputy secretaries, and under secretaries to the several Governments in India, except the secretaries, joint secretaries, deputy secretaries and under secretaries in the Army, Marine and Pubilc Works Departments,

2. Accountants-General,

3. Members of the Board of Revenue in the presidencies of Bengal and Madras, the United Provinces of Agra and Oudh and the Province of Bihar and Orissa.

4. Secretaries in those Boards of Revenue.

5. Commissioners of customs, salt, excise and opium.

6. Opium agent.

PART II.

OFFICES IN THE PROVINCES WHICH WERE KNOWM IN THE YEAR 1861 AS "REGULATION PROVINCES"

7. District and sessions judges.

8. Additional district or sessions judes and assistant sessions judges.

9. District magistrates.

10. Joint magistrates.

11. Assistant magistrates.

12. Commissioners of revenue.

13. Collectors of revenue, or chief revenue officers of districts.

14. Assistant Collectors.

FOURTH SCHEDULE.

Section 130.

ACTS REPEALED.

Session and Chapter.	Short Title.	Extent of Repeal.
10 Geo. 3, c. 47.	The East India Company Act, 1770.	The whole Act.
13 Geo. 3, c. 63.	The East India Company Act, 1772.	The whole Act, except sections forty two, forty-three & forty-five.
21 Geo. 3, c. 70.	The East India Company Act, 1780.	The whole Act, except section eighteen.
26 Geo. 3, c. 57.	The East India Company Act, 1786.	Section thirty-eight.
33 Geo. 3, c. 52.	The East India Company Act, 1793.	The whole Act.
37 Geo. 3, c. 142.	The East India Act, 1797.	The whole Act, except section twelve.
39 & 40 Geo. 3, c. 79.	The Government of India Act, 1800.	The whole Act.
53 Geo. 3, c. 155.	The East India Company Act, 1813.	The whole Act.
55 Geo. 3, c. 84.	The Indian Presidency Towns Act, 1815.	The whole Act.
4 Geo. 4, c. 71.	The Indian Bishops and Courts Act, 1823.	The whole Act.
6 Geo. 4, c. 85.	The Indian Salaries and Pensions Act, 1825.	The whole Act.

Session and Chapter.	Short Title.	Extent of Repeal.
7 Geo. 4, c. 56.	The East India Officers' Act, 1826.	The whole Act.
3 & 4 Will. 4, c. 85.	The Government of India Act, 1833.	The whole Act, except section one hundred and twelve.
5 & 6 Will. 4, c. 52.	The India (North-West Provinces) Act, 1835.	The whole Act.
7 Will. 4 & 1 Vict, c. 47.	The India Officers' Salaries Act, 1837.	The whole Act.
5 & 6 Vict, c. 119.	The Indian Bishops Act, 1842.	The whole Act.
16&17 Vict, c. 95.	The Government of India Act, 1853.	The whole Act.
17&18 Vict, c. 77.	The Government of India Act, 1854.	The whole Act.
21&22 Vict, c. 106.	The Government of India Act, 1858.	The whole Act, except section four.
22&23 Vict, c. 41.	The Government of India Act, 1859.	The whole Act.
23&24 Vict, c. 100.	The European Forces (India) Act 1860.	The whole Act.
23&24 Vict, c. 102.	The East India Stock Act, 1860.	The whole Act, except section six.
24&25 Vict, c. 54.	The Indian Civil Service Act. 1861.	The whole Act.
24&25 Vict, c. 67.	The Indian Councils Act, 1861.	The whole Act.
24&25 Vict, c. 104.	The Indian High Courts Act, 1861.	The whole Act.

Session and Chapter.	Short Title	Extent of Repeal.
28&29 Vict, c. 15.	The Indian High Courts Act, 1865.	The whole Act.
28&29 Vict, c. 17.	The Government of India Act, 1865.	The whole Act.
32&33 Vict, c. 97.	The Government of India Act, 1869.	The whole Act.
32&33 Vict, c. 98.	The India Councils Act 1865.	The whole Act.
33&34 Vict, c. 3.	The Government of India Act, 1870.	The whole Act.
33&34 Vict, c. 59.	The East India Contracts Act, 1870.	The whole Act.
34&35 Vict, c. 34.	The Indian Councils Act, 1871.	The whole Act.
34&35 Vict, c. 62.	The Indian Bishops Act, 1871.	The whole Act.
37&38 Vict, c. 3.	The East India Loan Act, 1874.	Section fifteen.
37&38 Vict, c. 77.	The Colonial Clergy Act, 1874.	Section thirteen.
37&38 Vict, c. 91.	The Indian Councils Act, 1874.	The whole Act.
43 Vict. c. 3.	The Indian Salaries and Allowances Act, 1880.	The whole Act.
44&45 Vict, c. 63.	The India Office Auditor Act, 1881.	The whole Act.
47&48 Vict, c. 38.	The Indian Marine Service Act, 1884.	Sections two, three, four and five.

Session and Chapter.	Short Title.	Extent of Repeal.
55&56 Vict, c. 14.	The Indian Councils Act, 1892.	The whole Act.
3 Edw. 7, c. 11.	The Contracts (India Office) Act, 1903.	The whole Act.
4 Edw. 7, c. 26.	The Indian Councils Act, 1904.	The whole Act.
7 Edw. 7, c. 33.	The Councils of India Act, 1907.	The whole Act.
9 Edw. 7, c. 4.	The Indian Councils Act, 1909.	The whole Act.
1&2 Geo.5, c. 18.	The Indian High Courts Act, 1911.	The whole Act.
1&2 Geo.5, c. 25.	The Government of India Act, Amendment Act, 1911.	The whole Act.
23& Geo.5, c. 6.	The Government of India Act, 1912.	The whole Act.

FIFTH SCHEDULE

Section 131. (3)

PROVISIONS OF THIS ACT WHICH MAY BE REPEALED OR ALTERED BY THE GOVERNOR-GENERAL IN LEGISLATIVE COUNCIL.

Section.	Subject.
16	Transmission of information by the Governor-General in Council to the Secretary of State.
33, the last twenty words.	Obedience of Governor-General in Council to orders of Secretary of State.
40 (1). . . .	Form and signature of proceedings of Governor-General in Council.
41 (1), the words "the Governor-General in Council shall be bound by the opinion and decision of the majority of those present".	Governor-General in Council to be bound by the opinion and decision of the majority of the members present at a meeting of the executive council.
41 (4). . . .	Restriction of powers of Governor-General in acting against the opinion of the majority present at a meeting of his executive council.
43(2). . . .	Orders by Governor-General to local Governments or Officers or servants during absence from his executive council.
43(3)	Suspension by Secretary of State in Council of the power to issue orders under section 43 (2).
44	Restrictions on power of Governor-General in Council to make war or treaty.

Section.	Subject.
45 (2)	Restrictions on power of local Government to make war or treaty; punishment of officers disobeying orders of Governor–General in Council under this sub-section.
47 (3)	Commander-in-Chief when to be a member of a Governor's executive council.
49 (1)	Form and signature of proceedings of Governor-in-Council.
50 (2)	Power of Governor to act against the opinion of the majority present at a meeting of his executive council.
50 (3)	Written communications, and signatures in such cases.
50(4) last twenty words	Restrictions on powers of Governor in acting against the opinion of the majority present at a meeting of his executive council.
51. first paragraph, the last twelve words.	Powers of member of Governor's executive council presiding in absence of governor.
51. proviso. . .	Governor's signature to proceedings of meeting held in his absence.
62 . . .	Power to extend limits of presidency towns.
104 (2) . . .	Commencement and exclusiveness of official remuneration of judges of High Court.
104 (3), (4) . . .	Payments to representatives of deceased judges of High Courts.
106	Jurisdiction, powers and authority of High Courts.
108 (1) . . .	Exercise of Jurisdiction of High Court by single judges or division courts.

Section.	Subject.
109	Power for Governor-General in Council to alter local limits of Jurisdiction of High Courts, etc.
110	Exemption from Jurisdiction of High Courts.
111	Written order by Governor-General in Council a justification for act in High Court.
112	Law to be administered in case of inheritance, succession, contract and dealing between party and party.
114 (2). . . .	Powers of advocate-general.
116	Power of Bishop of Calcutta to admit to holy orders.
118 (2)-so far it relates to the Bishop of Calcutta and archdeacons.	Commencement, exclusiveness and continuance of official remuneration.
118 (3)-so far as it relates to the Bishop of Calcutta.	Expenses of visitations.
119--so far as it relates to the Bishop of Calcutta.	Payments to representatives of deceased bishop.
120-so far as it relates to residence of the Bishop of Calcutta as such bishop or as archdeacons.	Pension.
124 (1). . . .	Oppression.
124 (4)-so far as it relates to persons employed or con-	Trading.

Section.	Subject.
cerned in the collection of revenue or the administrations of Justice.	
124 (5)-so far as it relates to persons other than the Governor-General, a Governor, or member of the executive council of the Governor-General or of a Governor.	Receiving presents.
125	Loans to princes or chiefs.
126	Carrying on dangerous correspondence.
127	Prosecution of offences in the United Kingdom.
128	Limitation for prosecution in British India.
129	Penalties.

Appendix.

The Government of India (Amendment) Act, 1916.

(6 and 7 Geo. 5, Ch. 37.)

An Act to amend certain enactments relating to the Government of India, and to remove doubts as to the validity of certain Orders in Council made for India. [23rd August, 1916.]

Be it enacted by the King's Most Excellent Majesty, by and with the advice and consent of the Lords Spiritual and Temporal, and Commons, in this present Parliament assembled, and by the authority of the same, as follows:—

1. (1) In section sixty-three of the Government of India Act, 1915 (in this Act referred to as "the principal Act"), shall be inserted the following sub-sections:—

"(6A) Rules made under this section may provide for the final decision of doubts or disputes to as the validity of an election."

"(6B) Subject to any rules made under this section, any person who is a ruler or subject of any state in India shall be eligible to be nominated a member of a legislative council."

(2) In sections seventy-four and seventy-six of the principal Act corresponding subsection shall be inserted, and shall be numbered (4A) and (4B) in section seventy-four and (3A) and (3B) in section seventy-six.

(3) This section shall apply to and shall validate rules and nominations made as well before as after the commencement of this Act.

2. (1) In section seventy-one of the principal Act shall be inserted the following sub-section:—

"(3A) A regulation made under this section for any territory shall not be invalid by reason only that it confers or delegates power to confer on courts or administrative authorities power to sit or act outside the territory in respect of which they have jurisdiction or functions, or that it confers or delegates power to confer appellate jurisdiction or functions on courts or administrative authorities sitting or acting outside the territory."

(2) In section eighty-four of the principal Act, after the words "Governor General in Legislative Council" shall be inserted the words "or a local legislature," and, at the end of the section, shall be inserted the following words:—

"A law made by any authority in British India and repugnant to any provision of this or any other Act of Parliament shall, to the extent of the repugnancy, but not otherwise, be void."

(3) This section shall apply to and shall validate laws made as well before as after the commencement of this Act.

3. After section ninety-six of the principal Act shall be inserted the following section:—

"96A. Notwithstanding anything in any other enactment, the Governor General in Council, with the approval of the Secretary of State in Council, may, by notification, declare that, subject to any conditions or restrictions prescribed in the notification, any named ruler or subject of any state in India shall be eligible for appointment to any civil or military office under the Crown to which a native of British India may be appointed, or any named subject of any state, or any named member of any independent race or tribe, in territory adjacent to India, shall be eligible for appointment to any such military office."

4. In section ninety-seven of the principal Act, after the words "British subjects" shall be inserted the words "and of persons in respect of whom a declaration has been made under the last foregoing section who are," and, after sub-section (2), shall be inserted the following sub-section:—

"(2A) The admission to the Indian Civil Service of a British subject who or whose father or mother was not born within His Majesty's dominions shall be subject to such restrictions as the Secretary of State in Council, with the advice and assistance of the Civil Service Commissioners, may think fit to prescribe, and all such restrictions shall be included in the rules."

5. An Order of His Majesty in Council heretofore or hereafter made under the Foreign Jurisdiction Act, 1890, empowering the Governor General of India in Council to make rules and orders in respect of conrts or administrative authorities acting for any territory shall not be invalid by reason only that it confers or delegates power to confer on courts or administrative authorities power to sit or act outside the territory in respect of which they have jurisdiction or functions, or that it confers or delegates power to confer appellate jurisdiction or functions on courts or administrative authorities sitting or acting outside the territory.

6. (1) India stock may, if registered for the time being as stock transferable by deed in manner provided by regulations made under this section, be transferred by deed.

(2) The Banks of England and Ireland respectively, with the concurrence of the Secretary of State in Council, shall provide by regulations for a separate stock register being kept for India stock which is for the time being transferable by deed, for the conditions upon which stock is to be entered in or removed from that register, for the mode in which the transfer by deed is to be carried out, and for the payment of any fees in respect of the entry or removal of stock in or from the register and the carrying out of any transfer of stock by deed.

(3) The provisions of all enactments relating to India stock which are in force at the commencement of this Act shall apply to stock transferable by deed in pursuance of this section as they apply to stock transferable in the books of the Banks of England or Ireland, or of the Secretary of State in Council, except so far as express provisions is made to the contrary by this section or by the regulations made thereunder.

(4) No stamp duty shall be payable in respect of any deed of transfer of India stock or any dividend warrant or register certificate relating to India stock.

(5) In this section the expression "India stock" means any stock created and issued, whether before or after the commencement of this Act, by the Secretary of State in Council under the authority of Parliament.

7. (1) The principal Act shall be further amended in manner appearing in the First Schedule to this Act.

(2) The enactments specified in the Second Schedule to this Act are hereby repealed to the extent mentioned in the third column of that Schedule.

(3) Nothing in this Act shall affect any right acquired before the commencement of this Act under any judgment or order of a court of competent jurisdiction.

8. (1) This Act may be cited as the Government of India (Amendment) Act, 1916, and the principal Act and this Act may be cited, together as the Government of India Acts, 1915 and 1916.

(2) This Act shall come into operation on the first day of September, one thousand nine hundred and sixteen.

(3) Where any enactment or word is directed by this Act, or by any Act for the time being in force, whether passed before or after the commencement of this Act, to be inserted in or added to the principal Act, or to be substituted in the principal Act for any other enactment or word, or where any enactment or word in the principal Act is so directed to be repealed, then all copies of the principal Act printed by His Majesty's printers after that direction takes effect shall be printed with that enactment or word inserted in or added to the Act, or printed therein in lieu of any enactment or word for which the same is substituted, or omitted therefrom, according as the direction requires, and with the sections and subsections numbered in accordance with the direction; and the principal Act shall be construed as if it had, at the time at which the direction takes effect, been enacted with that addition, substitution or omission.

(4) A reference in any enactment, whether passed before or after the commencement of this Act, to the principal Act shall, unless the context otherwise requires, be construed to refer to that Act as amended by any enactment for the time being in force.

SCHEDULES.

First Schedule.

Further Amendments of the Government of India Act, 1915.

Enactment to be amended.	Amendment.
The Government of India Act, 1915 (5 & 6 Geo. 5, c. 61).	
Section 3 (3). . . .	The word "British," where secondly occurring, shall be repealed.
Section 13 (1) . . .	For this sbu-section shall be substituted the following sub-section:— "(1) Where an order or communication concerns the levying of war, or the making of peace, or the public safety, or the defence of the realm, or the treating or negotiating with any prince or state, or the policy to be observed with respect to any prince or state, and a majority of votes therefor at a meeting of the Council of India is not required by this Act, the Secretary of State may send the order or communication to the Governor General in Council or to any Governor in Council or officer or servant in India without submitting it to a meeting of the council or depositing it for the perusal of the members of the council or sending or giving notice of the reasons for making it, if he considers that it is of a nature to require secrecy."
Section 13 (2) . . .	The words "or any of the matters aforesaid" shall be substituted for the words "or the levying of war, or the making of peace, or negotiations or treaties with any prince or state."

Enactment to be amended.	Amendment.
Section 21	At the end of this section shall be added the words "Provided that a grant or appropriation made in accordance with provisions or restrictions prescribed by the Secretary of State in Council with the concurrence of a majority of votes at a meeting of the council shall be deemed to be made with the concurrence of a majority of such votes."
Section 26	The words "twenty-eight days" shall be substituted for the words "fourteen days."
Section 27 (10) . . .	The words "or retiring" shall be inserted after the word "superannuation;" the words "and their legal personal representatives shall, for the purposes of gratuity" shall be inserted after the word "allowance;" and the words "the auditor and his assistants" shall be substituted for the word "they."
Sections 28 (1) and 30 (1).	The words "or personal," shall be inserted after the word "real," where secondly occurring, and the words "or otherwise" shall be inserted after the word "mortgage."
Section 28 (2) . . .	The word "two" shall be substituted for the word "three."
Section 63 (3) and 74 (2) .	The words "any office of profit" shall be substituted for the word "office."
Sections 64 (3), 75 (3) and 78 (2)	The words "or when questions are asked" shall be inserted after the words "any matter of general public interest."
Sections 67 (3) and 80 (3)	The words "or when questions are asked" shall be inserted after the words "at any such discussion."

Enactment to be amended.	Amendment.
Section 86 (1) . . .	The words "and a Lieutenant-Governor in Council" shall be inserted after the words "a Governor in Council."
Section 92 (3) . . .	The words "or special duty" shall be inserted after the words "is absent on leave."
Section 94	The words "or special duty" shall be inserted after the words "absence on leave," and the words "absence may be permitted" shall be substituted for the words "leave may be granted."
Section 99 (1) . . .	The words "in British India," where secondly occurring shall be repealed.
Section 106 . . .	In this section shall be inserted the following sub-section:— "(1 A). The letters patent establishing or vesting jurisdiction, powers or authority in a high court may be amended from time to time by His Majesty by futher letters patent."
Section 107, proviso . .	The word "law" shall be substituted for the word "Act."
Section 109 (1) . . .	The words "any British subject for the time being within" shall be substituted for the words "Christian subjects of His Majesty resident in."
Section 110 (1) . .	The words "Lieutenant Governor and chief commissioner" shall be inserted after the words "each Governor," and the words "executive council of the Governor General or of a Governor or Lieutenant-Governor" shall be substituted for the words "their respective executive councils."

Enactment to be amended.	Amendment.
Section 114 . . .	At the end of this section shall be added the following sub-section:— "(3) On the occurrence of a vacancy in the office of advocate-general or during any absence or deputation of an advocate-general the Governor General in Council in the case of Bengal, and the local Government in other cases, may appoint a person to act as advocate-general; and the person so appointed may exercise powers of an advocate-general until some person has been appointed by His Majesty to the office and has entered on the discharge of his duties, or until the anvocate-general has returned from his absence or deputation, as the case may be, or until the Governor General in Council or the local Government, as the case may be, cancels the acting appiontment."
Section 120 . . .	The words "Secretary of State" shall be substituted for the words "Chancellor of the Exchequer;" the words "Madras or Bombay" shall be inserted after the words "Bishop of Calcutta," where thirdly and fourthly occurring; and the words "to be paid quarterly" and the word "British" shall be repealed.

For the Fifth Schedule shall be substituted the following:—

FIFTH SCHEDULE.

Provisions of this Act which may be repealed or altered by the Governor General in Legislative Council

Section.	Subject.
62	Power to extend limits of presidency towns.
106	Jurisdiction, powers and authority of high courts.
108 (1)	Exercise of jurisdiction of high court by single judges or division courts.
109	Power for Governor-General in Council to alter local limits of jurisdiction of high courts, etc.
110	Exemption from jurisdiction of high courts
111	Written order by Governor General in Council a justification for act in high court.
112	Law to be administered in cases of inheritance, succession, contract and dealing between party and party.
114 (2)	Powers of advocate-general.
124 (1)	Oppression.
124 (4)–so far as it relates to persons employed or concerned in the collection of revenue or the administration of justice.	Trading.
124 (5)–so far as it relates to persons other than the	Receiving presents.

governor general, a governor, or a member of the executive council of the governor general or of a governor.	
125	Loans to princes or chiefs.
126	Carrying on dangerous correspondence.
128	Limitation for prosecutions in British India
129	Penalties."

SECOND SCHEDULE.

Enactments repealed.

Session and Chapter.	Short Title.	Extent of Repeal.
13 Geo. 3, c. 63 .	The East India Company Act, 1772.	Sections foty-two, forty-three and forty-five.
24 Geo. 3, sess. 2 c.25	The East India Company Act, 1784:	The whole Act.
26 Geo. 3, c. 74 .	The East India Company Act, 1786.	The whole Act.
9 Geo. 4, c. 74 . .	The Criminal Law (India) Act, 1828.	Section fifty-six, except so far as in force in the Straits Settlements,
5 and 6 Geo: 5, c. 91.	The Government of India Act, 1915.	In section twenty-six, paragraph (d). In section eighty-seven, sub-sections (2), (3), (4), and (5). Section one hundred and sixteen.

INDEX.

F

G

H

I

J

K

L

Q

U

V

W